THE
EVERYTHING
TRIATHLON TRAINING BOOK

From scheduling workouts to crossing the finish line—all you need to meet the challenge

Brent Manley and Lucia Colbert

Avon, Massachusetts

I dedicate this book to Donna, my wife and biggest supporter,
and to Steve Parker and Ray Dear, who run me
ragged on a regular basis.—Brent Manley

This book is dedicated to my Dad,
who has inspired me in everything I have done,
and to my husband and soul mate, Bert.—Lucia Colbert

An Everything® Series Book.
Everything® and everything.com® are registered trademarks of F+W Media, Inc.

Published by Adams Media, a division of F+W Media, Inc.
57 Littlefield Street, Avon, MA 02322 U.S.A.
www.adamsmedia.com

ISBN 10: 1-59869-807-9
ISBN 13: 978-1-59869-807-7

Printed in the United States of America.

J I H G F E D C B A

Library of Congress Cataloging-in-Publication Data
is available from the publisher.

This publication is designed to provide accurate and authoritative information with regard to the subject matter covered. It is sold with the understanding that the publisher is not engaged in rendering legal, accounting, or other professional advice. If legal advice or other expert assistance is required, the services of a competent professional person should be sought.

—From a *Declaration of Principles* jointly adopted by a Committee of the American Bar Association and a Committee of Publishers and Associations

Many of the designations used by manufacturers and sellers to distinguish their products are claimed as trademarks. Where those designations appear in this book and Adams Media was aware of a trademark claim, the designations have been printed with initial capital letters.

Interior illustration credits: Triathlon icons © iStockphoto / Paul Pantazescu, Illustrations © Eric Andrews.

This book is available at quantity discounts for bulk purchases.
For information, please call 1-800-289-0963.

THE EVERYTHING TRIATHLON TRAINING BOOK

Dear Reader,

There is something extraordinarily compelling about certain athletic endeavors. It is inspiring beyond words to see a competitor summon some indescribable something from inside to overcome seemingly impossible odds. We look on in awe and wonder, and dream of our own moments in the sun.

Most of us will never reach the heights that create legends, but in our own way we can experience something similar to the greatest champions as we draw just as deeply within ourselves to scale our own, albeit smaller, mountains.

The triathlon is an imposing test for someone who has never tried it, but if you believe in yourself and have the courage to try, you will never be the same after you cross that finish line.

You don't have to be first to experience an achievement that will last forever. You are about to become a triathlete. Congratulations and good luck.

Brent Manley & Lucia Colbert

Welcome to the EVERYTHING® Series!

These handy, accessible books give you all you need to tackle a difficult project, gain a new hobby, comprehend a fascinating topic, prepare for an exam, or even brush up on something you learned back in school but have since forgotten.

You can choose to read an *Everything*® book from cover to cover or just pick out the information you want from our four useful boxes: e-questions, e-facts, e-alerts, and e-ssentials. We give you everything you need to know on the subject, but throw in a lot of fun stuff along the way, too.

We now have more than 400 *Everything*® books in print, spanning such wide-ranging categories as weddings, pregnancy, cooking, music instruction, foreign language, crafts, pets, New Age, and so much more. When you're done reading them all, you can finally say you know *Everything*®!

QUESTIONS?
Answers to
common questions

FACTS
Important snippets
of information

ALERTS!
Urgent
warnings

ESSENTIALS
Quick
handy tips

PUBLISHER Karen Cooper

DIRECTOR OF ACQUISITIONS AND INNOVATION Paula Munier

MANAGING EDITOR, EVERYTHING SERIES Lisa Laing

COPY CHIEF Casey Ebert

ACQUISITIONS EDITOR Lisa Laing

SENIOR DEVELOPMENT EDITOR Brett Palana-Shanahan

EDITORIAL ASSISTANT Hillary Thompson

Visit the entire Everything® series at *www.everything.com*

Contents

Acknowledgments

The authors are indebted to certain individuals and groups who contributed to this book, even if they didn't know it at the time.

We wish to thank Ashley Hofeditz—runner, triathlete, and, most important, nutrition expert—for her help in setting us straight on several matters relating to eating and drinking for athletic success.

Thanks also to a former triathlon squad, dubbed Team We Shoulda Trained and captained by Scott Landreth, who helped open the exciting world of triathlons for Brent.

Thanks also to physical therapist Nanette Farris, whose invaluable advice about injury prevention and treatment made up key parts of this book.

Also, thanks to the Los Locos Triathlon Team for their input. Lucia's Wednesday running group also offered many helpful ideas.

Top Ten Reasons for Doing a Triathlon

1. The training is a great way to relieve stress in your life. Had a bad day at work? Blow off some steam with a tempo run.

2. There are lots of travel opportunities. Triathlons are organized in a lot of fun places to visit.

3. You will make new friends who share your interest in outdoor sports. Your tri buddies will be there for you in other areas of your life as well.

4. The triathlon is a great excuse to buy a lot of high-tech gear, fancy bikes, and state-of-the-art running shoes that you *really do need*.

5. The T-shirts are great, not to mention the medals and trophies for the den.

6. You often get to compete in the same field as—and learn from—some of the best triathletes in the world.

7. You get to eat "bad" stuff after the triathlon without guilt—at least for the afternoon. And don't forget the beer!

8. The cross-training is best for your overall fitness and will help you stay active while minimizing the risk of injury.

9. You will become really fit and more attuned to a healthy lifestyle. And you will probably lose weight, too.

10. In the competition, you will find out things about yourself you never knew, and you will be amazed. You'll say, "Wow! Why didn't I try this sooner?"

Introduction

▶ WARNING! THE FACT that you have picked up this book means you are interested in the sport called triathlon. There is a serious danger that you could become a triathlete. You could lose weight and become exceptionally fit while gaining muscle and the respect of your peers. Cross that triathlon finish line just once and you could become addicted.

Don't say you weren't warned.

The triathlon in North America can trace its roots to Southern California, where the first three-sport race—swimming, cycling, and running—took place in the fall of 1974. From that start, the sport has grown by leaps and bounds.

USA Triathlon (USAT), the governing body of the sport, estimates there are more than 2,000 multisport races in the United States each year. Membership in USAT is approaching 100,000. Worldwide, the number of triathlon participants is estimated to be in the hundreds of thousands annually.

A major impetus for the recent growth of the sport was the debut of the triathlon in the 2000 Olympic Games in Sydney, Australia. Today, one of the most popular formats for a triathlon is the Olympic-distance triathlon of a 1,500-meter swim, 40-kilometer bike ride, and 10-kilometer run.

Like the marathon in running, triathlons are now more accessible to amateur athletes, who make up a larger part of the triathlon scene each year. There are many races with shorter distances, known as "sprint" triathlons, for those new to the sport.

You may be asking why you need a book to get started in this sport, or to make improvements from your first triathlon. Preparation, of course, is the key to execution, and few people instinctively know proper techniques and the best plans for integrating the training for the three sports in such a way that they complement each other. You need guidance, and having plans laid out for you and explained can only improve your chances on race day.

Most triathletes have lives apart from the competition, and the training programs in this book allow for you to still be a spouse, parent, and dependable employee while preparing for race day. When the big day comes, you will be ready physically and mentally if you follow the advice in this book.

The triathlon is known as an endurance sport, and the designation could not be more appropriate. To get ready for your big day, you will have to endure early mornings at the pool and tough rides and runs, sometimes in adverse conditions. You may have setbacks in your training with injuries or illness. It's an odyssey that, by comparison, might make the actual race look easy.

The training is not all misery, however. It will be exciting to experience the inevitable gains in fitness, and who wouldn't be happy to see the pounds melting away? If you find some fellow trainees to join for workouts, the camaraderie you share will more than make up for the rigors of the training. Making friends as you prepare for your triathlon will be the gift that keeps on giving.

Neither the race nor the training is supposed to be easy. Where's the feeling of accomplishment if you don't have to push yourself?

The triathlon, especially if it's your first, may be the hardest thing you ever do. Chances are you will also look upon the moment that you cross the finish line as one of your finest hours.

CHAPTER 1

Getting Started

Well, here you are—about to start a journey unlike any other you have experienced. For all but a few, it will seem overwhelming just to consider what lies ahead. You might be a runner anticipating your first-ever competitive swim. Perhaps you are a biker with little experience in the other two sports. So step back, take a deep breath, and tell yourself: no more stalling. It's time to get going.

Why Compete in a Triathlon?

Only you know why you decided to give this exciting sport a try. Perhaps you have friends who compete and heard them talking about a race. Maybe you saw a triathlon on television and thought it looked like fun. Most runners at some time will be advised to do more cross-training, and what could be better for that objective than a competition that *requires* you to vary your training.

Athletic competition in many ways is its own reward. It is very satisfying, for example, to complete a 10-kilometer run in difficult conditions. You don't even have to win to feel good about crossing the finish line. At some point in a tough race, you probably had to call on something within you to finish, or you had to fight off a message your body was sending you to slow down or stop.

Do not think of a triathlon as three individual sports—swimming, cycling, and running. A triathlon is one sport with three separate phases. You don't get credit for any of them unless you complete all three.

Confidence Builder

There is no question that it is difficult to complete a triathlon, especially the first time, even one of relatively short distance. The difficulty factor is multiplied if you started without much experience at any of the sports. Then again, if it was easy, who would want to do it?

Yes, it's hard to prepare yourself for the challenge, and you will be testing yourself as never before when you hit the water in your first triathlon, but with the right training and the will to stick to a schedule, you can do it. You won't be asking your body to do the impossible.

Because completing a triathlon is challenging, you will feel a sense of confidence when you finish that you might not have known before. What seemed light years away when you started is now part of your personal history. How cool is that?

Expanding Horizons

Most people come to the triathlon with experience in just one of the sports, principally either running or cycling. As you work on the other sports, it will be exciting to know you are growing and moving into a new class as an athlete. You will be opening a whole new chapter, perhaps more than one, in your athletic history.

When you start your training, it may seem that getting to the finish line of the actual event is just a dream. As you improve as a swimmer, biker, and runner, you will realize that you have what it takes. That's a great feeling.

FACT

Many triathletes have been inspired by the enduring legend of Julie Moss, who led the 1982 Hawaii Ironman Triathlon nearly all the way before cramps and dehydration in the severe heat nearly shut her down close to the finish. She fell several times but became a folk heroine by crawling several yards to the finish line. A video of her heroic feat is still widely circulated today.

Easier on the Body

One reason that coaches urge athletes, especially runners, to cross-train is that it saves wear and tear on the body. Swimming, in fact, is an ideal cross-training activity because you don't experience the pounding that you do when you run, but you still get a very useful cardiovascular workout as you make your way back and forth in the pool. You will probably find when you jump into the pool for the first time that there is nothing easy about negotiating the 50 meters down and back in the pool, but it won't give you shin splints or runner's knee. Similarly, biking also provides a good workout for your heart and lungs without beating up your legs.

In Focus

As you move from one sport to the other in your training, you will learn the art of focusing on what you are doing—and only what you are doing.

Learning this skill will be of immense value to you on race day. When you enter the water on the swim portion of the triathlon, you want to have your mind on getting around those buoys and out of the water. You do not want to be thinking about anything but the strokes that will get you from point A to point B.

As you train, you will concentrate on, among other things, perfecting your stride as you run, keeping low on the bicycle to decrease wind resistance, and learning long, slow strokes as you swim. Whatever you are doing that particular session is the only thing you will be thinking about.

QUESTION?

Why is running so much harder on the body?
It is estimated that every step you take as you run makes an impact on your body equal to up to six times your body weight. This puts stress on the bones and joints, especially when just starting out. Swimming and cycling are low-impact activities; running is a high-impact sport.

How Triathlons Work

Triathlons may feature different distances and venues, but each is organized the same way: swim first, then cycle, then run. The swim will have the most variety as it can occur in a lake, ocean, or even an indoor pool. In a typical triathlon, you will be riding your bicycle on a paved road. Most rides will be out and back, but a loop course is possible. The run will be basically the same—out and back or loop, also on a paved road. Some of the run course might be on a trail or off-road surface, but the cycling part will not be unless your triathlon is specifically an off-road event.

Waves of Swimmers

There are two different ways to start the triathlon swim. The most common is the wave start. In a wave start, groups of triathletes assemble on the edge of the lake or ocean and all enter the water together when a siren sounds or a starter gun goes off. The size of the group depends in part on the size of the entrance to the body of water. Groups can be thirty swimmers or up to fifty or sixty if there is plenty of room.

Many road races allow runners taking part to register the day of the race, some even minutes before the start. Don't expect to do that with a triathlon. Almost all triathlons require preregistration, some with deadlines days before the event. This is because many have only a limited number of slots available, and it's much more complicated to organize a triathlon than a road race.

In a wave start, the first group is usually made up of the fastest swimmers, typically the male "pro" triathletes. This is not unlike the way some large marathons are organized with the elite runners starting out a few minutes ahead of the rest of the pack. If you are participating in a smaller triathlon, you probably will not see this configuration.

In any event, the wave start will have several groups, determined by the race organizers, each entering the water together in turn with a wait of a minute or so before the next group gets started. The last groups to enter the water in a wave start are usually the relay participants and younger swimmers.

Right on Time

The other way of starting the triathlon is by a time trial. In this format, swimmers stand in single file at the edge of the water, starting their swim on cue, with a delay of three to five seconds before the next swimmer starts. The swimmers stand in line in the order of their race numbers, which are displayed on their swim caps and written on their arms and legs with waterproof marker.

Number one, usually the favorite to win the triathlon, goes first, followed by number two, and so on. Time trials can include age groups, with each participant in a particular group standing in line according to his number, starting with the lowest.

In a time trial, the swimmer's race number and time of the start are noted so that person's total time can be calculated from the point of entering the water to crossing the finish line in the run.

It is not unusual for a triathlon to use both formats for starting the swim, with the elite athletes beginning in a time trial and others, especially relay participants, in wave starts by groups.

QUESTION?

What if I'm in a time trial start and I miss my turn?
You won't be disqualified, but when your number comes up once the time trial has begun, your time will start then. If you were in the port-a-john when your number came up, you would have to go to the back of the line, however long it is, and wait. As you can imagine, such a lapse could be very costly, not to mention embarrassing.

A Matter of Timing

There are two ways to time the participants in a triathlon: with regular time-calculating machinery augmented by human observation or by computer chip. Larger races use the chips. The chip is a small plastic device with a transponder inside. On the transponder is information that identifies the participant. By using special mats that receive the signals from the chips and send them to a computer, race organizers can tell when each swimmer entered the water and emerged at the end of the swim, when that participant started the cycling portion and when it was completed, and when the run began and the runner crossed the finish line. The mats that receive the information are placed at strategic points on the various courses, picking up signals from all competitors as they pass over them.

Chips in road races are usually attached to the shoes of the runners. In a triathlon, the swimmers won't be wearing shoes, so the chips are attached to a Velcro strap that goes around the wrist or ankle. Relay participants will hand off the strap to their teammates at each point in the competition. In a large race, the chip allows race organizers to post up-to-the-minute progress of each athlete on a website so that friends and family can follow the progress of the athletes.

It wasn't designed specifically for that purpose, but one of the benefits of chip timing for races is that organizers can set up mats at points designed to assure that each competitor completes the required distance. It is impossible for race organizers to police every single participant, and the chip provides a bit of insurance that everyone is playing fair.

Who Are You?

Triathlon organizers go to great lengths to make it easy to identify everyone who is taking part. That's why your swim cap has a number on it, why you are required to wear your race number out front on your singlet (a garment similar to a tank top) or your running shorts when you cycle and run, and why some races require you to lash race numbers to your bicycle in easy-to-spot locations.

Why is the swim the first event in the triathlon?
It's a matter of safety. It would be very dangerous for athletes fatigued from running and/or cycling to get into the water for a swim of even 300 yards, much less a mile or more.

This is especially important when the timing is done by humans instead of by computer. Spotters need to be able to tell who just got out of the water, started biking, and finished running. There are strict rules in triathlons, and judges must be able to identify competitors who break the rules.

When you show up for the race, someone will write your race number on your arms and legs. They might also write your age on your calf so that when you are running and someone comes up behind you, that person will know whether he is competing in your age group.

Most triathlons are set up so that the transition areas are near each other. As swimmers come out of the water, they usually don't have far to go to find their bicycles, just a few feet in many cases.

The bikes will all be in racks with numbers matching the athletes' race numbers. Swimmers will put on shoes and helmets, walk their bikes to the mount/dismount area, saddle up, and take off. When they return to the mount/dismount line, they get off, walk their bikes back to the racks, change into running shoes if necessary, and take off on the run.

The time it takes to change clothes and walk the bicycles around all counts in a triathlete's total time. You can read about transition efficiency in Chapter 14. The triathlon is completed when the athlete crosses the finish line.

What You Can Learn from the Pros

If you go to a triathlon of any size, you will usually see twelve to fifteen men and ten or so women who are in the pro or elite category of the competition. These are exceptional athletes who qualify for a pro/elite card from USA Triathlon by placing well in triathlons. Naturally, the pros are attracted to the larger races where prize money is typically available for the top professional finishers.

QUESTION?

What if I'm an amateur competitor and I beat a pro?
You get a good feeling in your heart, perhaps local bragging rights. What you don't get is money. You must have a pro card to cash in on a great performance.

You can learn a lot from watching the elite athletes in any sport, and triathlons are no different. If you just stand by and watch, you will notice that the pros are very smooth in the transitions. They know that an extra few seconds changing from swim mode to biking mode can mean the difference between winning and coming in second.

Don't forget, the winners are not necessarily the ones who cross the finish line first. The competitors don't start together, so the winner is the one with the lowest cumulative time in the three disciplines. An expert triathlete will usually spend about one-third as much time in transition as the typical competitor.

The pros have the best equipment, and while that's important if you take the whole triathlon adventure seriously, you should probably hold off on purchasing that ultracycle until you know you're going to stick to the sport.

FACT

You can spend a lot of money on your triathlon bicycle. An extremely light, high-tech, state-of-the-art cycle could easily set you back $5,000 or more. Make sure you are truly committed to the sport before you put that kind of charge on your credit card at the bike store.

The pros know the rules. For example, you can be disqualified for drafting—riding directly behind another cyclist to cut down on the wind resistance you have to face—in the cycling part of the race. On the other hand, drafting as a swimmer is perfectly legal and is recommended. One caveat: you have to trust that the swimmer ahead of you will follow the course. If he goes off course, so will you. As a beginning triathlete, you will be better off focusing on where you need to be in the water rather than trying to cut corners by drafting. Save that strategy for future races.

Better Plans

The pros know the opposition and are aware who is strong in which areas, and they plan accordingly. A triathlete who is very strong as a runner will not be concerned about being slightly behind after the swim and cycling phases. You can learn from this—even if your only goal is to finish—by not stressing if part of the triathlon doesn't go well. You can still excel in your best area and finish feeling confident.

Pros know how to train. They adopt training schedules and stick to them. They use heart rate monitors to be sure they are training at the proper intensity with each workout. More detailed information on that piece of equipment can be found in Chapter 10. You don't have to be a pro to benefit from using one.

You Will Be Glad You Did It

By the time you cross the finish line in your first triathlon, you will have many reasons to be pleased with your decision to undertake this challenge. You will have a feeling of accomplishment and new confidence, no matter how long it took you or where you finished in the standings. You will be a winner and will be acknowledged as such. You may be surprised at how supportive even the top athletes can be for those who dare to undertake such an ordeal.

Along the way, you will gain something even more rewarding. You will discover that you have joined the triathlon "family" and will enjoy all its rewards. In general, triathletes are very good about sharing tips and helping others to get better. The veterans remember what they went through when they were starting out, and most are willing to support you in any way they can.

You will make new friends, find new training partners, and at the post-race party you will get to eat and drink whatever you want without feeling guilty. After all, you just did something remarkable. You should have a reward for that.

Inspirations

If your first triathlon is a larger one, you may be surprised at how many "older" people are participating. It is not uncommon to see men and women in their sixties and seventies out there swimming, biking, and running with people who could be their grandchildren.

They won't be among the swiftest and most athletic of the competitors, but they will inspire you with their determination and grit. Perhaps you will see yourself as one of these troopers a few years down the road. These are the anti–couch potatoes.

Understanding the Challenge

The message that it's not easy to complete a triathlon has probably sunk in by now, but there are some details worth noting that could help you prepare for the challenge ahead—or at least give you a better idea of what's coming.

For starters, even if your debut triathlon is a sprint distance, you could be looking at a sustained period of exercise approaching two hours. If you are relatively new to athletic competition, two hours will almost certainly represent the longest event of your life.

Once you have finished, you may look back and wonder where the time went. While you were on the course, it might have seemed as though it was never going to end, that the finish line was getting farther away instead of closer as you struggled along. Just be aware that your first triathlon will contain some surprises, including how long it takes you to finish it.

You are also likely to experience more fatigue than you expected. You may have trained reasonably well in the three sports, but it's unlikely any of your workouts lasted as long as your first triathlon will. Be prepared for some surprises.

Breaking a Sweat

There may also be weather issues to consider, and it will be toughest when heat is the problem. The weather can be fickle, but most race organizers have information on their websites about the average high and low temperatures for race day. When high humidity is mixed in, the combination can be potentially lethal. There are many Internet sources of information for average temperatures in various locales. High heat and humidity could make your first triathlon a memorable occasion for a bad reason, exactly what you don't want.

FACT

When the temperature is 80°F and the humidity is 75 percent, the heat index—how hot it feels in the shade—is 84°F. Any time the temperature is in excess of 80°F, it is cause for concern. Exposure to direct sunlight can increase the heat index by up to fifteen degrees. Extended physical exertion in conditions like that can be extremely dangerous.

The bottom line is that you would be wise to avoid any race where the temperature projects to be 80°F or higher. Also, be aware that you probably will not be among the first to start, meaning that you may be finishing your run two, three, or even four hours after the first swimmers enter the water. So don't make your decision about your race based on the expected temperatures at 7 A.M. or 8 A.M. Check to see what the conditions might be at noon or later.

Goose Bumps

Just as heat can be a factor, so can cold. In some locations, April and May can be very chilly. Cold weather, at least to a point, is usually welcomed by runners in road races. It's the heat that really wipes out competitors in road races. A cold spell, however, can become a major issue for triathlon participants, particularly regarding the water.

Triathlon rules permit wetsuits—insulated rubber suits that cover your body from the neck to your ankles—when the water temperature is 78°F or lower. Wearing a wetsuit makes you more buoyant and keeps you from feeling like you're freezing in the water, but it can also be cumbersome. For more on wetsuits, see Chapter 8.

Take Your Goals Seriously

Cautions about how difficult a triathlon can be are not meant to scare anyone away from trying a sport with many rewards. It is important, however, for you to be serious about your training. Being ill-prepared for your first triathlon will result in a miserable experience. Your first triathlon might well be your last. Looking at it from a positive point of view, adequate preparation will assure that you enjoy the event

You won't feel good about yourself if you go out there and flounder around, struggling through each sport. Veterans know the difference between someone who is just having a bad day and a person who came to the race without the proper preparation. If life seriously gets in the way of your training, put off your first triathlon or try to get on a relay team. You want to be ready when you do your first.

Don't Panic

These stern messages about training properly do not mean that you are doomed if something happens that keeps you from doing a scheduled workout. It's not the end of the world, especially if the workout you missed is in your best sport. You don't want to make a habit of skipping workouts, but missing one now and then is not a big deal.

It's worth noting, too, that if you miss a workout, don't try to make it up unless you consider it absolutely vital to your training, for example, if it's in your weakest sport. Trying to compensate for a missed workout could easily disrupt your training schedule, and you will put yourself at risk for injury if you try to pile on too much in one day.

Marathon runners are often cautioned to "respect the distance," a way of saying that a person who dares to try a 26.2-mile run should know what he is getting into and that the training for the race should be adequate for the challenge. The same is true of a triathlon, even one with shorter distances. Respect the race. Train properly.

Downtime

It's human nature to think that if four days of training a week are good, then seven must be ideal. Too bad there isn't an eighth day! Get that notion out of your mind right now, especially if you are new to physical activity. Even top athletes build rest days into their training schedules, and they know why it's important.

Exercise and strength training tear down your muscles. They grow stronger in the process of being rebuilt. That's the wonder of the human body. If you never give your body a chance to rest, the rebuilding process won't occur or it won't be as efficient. Injury is the inevitable result of nonstop training.

Those who are new to sports should have at least one day a week with no exercise at all. If you schedule only one day of complete rest (doing little or nothing), you should avoid hard workouts two days in a row. Any time you have an intense workout, it should be followed the next day with something easy—or even a day off if you do not feel fully recovered

Committing the Time

Unless you won the lottery or are retired, you probably have a full-time job. If you also have a spouse and children, you already have considerable demands on your time.

Before you commit to the training necessary to complete a triathlon, you should take a good look at your typical weekly schedule.

What it takes to train for a triathlon is vastly different from what is required of someone taking up a single sport. If you are getting into running, you might have a couple of weight-training workouts a week to gain some strength, but mostly you will just have to find time to get out and pound the pavements or trails at various speeds four or five times a week.

When the triathlon is your goal, you have three times the demands, and your training venues will be separate, which translates into more travel time for those sessions. You should plan on adding ten to fifteen hours a week to your schedule for your triathlon training. Is this realistic for you? Your triathlon training will be stressful enough, especially if you are new to the sport. The last thing you need is more anxiety from trying to meet impossible demands on your time.

CHAPTER 2

Picking Your Race

Once you have decided to take the plunge and train for a triathlon, another important choice will be the race itself. There will be many to choose from, especially if you are able to travel to the competitions. For beginners, shorter distances are strongly recommended. No runner ever made his first race a marathon, nor should you overreach in your first "tri." A reasonable target will help assure success.

Mini Triathlon or Olympic Distance?

If you are coming to the triathlon with a history of strong athletic competition, and especially if you are a good swimmer, you may be a good candidate for an Olympic-distance triathlon, also known as a standard triathlon. Many skilled athletes look to the triathlon as a challenge worth meeting, and the best of them can actually earn a living as triathlon professionals. Imagine putting that occupation on your resume. It's a whole different situation if you are not a seasoned athlete or if you are very inexperienced in one of the disciplines, especially swimming. In that case, you should start with baby steps. That usually means a competition with shorter distances.

FACT

Before the triathlon became part of the 2000 Olympic Games in Sydney, Australia, the "standard" triathlon format was known as the international distance. Now it is known as the Olympic distance. No doubt the addition of the triathlon to the Olympic Games is at least partly responsible for the surge in interest in multisports events.

Do not be turned off by triathlons that are organized primarily or solely for beginners, often called "newbies" by veteran triathletes. If you are a beginner, that's the kind of race you should look for.

Sprint to Success

An Olympic-distance triathlon will always be the same: swim of 1.5 kilometers (.93 miles), 40K bike ride (24.8 miles), and a 10K run (6.2 miles). The Ironman Triathlon consists of a 2.4-mile swim, 112-mile bike ride, and a 26.2-mile run. If you are a beginner, don't even think about the Ironman or its cousin, the Half Ironman, at this point.

By contrast, the so-called "sprint distance" is not standardized and can feature a swim as short as 300 yards, but more and more organizers of sprint triathlons are choosing a half mile (750 meters) for the swim, 12 miles (20K) for the bicycle ride, and a 5K (3.1 miles) run. These distances are doable for just about anyone with ten to twelve weeks to train and the will to devote to it. These are the races first-time triathletes should target.

The Swim's the Thing

As you begin planning for your first triathlon and reviewing the various races in your area, focus on the length of the swim. For most new triathletes, the swim competition will be the most difficult segment. The shorter the swim portion of the race, the greater the chance that your first venture into this new world will be a positive experience.

A "sprint" triathlon does not meant participants have to go all out in the race. It's just the triathlon world's way of indicating a race with comparatively short distances.

A good way to determine whether you can handle a half-mile swim in a triathlon is to test yourself in a pool. Visit your health club and see if you can swim without stopping for twenty to thirty minutes. If you can do it or come close, you are on your way.

It is important to keep in mind that no matter how well your swim training went in the pool, when you start the race you will find yourself in an entirely different environment as you compete for space in the water and try to avoid other swimmers.

The key point is this: if you get in trouble in the cycling or run portion of the race, you can stop and deal with your problem, walking for a stretch or coasting on your bike. In fact, if you have problems in the third phase (running), you can walk in if you must. You will do what you must to avoid having to quit.

Once you're in the water, however, your options for dealing with trouble are severely limited. That's not to say that triathlon organizers don't take safety precautions. They do. The umbrella organization—USA Triathlon—is very safety oriented, and no one can participate in a triathlon without the requisite insurance. Even considering how committed to safety everyone will be, if you have difficulty in the swim and have to be pulled out of the water into a boat by one of the course monitors, your race is over.

Close to Home or Long Distance?

The triathlon season is generally guided by the weather (cold is not good), so the season in most areas runs from April through September. If you live in a relatively populous area, there are probably a variety of triathlons in your city or pretty close to you. Most triathlons take place in parks because of the need for a body of water and the space to set up cycling and run courses. For ease of managing the whole experience, staying close to home will probably work better for you as you plan your first triathlon.

FACT

USA Triathlon, the national umbrella organization for triathlons, lists nearly 500 triathlon clubs as USAT members. As expected, there is a concentration in Sun Belt states such as California, Texas, and Florida, but there is heavy representation in several states above the Mason-Dixon Line as well.

Training Buddies

One major reason for setting your sights on a hometown race is that it will allow you to train with local athletes who are also planning for that triathlon. If you are lucky enough to fall in with a group of beginners training for the same race, you will share the camaraderie and excitement of the training. It will make the whole experience seem much less daunting.

If you select an out-of-town competition, you might not find training partners who are on your schedule. Of course, many triathlons take place in resort areas—there are lots of them in Florida, for example. You might consider planning a family vacation around your big race. That could get the family invested in your training, which could be a big factor in how well your training goes.

Psychological Boosts

A major benefit of training with others, especially those of more or less equal ability and experience, is that socializing while running or biking decreases the perceived effort significantly, meaning a better attitude toward workouts and more effective training.

Further, if it's just you scheduled to get in a 4-mile run at 5:30 A.M., you might swat that alarm clock and roll over for a bit more sleep. If you are meeting a couple of friends at the park for that early-morning tempo session, you are much more likely to keep to your schedule. Training buddies can be motivators.

If there is a triathlon club in your area, chances are the organization has a beginners' program. This is one way to find training partners, who can have a huge influence on the outcome of your training. Many cycling and running stores organize group activities, another way to meet potential training friends.

Examining Course Details

If at all possible, scope out the racecourses for your first triathlon. This is another reason to select a triathlon close to home, but larger races will have websites with detailed descriptions of every aspect of the race.

Runners will tell you that once they have traversed a course a couple of times, it seems shorter. It sounds strange, but it's true. If you know certain landmarks on a 10K course you are running, you can break the distance up into smaller segments. The process of running from one segment to the next seems to shorten the distance. It's a mind game, to be sure, but getting your head right is essential to successful competition. Naturally, the same is true of the cycling course.

See for Yourself

If you have selected a triathlon in your city or nearby, make it a point to find out as much as possible about the courses. Invest some time and drive out for an in-person look. In the case of a hometown triathlon, you might even be able to do some training runs or bike rides on the courses that will be used. Knowing the courses like the back of your hand will give you an advantage. It won't necessarily mean you are going to win, but it will greatly increase the chances that you will have a good experience your first time out.

Every race has course details available in registration literature or online. It will not be as easy to visit and practice on the swim portion of the triathlon, mainly because the course markers are rarely laid out more than a day or two in advance. Still, it cannot hurt for you to have a look at the body of water in which you will be swimming. The more you know about the courses, the more relaxed and confident you will be on race day.

QUESTION?

Has anyone ever organized a triathlon indoors?
It's not unusual for a health club to sponsor an indoor triathlon. The swim takes place in the facility's pool, the bike portion is recorded on a stationary cycle, and the run can be on an indoor track or a treadmill.

Trouble Spots

Another benefit of checking out your triathlon courses is that you can become aware of potential danger zones. Most race directors try to have physical defects in the road fixed before the race, but there may be spots on the bike course, such as a tight curve, that pose potential hazards. It also helps to know if there are any significant hills. You will want to find out whether the road will be closed to regular traffic or if the bikers will be sharing it with cars and trucks. There will be barriers, usually traffic cones, to keep the motorized vehicles from interacting with the cyclists, but it can't hurt for you to know all the conditions of the cycling segment.

No Surprises

It's not unheard of for riders to encounter other problems, such as aggressive dogs, on their courses. If you do nothing more than drive the course in your car, you may discover something better known ahead of time than coming to you as a complete surprise during the race.

Many of the same issues are present for runners, especially regarding hills. If you know there are a couple of major hills on your run course, you can conserve your energy at the right times to be ready for them. The fewer the number of unknowns, the better your race will go.

Other Options: Relay or Duathlon

The triathlon is not the only multisport event out there for those who are looking to expand their athletic horizons. If you don't feel you can get up to speed in all three sports in time, or if you prefer to test the proverbial water one toe at a time, try to participate in the triathlon on a relay team. Pick the part of the race you feel confident in doing and get a couple of teammates who can do the other disciplines. In other words, if you feel that you can handle the run with no problem, try to find a swimmer and a biker to join you.

Luckily, you don't necessarily need two more people. A relay team can be two people: one member competes in two of the events, and the other person does one. So if you don't feel you can master the swim part of the race in the allotted training time but feel good about running and biking, try to recruit a competent swimmer.

Relay teams are common at triathlons, and they come in three flavors: men's, women's, and mixed. Some triathlons also have a master relay team category for participants forty years old and older.

Relay team members compete in the same order—swim first, then bike, then run—but they must hand off a wristband or computer chip at each transition point. As with individual competitors, the lowest time wins. It is fun to participate in a triathlon on a relay team in part because it expands the social aspect of the event for you and is very satisfying to feel that team spirit.

In the Arena

One advantage of participating in the triathlon on a relay team, especially if it is your first time to compete in such an event, is that you will experience the triathlon first hand. This could be very helpful to you in a number of ways, not the least of which will be psychological.

You won't be taking part in each race, but you will see how a triathlon works and how the veteran triathletes handle themselves and prepare for the competition. If you are competing in only one part of the race, you will have a chance to watch the others and learn something in the process. You may even see some mistakes that you can avoid in the future without having to make them yourself.

Be very careful about making your debut triathlon in an event that has an ocean swim. If the water is choppy or rolling on the day of the race, you can experience extreme disorientation. Play it safe—stick to the lakes.

You may not be competing as an individual, but when you hit the lake, the bike course, or start your run, you will be out there swimming, riding, and running with the best. That alone will boost your confidence for the time when you take on all three events by yourself.

Also, if you plan on doing all three sports in the same triathlon in the future, you will have gained the experience of one or more parts of the course in advance. You will know what to expect next time and you will be able to plan for it.

It Just Takes Two

The duathlon is a good option for an aspiring triathlete who does not feel completely confident in the swim portion of the race and doesn't want to recruit or be part of a team. In a duathlon, competitors start with a run, then hit the bicycle, followed by another run. A typical duathlon starts with a 5K run, followed by a cycling stage of 18 to 20 miles, then a second 5K run. It's not unusual for such a race to be off-road, that is, on trails.

Participating in a duathlon won't take the place of the triathlon, but it will introduce you and your body to the rigors of competing in two sports rather than just one. Also, after the cycling portion of the duathlon, you will at least get a preview of what the second two stages of the triathlon are like.

Planning for Proper Training

You are gaining an understanding of the rigors of training for a triathlon, and you realize that your life is about to undergo some significant changes. If you are single and truly unattached, charge ahead and good luck!

If you have a family, now would be the time to consider how this new regimen is going to affect them. You can avoid a lot of stress by getting your spouse—and perhaps your children—to buy into your plans. It will help if your life partner is also an athlete. That will mean there is a greater chance that your spouse will understand why you want to test yourself this way and why you want to spend so much time preparing for it. Even better, if it's just the two in the household, you might both undertake the training and enjoy it together.

QUESTION?

What if I have only twenty minutes for a run that I had scheduled for forty-five minutes?
Go ahead with your run. A twenty-minute workout beats no workout every time. Life will get in the way of your training now and then. Make the most of the time you have.

If your spouse is not into participating in athletics, explain that your new goal is important to you, and don't forget to be honest about how much time it is going to take. Explain also that on occasion you will be too tired from training to participate in some of the normal and expected family activities.

Good Timing

You can alleviate some of the pressure created by conflicts between your training needs and those of your family with clever scheduling. The more workouts you can plan for early mornings and during your lunch hours, the more time you will retain for your family during the evening. It will also help if you can find training facilities—a health club or running and biking courses—close to home, cutting down on the time you spend going to and returning from your workouts.

Don't panic or grumble if a family crisis or obligation interferes with a workout. Interruptions are inevitable and will not significantly affect your training so long as they are held to a minimum.

Don't focus so intently on your triathlon training that you forget you have a family and friends. The triathlon and training for it are supposed to be sources of good feelings, not ill will.

A thirty-minute run during your lunch break at work can be a very beneficial workout in your triathlon training. The same goes for a short swim. Both fit in with your overall plan to have easy workouts that complement more intense sessions.

It will also be beneficial if you limit your weekend workouts to one day, perhaps on Saturday morning. That leaves all day Sunday for family time. You will be able to give your spouse and children the attention they want and need, and they will feel better about losing you to your quest at other times.

CHAPTER 3

Building a Base

The foundation upon which you will build your training for your first triathlon is known as the base, which is your current fitness level. If you are attempting a triathlon with no previous experience in athletic pursuits, you will have more work to do to establish a level of fitness sufficient to give you a chance to get through the rigors of training, followed by the achievement of your objective of finishing a triathlon.

Assessing Your Fitness Level

To help you judge whether you are fit enough to attempt a triathlon it is necessary to put the issue in context. A person might be incapable of running a marathon yet able to run a 5K in twenty minutes. That individual is definitely fit.

Fortunately for those venturing into the new territory of the triathlon, the unique demands of that sport lend themselves to quantification, at least in a general sense. You can use the following to help you decide where your position is in the fitness spectrum.

In the process of trying to measure your fitness in swimming, running, and cycling, do not go all out at any point in any of the activities. Your pace in each should be vigorous and sustained but not full speed. You will tire much too quickly if you open the throttle all the way, and you will risk injury as well.

Numbers

Assuming you have some experience in athletic pursuits, you are probably in reasonably good shape to begin training for a triathlon without additional base building if you can:

- Run 3 miles in less than thirty minutes without walking.
- Ride a bicycle at a sustained pace for forty-five to sixty minutes in relative comfort or without undue exertion.
- Swim 500 to 1,000 yards in relative comfort without extended breaks.

As a test, try each of these activities. For the run, find a level surface with few turns—a mile and a half out and back would be ideal—and try to avoid running in hot weather. That will exacerbate any natural fatigue you might feel. If at any point you become uncomfortable, stop and take note of how far you have run. For example, if you run out of gas at the 2-mile mark on your run, you can figure you are about two-thirds of the way to making the grade in that discipline.

For your bike test, try to find a long stretch of road with a wide shoulder. If your community has streets with bike lanes, that would be an ideal venue for your road test. As with the run, look for a level surface.

Try to maintain an even pace without coasting. If it is feasible, have a friend or family member follow along in a car so that if your ride becomes difficult you can stop (noting your distance), load your bike, and return home without undue stress.

FACT

Swimming pools where athletes train are basically the same size, and most are 25 yards long. A mile is 1,760 yards, so to do a 1-mile swim you would have to swim from one end of the pool to the other and back again thirty-five times.

The swim test is less complicated than the other two. Simply get into the pool and see if you can go 500 or 1,000 yards with few or no rest breaks. It is okay to take a breather for a few seconds after each length, but to have a fair test you should try to keep the breaks to a minimum.

Don't worry if you make it only half way in one or more of the activities. Not being able to meet the standards laid out here does not mean you should scrap your plans for a triathlon. In fact, you can use the data you collect from these tests to measure your progress as you train.

Starting Out with Little or No Experience

If you have decided to give the triathlon a whirl with little or no background in athletic competition, congratulations on your decision to abandon your sedentary lifestyle. You are about to embark on a journey that could improve and extend your life. People who exercise regularly find it easier to maintain a healthy weight and good blood pressure. They sleep better, live longer, are sick less often, and are more productive at work. Now that you're off the couch, if that's where you're coming from, there are some things you need to know about getting started with your training.

What's Up, Doc?

If you are new to the whole athletic scene, make an appointment to visit your family physician. Discuss your plans and let your doctor check you out thoroughly to make sure you are ready for the physical exertion you will experience in your training and in the race.

If you are lucky, your physician will know something about athletics, perhaps even be a participant, and will be more attuned to what to look for in checking you out. The key is to be sure that there are no surprises waiting for you in this new activity.

Slow and Steady

If you are relatively new to athletic pursuits, you must understand that it will take your body some time to adjust to the new stresses you will be putting on it. Especially where running is concerned, your muscles and tendons will not used to the strain they are about to experience. Of the three sports you will be undertaking, the run will be the one with which you must use the most caution.

Do not be alarmed if you experience muscle soreness at the outset of your triathlon training. That is normal as your muscles and tendons adapt to the strain of new activity. You can also expect an increase in fatigue, and you might require a bit more sleep to cope.

Be a Tortoise

If you are brand new to physical activity or returning after a long period of little or no exercise, you must start slowly. Especially with running, you should follow a beginner's plan as outlined in the next section. You might find such a regimen boring and unnecessary. You might find yourself wanting to break into a sprint at times, but taking it easy will prevent injuries that could end your quest for triathlon glory before you even get started. No matter how confident you are that you can conquer the run without problems, you should follow a plan to ease into the new activity.

QUESTION?

Why do I have to have running shoes for my training? Won't any sneakers do?
Good running shoes are made specifically for the way your feet interact with the ground. They come in different designs to cater to a variety of runner profiles, including large runners and those with different arches (from high to low). Running in shoes not designed for the sport is asking for big trouble.

Walk and Run

If you are an inexperienced runner, don't simply charge out the door and run at full speed until exhaustion takes over, which will happen usually very quickly. Start off slowly with a minimum of two weeks in a combination of running and walking, alternating a couple of minutes of each in sessions of no more than twenty minutes.

As you go, you can build from twenty minutes, working up to running for longer stretches and with less walking. Your body will tell you when you can increase the time and distance. The key is to gradually introduce your muscles, bones, and tendons to the stresses of running.

Be Safe: Don't Do Too Much Too Soon

You have just completed your first run of a mile without walking. You're a bit tired, but you feel great. You feel confident. You start thinking that if one mile is good, why not three or four, or more?

Be careful—you are about to fall into a trap that is common for novice athletes, especially those new to running. More at this point is not necessarily better, and it's important for you to stick to your program.

Suppose after your successful run of 1 mile you decide to go 3 miles on your next run. Perhaps your 20-mile bike ride was a breeze, so you decide to try and ride 40 miles next time. Will these actions advance your training to a degree commensurate with the increases?

They will not. You might get through that run or cycling session on adrenaline and determination—some might call it stubbornness—but the extra strain will not be beneficial. A more likely result of your folly is that you will hurt yourself, which will retard your progress instead of advancing it.

FACT

Unless you have some really good genes, expect the gains from your training to be gradual. Two of your major assets as you work toward your goal of triathlon readiness will be patience and the discipline to stay with your plan.

It is perfectly normal for you to want to do more when things are going well. You are discovering how exciting it can be to test yourself and succeed, and you can't wait for your next workout. In the excitement of the whole experience, it's easy to forget that you can do more harm than good by overdoing it.

Swimming does not produce the impact on your body that running and, to a lesser degree, biking can, but you can overdo it in the pool as well. Restraint is the key word here.

Wanting More

A major reason that new athletes overtrain is that they don't see progress fast enough. Even veterans can fall into that trap, and the resulting additional stress only adds to the negative energy that hampers training even more.

As you get into your training, it may seem at times that you have stayed at a certain level for a long time. Perhaps your goal is to be able to run a mile in eight minutes, and you just can't seem to cover the distance much faster than nine minutes. Is the solution to run twice as much or do your workouts twice as fast? No, and the likely results of overdoing it have already been covered.

It is normal for your training to progress in plateaus. You may be surprised and a bit chagrined at the time it takes you to go from one level to the next. It is worth noting that even the elite triathletes spend years progressing from level to level. Don't be discouraged if you feel that your progress is slower than it should be. Wait for the breakthroughs. They will come.

ALERT!

The symptoms of overtraining are easy to spot. The principal signs of overdoing it are an elevated heart rate, excessive muscle soreness, chronic fatigue, difficulty sleeping, loss of motivation (translation: burnout), and increased susceptibility to illness, especially colds. Any or all of these symptoms can indicate overtraining.

One way to assure that your training progresses is to get adequate rest. This is especially important after an intense workout. Your body becomes stronger in the process of rebuilding muscles that have been broken down by the stresses of training. The rebuilding process occurs best when the body is at rest. If you never give your muscles a break, they will not rebuild efficiently. The results can be injury and burnout—or both.

A good buffer for muscle soreness is swimming. It is a low-impact activity that you can do with a lower heart rate. Swimming is a great way to flush toxins such as lactic acid from your system the day after an intense running or cycling workout.

Improving Your Weak Areas

The majority of new triathletes come to the sport as runners, and it's not uncommon for bikers to make the transition to multisport competitions. A much smaller percentage of beginners have only swimming as their athletic backgrounds, so that aspect of the triathlon is likely to provide the greatest challenge to most new competitors.

Being a poor or below-average swimmer does not have to mean you should take on some other challenge. There are ways to get yourself to the point where you feel the swim segment won't be your undoing, and with proper assistance, you can even make it a strong point.

ALERT!

Few people instinctively know the right way to swim. In that sport, technique is everything. The best way to get better as a swimmer is by enlisting the aid of a coach. A coach often works with a group, watching each swimmer in turn and offering tips for better technique and form. Fortunately, most facilities with big pools also have programs that include coaches as part of their master swim classes.

As a runner, you train yourself to move in short steps with quick foot turn-over. Long strides are inefficient and waste energy. A good rule of thumb for running is about 180 steps per minute.

In the pool, your goal is a long stroke that carries you a greater distance. At the start of a triathlon, you might see a group of twenty-five to thirty expert swimmers seemingly in a frantic scramble, thrashing about as they try to get ahead. Once they settle down, however, the strokes are long and smooth, not short and choppy. They literally glide through the water. Good swimmers don't stay in the flailing mode for more than a few seconds.

Repetition, Repetition

If swimming is your weakest area and you have the time leading up to the triathlon season, hit the pool five days a week, even if it's just for short workouts, say twenty or thirty minutes at a time. You don't want to do that much swimming when you are in full triathlon training, but the repetition will make you feel more confident where you need that feeling the most and leave you better prepared to take on your new challenge.

Rolling Along

If you feel least comfortable in the cycling part of the triathlon, you can gain confidence with training on hills. Riding your bicycle on hills is similar to weight training, and you don't want to do a lot of that during the triathlon season. As with running, hill workouts add a lot of leg strength, which you need in both sports.

If you haven't done a lot of riding, you may be surprised at how tough it is to negotiate a hill on a bicycle. With each workout, however, it will get easier, and your confidence will grow.

As with training for any sport or endeavor, there will be days when things just don't go well: everything seems to be a struggle, or fatigue overtakes you sooner than you expected. You can't let these minor setbacks get you down. Learning to shrug off the bad workouts instead of obsessing about them is part of your growth as an athlete.

Proper Training Venues

Now that you have committed to a regimen of training and have been cleared by your physician to participate, your next step is to find the right places to do your workouts. The swim part is easy. You have to find a pool long enough to swim your laps. With rare exceptions, the pool in your back-yard won't be 25 yards long, which is what you need.

That leaves you with the health club or fitness center. Most of them have pools and, even better, masters swimming programs. Fortunately, the swimming programs are not terribly expensive, usually $25 to $30 per month, and the costs include a coach. You will find out in Chapter 8 how important a swim coach can be.

A typical masters swim program takes place in the early morning. You may grumble about having to get out of bed before dawn during the week, but on the plus side, you will get one of your triathlon training workouts out of the way before you head for work.

Another plus for joining a masters swim program at a health club is that it probably will have a lot of the equipment you will need for your swim workouts—buoys and kickboards, for example—so you won't have to buy them yourself. Some may have fins, but don't count on it. Plan to buy your own.

If you are a college student, check to see if your school has an indoor pool and a swimming program. It's likely the answer is yes.

Run for It

You will have lots of options when it comes to the venues for your running workouts. In a pinch, of course, your neighborhood probably qualifies so long as you don't live on a heavily traveled street. You can map out specific distances relatively easily so that, if you are pressed for time, you can throw on your running clothes, head out the door, and complete your workout without having to think about it too much.

If you have access to a lake, you can consider doing some of your swimming workouts there, but the vast majority of your swim training should be in a pool as part of an organized program. Pool workouts are safer and more productive because nearly all of them are done under the supervision of a coach.

If your neighborhood streets are composed of concrete, use that option only if you are desperate and only for a very short distance. Concrete is the worst surface for running you are likely to encounter (steel is harder than concrete, but you would encounter that surface only on a ship). The admonition to avoid concrete applies equally to sidewalks, of course. They are almost always concrete.

Concrete is ten times harder than asphalt or macadam. If you consider that the impact of one stride can be up to six times your body weight, you are courting injury in a big way if you do more than an occasional, very short, run on concrete. Stick to a track, dirt, or asphalt.

The best surface you will probably find for running will be a track. There may be one available to you at your local high school or college. A track is typically an oval of 400 meters, so four loops would be a mile. The track surface is soft, with good traction, and is ideal for speed workouts.

If you are doing a long run, however, it can be very boring to go around and around in a circle on a track. For longer runs, the best surface will be a trail. The dirt surface is much easier on the legs and joints than even asphalt. A trail will almost always be more scenic and peaceful than a city street, and you don't usually have to watch out for cars and trucks.

ALERT!

Trail running is enjoyable because of the scenery and the forgiving surface, but there are caveats: Many trails have tree roots and stumps that can send you flying if you don't watch out for them. There may also be insects or wild animals to deal with. Just be aware that it's a lot different from road running.

Your pace will be slower on a trail because of all that you have to watch out for, and there can be a lot of zigging and zagging on your course, but the workout will be better because it's a bit more difficult.

Your main concern will be finding safe places to run, including at least one venue with some hills. Hill workouts strengthen the legs and are absolutely necessary if your triathlon run includes hills.

Pedal Mettle

When selecting a course for your cycling workouts, safety is the number one concern. Consult your local bicycle shop for information on riding courses. The bike shop owners will know several, and they will probably have some organized rides you can take part in as well.

When searching on your own, look for wide roads without heavy traffic. In many areas, roads and city streets have bike lanes. At the very least, look for wide roads with good-sized shoulders or breakdown lanes. Avoid two-lane roads with no shoulders.

Some cities have greenways—paths set aside exclusively for runners, walkers, and bikers. Check to see if there is one in your area. Many communities have also made running and biking paths out of abandoned rail beds. These are ideal for running and cycling.

On days when the weather interferes with your bike training, you can get a good workout on a stationary bike at your fitness center or at home. All stationary bikes indicate mileage and calories burned, and many have programs that simulate hills and other variables. It's not exactly the same as your regular ride, but it's a great alternative when it's raining outside or if the roads are iced over.

Another indoor option is a fluid trainer, a stationary platform that your bike sits on that allows the rear wheel to rotate as you pedal. You can adjust the resistance as you go to simulate a variable terrain.

Do your bicycle training in group rides as often as possible. Besides being more enjoyable because of the social aspect, a group ride is safer. For example, a group of fifteen to twenty cyclists is easier for drivers to see than one or two on their own. When it comes to cycle training, there really is safety in numbers.

Developing a Training Schedule You Can Stick to

It will help a lot if you can settle on a regular schedule and get into a routine. For example, you could schedule your swim workouts for Monday, Wednesday, and Friday, with bike and/or run on Tuesday and Thursday, and have an extended workout such as a long run on Saturday. Your rest day would be Sunday.

Naturally, the availability of some elements of your training will dictate how you schedule others. For example, you might need to fix your training schedule around the swim classes, the one thing you probably won't be able to control.

Do the Math

The key to figuring out a schedule is to add up all the time your training will take during the week and see how that fits in with your life. The ideal weekly training regimen would be three swim workouts, two short runs and two short bike rides, and a longer ride and run on Saturday. That gives you three workouts at each sport during your typical training week, including the extended session on the weekend. During the week, you can do the rides and runs together or separately, whichever fits your schedule better.

For many people, three of each during the week won't be possible, and it may be more realistic to do two of each with a possible third swim if that is your weakest sport. Here's how to figure the time involved for two runs and two rides plus three swims during the week.

You can get a good workout with a 3-mile run, and at a normal pace that's about thirty minutes, probably a bit less for most. Unless you are running in your neighborhood, you will spend perhaps twenty minutes each way going to and from your run. That's an hour and ten minutes.

Your swim workouts should be thirty to forty-five minutes. Giving yourself twenty minutes each way going and coming, that's another hour and ten minutes to an hour and twenty-five minutes.

Except for biking in your own neighborhood, the cycle workouts will take a bit longer because you will be racking your bike before you leave and after your workout. Add another ten minutes. If you ride for an hour during the week, that's nearly two hours for the bike workout.

You can combine the bike and run workouts by riding for an hour and following that with a thirty-minute run. In fact, that's a good workout that will help you prepare for the real action of the triathlon. You should do this workout, called a "brick," at least once a week when you start out, moving to twice a week when you get used to the training regimen. Adding it up, then:

- Three swim workouts at one hour and ten minutes—or three hours and thirty minutes (includes travel time of twenty minutes each way) for the week
- Two bicycle-run workouts at two hours and twenty minutes each (including travel time)—or four hours and forty minutes
- Total training time Monday through Friday: eight hours and ten minutes

That does not count whatever you do on the weekend, which will almost certainly be at least two hours and likely more.

You may need to try this schedule for a couple of weeks to see if you can manage it. Do not be afraid to make adjustments, possibly cutting out one of the swim workouts or shortening your bike workout a bit.

Also, remember that life is going to give you some rest days, be it family obligations, emergencies, or the weather. Do not panic over lost workouts, and don't feel your training is going south because you had to miss a workout. That does nothing but add stress to something that you are supposed to be enjoying.

QUESTION?

If I become ill while I'm training, is it okay to just keep going?
It depends in large measure on the illness. You can probably train through a mild cold, but if you have fever, forget training until the fever is gone. You'll only make yourself sicker and end up taking more time off.

The Advantages of Group Training

Triathlon training is work, but there is no rule that says it can't be fun. You are much more likely to really enjoy the hard work if you schedule as many of your workouts as possible in group settings.

Many of your swim workouts will be in masters swim classes, so those will naturally be in groups. Interaction is more difficult because of the way the swims go, but you can still make friends and enjoy some postworkout camaraderie. If you are in a lane with several swimmers, your workout will probably be better as you strive to keep the person behind you from catching up.

Togetherness

Group runs and cycling sessions offer many advantages, including the very important aspect of safety. When you are biking in a group, you are much less likely to have an unpleasant interaction with a car or truck. Bikers who are hit in traffic are almost always alone.

The social aspect of group runs and rides can be very important. It's not unusual for a group to finish a ride or a run and then head for the coffee house or pub for some relaxation. If this is common for your group, you will look forward to the training sessions rather than dreading them, a major plus for your outlook on the whole process.

FACT

The best way to find out about the triathlons or other events you are considering is to ask someone who has been there, done that. If you train regularly with a group, it's likely someone has participated in a triathlon you are considering. Ask for an unbiased review to see if you want to go through with your plans.

Motivators

Runners and bikers tend to gather in groups of similar abilities, but there will always be one or two who push it just a bit. That can mean slightly more intense and more effective workouts.

On the other hand, if you are having a bad day and are lagging behind, there will usually be someone who will hang with you. That's a big morale booster.

A key element to any successful training program is rest, and your schedule should incorporate rest weeks. That doesn't mean no training. You can have an active rest period by following three weeks of regular training with a week of significantly less intense training. This will help ward off stress, injuries, and burnout.

You will often get energy from the group that can make the difference between a poor session and a productive workout. Most cities of reasonable size will have running, biking, and triathlon clubs, and each will offer group activities. Many sports retailers, particularly running and biking shops, have group runs and rides, plus information about others.

If you train frequently with a group, you will learn from the more experienced riders and runners. You can get tips on better training or racing, and you will learn about new equipment, better nutrition, and different workouts that can add variety to your training. In the end, the top reward for training with others will be the friends you make.

When Group Training Isn't an Option

Training with a group is an excellent way to really enjoy your training. Time literally flies by when you are running or riding in a group. It will not always be possible for you to train with others, and when schedules conflict or the group session is canceled for some reason, don't dwell on the negative. Use the opportunity for training on your own to build your confidence.

You can of course, head for the health club to ride a stationary bike if your group ride fell through. Another option at the club might be a spin class, where you mount a stationary bike that uses a flywheel that requires constant pedaling so you can't coast. It's a tough but very effective workout, and you can usually just jump into a spin session at the last minute as long as there is a free bike.

ALERT!

A good way to cope with being alone on a solitary workout is to listen to music or the radio on a portable device such as an iPod. This is acceptable if you are running on a trail or in a park without vehicular traffic, but it is not safe on a city street. Never, ever, use such a device while cycling.

On a solitary run, use the time by yourself to visualize your race. See yourself coming out of the water, zooming down the road on your bicycle, and triumphantly crossing the finish line at the end of your run. Visualization is an important part of athletic success.

If you are on your own, try to find a trail or park where the scenery is attractive. Use the quietude to have an enjoyable rather than stressful workout.

CHAPTER 4

Competing in Your Twenties and Thirties

It's not important what motivates a person to undertake an athletic activity. For many sports, triathlons included, it's the participation that matters. Triathletes come in all sizes and shapes, and just about all ages. When it comes to success, a definite advantage goes to the younger athletes. They can train harder and longer with less risk of injury. And there's always that youthful enthusiasm.

When You're Just Coming Off the Couch

Not all couch potatoes are men in their fifties with beer guts and bald heads. No age group has a monopoly on inactivity. Fortunately, fitness and health have more of a cachet in recent times as study after study reveals the risks of obesity and the rewards of an active lifestyle. If you are a young person (in your twenties or thirties) coming to triathlon competition with no previous athletic experience beyond perhaps the company softball game, start with the four-week Prep for Absolute Beginners schedule in Chapter 11 before tackling the twelve-week Beginner Triathlon Training schedule.

You may be young, but you still need four weeks just to get your body used to the stress of physical activity. Your muscles and tendons, not to mention your cardiovascular system, need that amount of time to adjust to the rigors of training. If you can get through the basic running program outlined in the Prep for Absolute Beginners and feel ready for more, you can then start the Beginner Triathlon Training schedule.

A beginner's running program for the formerly sedentary should start with a ten- to twenty-minute routine consisting of two minutes of easy running, followed by two minutes of walking. Alternate the two through your first run. Gradually increase running time and decrease walking time to a comfort level during a thirty-minute run.

You will also want to start getting used to swimming. Start by just trying to make it from one end of the 25-yard pool to the other without stopping. Rest when you get to one end for as long as you need to, then swim back. Keep it up for fifteen to twenty minutes. Gradually increase your time in the pool and shorten your rest breaks.

For bikers, start with rides of twenty to thirty minutes, coasting when you need to. Your main goal is to get used to the seat and your position on the bicycle.

Reliving the Past

If you are a former high school or college athlete who has been on the couch for a number of years, you are in a vastly different situation from the aspiring triathlete who has never experienced competition. You will begin triathlon training confident that you can master the disciplines necessary to compete. Perhaps you will even excel. There are dangers for you, however.

Perhaps you ran a twenty-minute 5K in college but have been inactive for several years while you made your way up the corporate ladder or started your own business. If you begin your training with the idea that another twenty-minute 5K is right around the corner, you could be in trouble before you start.

In fact, if getting back to a fast 5K is all you're really interested in, you should probably consider just making that goal and saving the triathlon for another time. In the sense that you must also start slowly and go carefully, you are not much different from the person who has triathlon hopes but no experience at all.

Sports massage can be very beneficial to someone who is taking up a physical activity for the first time. A good massage practitioner can help alleviate soreness and increase flexibility to help prevent injury.

Former athletes must keep in mind that it will take a lot of work to regain former levels of athletic ability—if it's possible at all. Keep your focus on the big picture and the little things will take care of themselves.

Even if you were pretty hot back in college or high school, if you have been inactive for an extended period, it will be a shock to your system when you start training again. If you are young enough and train properly, you can get back to where you were, or close to it, as long as you use good judgment. It will be in your best interest to be conservative.

What to Focus on First

If you have had previous experience in competition, chances are it was as a runner or biker. That would leave swimming as your weak area, and that is where you should concentrate your initial efforts.

If you are brand new to athletics, it may be difficult for you to determine which area needs the most work. Few people know intuitively the proper ways to swim, so instruction on technique is vital to your success, possibly even your safety, during the actual competition. The biggest gap between what you know now and what you need to know will be in the swimming part of the race.

That said, each of the sports will present its own set of intangibles and mysterious elements, so the proper overall focus will be to get comfortable with the distances for each sport. You may be able to do a 5K run, but can you do it after swimming 750 meters and biking for 20 kilometers? Your goal in training should be to gain the confidence that you can complete each of the three disciplines.

Training Smart: Different Plans for Different Goals

A runner who is training to run a marathon for the first time is almost always advised that the goal should be to finish—period. Higher aspirations can wait until marathon number two or beyond.

The same is great advice for a first-time triathlete. Setting a time goal for your first triathlon is like starting a book by reading Chapter 2. You don't know how you are going to react to this brand new experience, so don't put pressure on yourself that is unnecessary.

If you decide at the finish, or perhaps a day or two later, that you really enjoyed the experience and want to do lots more triathlons, you can get to work on time goals, using your first times as a basis for comparison. Just enjoy the first one.

Remember, this is supposed to be a fun experience, and that includes the training. That's not to say you are going to be dogging it and just lollygagging through your training, but it will be less intense as you focus primarily on getting comfortable with the distances you will cover in the swim, bike, and run. The triathlete newbie will also be less concerned about missing a workout.

With a goal of completing the triathlon, you will not need to do any really intense workouts, such a speed sessions on a track. You can, however, add some speed work to any of the sports to break up the monotony of the drills. So long as you add these higher-intensity workouts judiciously and infrequently, they are unlikely to do harm. It's worth noting that just because your only goal is to finish does not mean you won't finish well in your age group. Anything in the top 50 percent would be an outstanding achievement for a first-time triathlete.

In any triathlon, there will be elements of the competition you have control over and those that you don't. You have control over your effort, your speed, and your determination to finish. You do not have control over the weather, the venue conditions, or where you place in the race. Worrying about what you cannot control only heightens your anxiety and adds undue stress.

Dial It Up

If you do have a specific goal in mind for your triathlon—perhaps you have participated before—you will be practicing to complete the distances in the time you have targeted. Of course, you will have to integrate your training to account for the fact that you will be doing three sports instead of just one, and it is highly unlikely that you will be able to train under the actual triathlon conditions (swim, bike, and run all in one session).

You can, however, train to run the triathlon distance at your goal time after biking the triathlon distance. In fact, the bike-run session is a recommended part of the training regimen, known as a brick. Chapter 11 contains charts of schedules for triathletes who are training with specific time goals in mind.

FACT

In triathlon-speak, a "brick" is the term for a bicycle workout followed immediately by a training run. The origin of the term is lost in the lore of the sport—there are multiple stories about how it arose—but one explanation is that a brick is what your legs feel like after the double workout.

Learning to "Read" Your Body

It is normal to have some pain while training for any competitive sport. In fact, at the start of training season, a veteran athlete looks forward to a bit of muscle soreness as a sign that the body is working its way back to a certain fitness level.

ALERT!

The pharmaceutical industry has created many pills that effectively manage pain, and these drugs are useful in many circumstances. Using a pain reliever to get through a workout when you have a serious injury will only make it worse, sending you to the sidelines, sometimes for an extended period.

Only the easiest of workouts will be pain free. The stress of pushing your muscles and tendons to another level, which is how you gain in strength and endurance, will bring some discomfort. For example, if you are doing some hill training, running or biking, it's going to hurt as you push yourself up that incline. If your swim session is focused on increasing your speed, your shoulders will be burning as you get to the end of the pool each time.

All that is normal. It is an entirely different matter when you experience unexpected or sharp pain. When that happens, the alarm bells should start going off. It is a mistake with potentially serious consequences to ignore acute pain or to train through it.

Whatever you are doing, if you feel a sharp pain, stop your activity. Walk if you are running, coast if you are biking, get to the side of the pool (or out of it) if you are swimming. Give yourself a few minutes, then resume whatever you were doing. If the pain persists, give up on that workout. With all but the most serious injuries, you can push through, ignoring the pain, but at what cost?

Pain in the hip area can be indicative of a stress fracture. Running on that kind of injury will only make it worse. You could end up on crutches for months.

QUESTION?

I don't have sharp pain, but I'm sore all the time. What does that mean?
It is likely that you are overtraining, a common problem for athletes. You should make adjustments to the intensity and/or duration of your workouts, and consider eliminating one workout a week for a couple of weeks. It won't hurt your fitness, and it will keep you fresher.

As you get into training, you will learn to distinguish between the aches that are simply strain on the muscles and tendons and the pain that is the first sign of a potentially serious injury.

Pound for Pound

By far, the triathlon sport most likely to produce injury is the run, mostly because of the pounding the body takes from the impact of each step. Runners also have IT band problems, but there are many other potentially serious injuries and chronic conditions to deal with, including runner's knee, shin splints, and plantar fasciitis. Chapter 13 has detailed information about recognizing and dealing with the most common injuries.

The most common problem for swimmers is in the shoulder area, primarily the rotator cuff. A biker can have problems with the iliotibial band, a long tendon that runs down the side of the leg from the hip to just below the knee. It helps stabilize the knee and can become inflamed from overuse and failure to stretch.

Don't Do It Yourself

When that sharp pain doesn't go away with a brief break from your activity, and when it comes back even after a couple of days off, you may be dealing with a potentially serious issue. Sometimes rest and ice will do the trick, even extra stretching in some cases. If the recommended treatments don't bring relief, your best move is to find a physician, preferably one who knows sports injuries. A sports specialist will more easily diagnose your problem and prescribe the most effective treatments. More important, a sports doctor will also detect the more serious problems that, untreated, can lead to long periods of inactivity.

Consider Plan B

Don't give up on your triathlon if you come down with an injury that keeps you from training for one of the sports. You might still be able to compete on a relay team. Joining a team will help you keep your incentive to continue the training you are able to do, and you will have the fun of participating in the triathlon.

Balancing Training with School, Family, and Career

In many ways, athletes in their twenties and thirties have more to deal with than their older counterparts. Many young triathletes will be trying to fit training into a life that already has plenty of demands—work, young children, even school.

Trying to fit triathlon training into your already-crowded schedule can add a lot of stress to your life. That's why you were advised earlier in this book to make sure you have the time to devote to this new pursuit.

There are a few tricks to help you cope with the extra demands on your time. Start with the job. Perhaps your employer will allow you to come to work thirty minutes later two or three days a week, maybe even every day. That will give you time to complete some of your workouts early in the day.

Not having to rush home after work every day and then rush to do a run or bicycle ride will relieve a lot of pressure. Most swim workouts take place in the early morning, and if you can find a running buddy who will meet you a couple of days a week, you will be able to get a lot of good training in before heading for work.

To avoid rebellion at home on the part of your children or spouse, schedule only one weekend day for triathlon training. Stay home and meet your family obligations on the other day. You need a rest period anyway, and relaxing with the family is a good way to recharge the batteries for your next workout.

Consider involving the kids in your training. For example, take them along with you for one of your runs and let them ride their bikes with you as you go. Or take them to the track and ask them to count your laps as you run, with a stop for ice cream on the way home.

You might also look for a triathlon that features two distances, including a shorter one for novice triathletes. Your spouse might be up for one of those, and there is always the option of a relay team for your loved one. You can check with the race director to see if your spouse could be added to a team. That is an ideal way to involve your partner in the event.

Many triathlons take place in vacation destinations. Sign up for one of those and plan on taking the spouse and young ones with you. That will give the whole family a vested interest in the success of your training.

If you are a college student, your schedule will be more flexible. You can book your classes to provide more time in the morning to get your training in, and chances are you will have access to a swimming pool, weight room, and track for running.

The key for everyone is to avoid obsessing about the training. Interruptions in training are going to happen, so don't panic over a missed workout or two. If you miss more than a few workouts, however, you should probably reassess your plans. Losing your entry fee will be insignificant compared to the misery of taking part in a triathlon on grossly inadequate training. Keep your perspective. If you can't get ready, wait.

CHAPTER 5

Competing in
Your Forties and Beyond

As you age, your body changes. You lose flexibility
and muscle mass. Your ligaments and tendons are
less elastic. You recover more slowly from workouts
and injuries. So what's an aging athlete to do? Give
up? Head for the couch? Don't even think about it. As
long as you train smart and have realistic goals, you
can keep on keepin' on well past forty.

Key Issues for Aging Athletes

If you have maintained an active lifestyle into your forties, no one needs to tell you that your body has been changing over time. You have experienced it. You know that a day off between workouts is essential to prevent injury. You know that when you do hurt yourself, it takes longer to recover. Things hurt that never used to.

You haven't lost your motivation to stay fit and compete, but you know that you can't train the way you once did. You would rather slow it down and be conservative than end up sitting out a racing season because you overdid it and injured yourself.

New athletes who are younger were cautioned earlier in this book to go easy, especially at first. That applies even more to those who are trying to become athletes for the first time in their forties or beyond. No one is saying you can't do it. Just be careful.

FACT

One's VO_2 max is usually measured in terms of milliliters of oxygen per minute per kilogram of body weight. A typical club athlete has a VO_2 max of 70. For an elite athlete that number will be 90 or higher. By way of comparison, the VO_2 max for a typical thoroughbred horse is 180.

A Natural Process

There are ways to slow down the aging process, but it is unstoppable. It is just nature at work. You can fight back and stay fit if you don't try to do at forty-five what came easy to you at twenty-five.

One of the first things to change in your body is its capacity for processing oxygen during a time of physical exertion. The measurement of how much oxygen your body can process during a specified period of exercise is expressed in terms of *VO_2 max*, which stands for maximal volume of oxygen. Your VO_2 max will have a big influence on your performance in athletic endeavors such as a triathlon.

Your maximum heart rate usually drops as you age, meaning that when you are really pushing it, the blood carrying oxygen through your system will not circulate as rapidly as it once did. This will affect how fast you can run, swim, and cycle—and it's one reason race organizers have competitions within age groups. It would not be fair to pit a fifty-year-old against a twenty-five-year-old. If the two had similar ability and training, the twenty-five-year-old would win every time.

It's Cellular

As you age, your body does not repair and regenerate cells as well as before, and there is higher free radical damage. Exercise produces free radicals, which are molecules with single unpaired electrons in the outer shells. Free radicals are blamed for damage to cells, called oxidation, another way of describing the aging process.

FACT

As the term *oxidation* implies, the process involves the interaction of oxygen with something else. When metal oxidizes, you get rust. When a slice of apple turns brown, that's oxidation. In your body, free radical production is the result of the interaction of oxygen with your tissues.

Free radicals come from your body's production and use of adenosine triphosphate, more commonly known as ATP. That substance is the immediate source of energy for muscle contraction. Without it, the muscles won't work. The body makes ATP from glycogen, the sugar that is stored in your liver and muscles. You need ATP, but it leaves free radicals behind. Dealing with them is important for everyone, and in particular for athletes. Chapter 12, focusing on nutrition, will provide you with ammunition to fight free radical damage.

Not So Strong

Another change you will experience as you age is a loss of muscle strength and power. It is for this reason that strength training is given its own chapter (Chapter 6) in this book.

You have more than 600 muscles in your body, all connected by tendons, fascia, and other tissue. Some of your muscles are fast-twitch, the ones that help you run fast. The others are slow-twitch, the muscles you use to run long distances.

Fast-twitch muscle fibers don't turn into slow-twitch fibers. Without adequate training, fast-twitch muscles simply atrophy. It is vital for an older athlete to maintain proper training to keep from losing fast-twitch muscles.

Flexibility is a key issue for older athletes, mainly because they have less of it than their younger counterparts. A tendon is the fibrous tissue that connects a muscle to a bone. A ligament runs from bone to bone. Ligaments and tendons in older athletes are less flexible and more prone to injury. Neither has a copious blood supply, so when they are injured it takes longer for them to heal.

Take It Easy

If all this sounds as though the forty-plus athlete is heading for disaster just getting out of bed, it is not intended to. These admonitions are meant to remind you that you do not have the body of a twenty-year-old any more, and you should behave accordingly. That means more days off during training season, more easy days, and fewer intense workouts.

If you make your triathlon preparation a slow and steady process, you might actually beat out some of the young Turks who went all out in their training every session and ended up injured.

Realistic Goals

As an older athlete, you have had more life experience than the younger competitors. Perhaps you are a successful businessperson, chief executive of your own company, or a partner in a law firm. You are used to winning simply by applying yourself and working hard.

Unless you have a strong background in athletics, don't expect to scale the heights in your first stab at a triathlon. All the determination you can muster will not necessarily get your new-to-athletics body in shape to win your first time out.

Set your sights on a shorter distance for your triathlon, and be happy to finish. Don't worry about where you place, and don't try to compete with the younger athletes.

Baby Steps

Don't turn your nose up at a "baby" triathlon such as a sprint distance aimed at newbies. You don't have to conquer Mount Everest on your first attempt to be successful. There is no shame in thinking small for your debut. You don't even know for sure that the three-sport event is right for you.

You can be more ambitious next time out if your first shot goes well. It's okay to dream of the Ironman Triathlon, but start with the sprint version.

As an older athlete just starting to train for a triathlon, you will enjoy your preparation more if you can find a few other aspiring athletes roughly your own age. You will relate to them better, and the training pace will be more comfortable for all of you.

Memories

If you are returning to athletics in your forties or fifties after a long layoff because of career and family issues, don't get caught in the trap of trying to regain past glory. Your body simply won't do what it once did, and perhaps you don't remember the past as well as you think you do. This thought, "The older I get, the better I was," might apply to you. Be realistic.

Basic Training

If you are a nonathlete, don't think about your first triathlon unless you can give yourself twelve weeks to get ready for it. If you don't have a good base of running and biking, make that sixteen weeks.

It is not realistic to think you can undergo the stress of the training and the race without first getting your body used to it. That process will take longer with older athletes, especially those who have not been active in years.

You are to be commended for daring to compete in a triathlon. You will enjoy the training and the actual event more if you prepare properly.

A Different Training Schedule

Whether you like it or not, if you are older than forty, you are considered an "older" athlete. There's a reason that the masters category in races starts at forty. Competitors older than fifty years old go into the grand masters group. Sounds ancient, doesn't it?

Well, forget about all that. You are what you are, and if you want to get into triathlon competition, you are going to have to go by different training rules.

You will need more time off between workouts because it takes you longer to recover. You should do more strength training to maintain the muscle mass you lose as you age. You will limit the high-intensity workouts to guard against injury. That said, you will not forsake all hard workouts.

It's in the Intervals

All older athletes need more interval training, and a triathlete in training should practice intervals in swimming, biking, and running.

An interval is a run of set duration—an hour is typical—with planned increases in speed throughout. For example, on a 400-meter track, you do a warm-up mile (four loops), then pick up your speed to high intensity, but not all out, for two loops or 800 meters. Dial it back down to a jog for the same distance, then do another 800 meters at a hard pace.

What is happening with your body is that in the hard part of the run, you are in oxygen debt and your body is burning glycogen for fuel. In the recovery part of the run, when you are jogging, your body is making an adaptive response to the workout, creating more capillaries to carry blood (and therefore oxygen) to your system. You are increasing your aerobic capacity and training your body to run hard.

This will come in handy during your triathlon, probably not your first one, but later when you are competing for an age-group prize. You will have that extra oomph needed to achieve your goal.

FACT

Interval workouts don't necessarily have to be measured in distance. You can do intervals by time as well. For example, on a one-hour run, pick up the pace to a hard (but not all out) level for ninety seconds, then slow down. It is advisable for you to start with four or five of these "pickups" and work up to ten in a one-hour session. Always follow with a slightly slower pace than the overall run for another couple of minutes.

Intervals are more important for you as an older athlete because doing the same workouts you did when you were thirty will not produce the same results now that you are forty-five. You will also want to practice intervals on your bicycle and in the pool, following roughly the same plan—a short burst followed by a slower pace.

You will be surprised at the results these workouts will produce, but use caution. Your training the day after an interval session should be easy. Complete rest on occasion is advisable.

It should also be noted that interval workouts are more important for triathletes who are training to be competitive. For first-timers or for those who just enjoy taking part, intervals are not as important, though an occasional session won't do any harm. It's good to push yourself now and then, and a schedule with nothing but easy workouts won't be very challenging or interesting.

Getting a Lift

Some of your training will be seasonal. You won't, for example, be doing intervals year round. You will surely be injured if you overdo the hard stuff.

One regimen you should follow year round is strength training. As you age, you lose muscle mass, and the best way to combat that is to hit the weight room on a regular basis. As a result, older athletes need to focus more on strength training. There are other ways to strength train, and they are covered in Chapter 6.

How to Deal with Longer Recovery Times

An older person is supposed to be wiser than an impulsive young pup. Be sure you retain that trait when it comes to your triathlon training.

After a workout, rest is how your body grows stronger. It uses the downtime to rebuild from the stresses of your training. You may feel great after a workout as the endorphins kick in, and you can't wait for the next training session. Do yourself a favor. Wait.

If you follow one hard workout with another, your body will not have a chance to rebuild damaged tissue. Eventually, it will start breaking down rather than regenerating. The bottom line will be injury. You may have to force yourself to go easy the day after an excellent workout, but common sense must rule or you will find yourself in trouble.

QUESTION?

Are there alternatives to complete rest after a hard workout?
Yes, you can engage in "active rest" the day after a vigorous workout. A typical active rest session would be an easy bike ride or a swim at low to moderate intensity. What you don't want to do at any intensity level is to run. Even an easy run can be hard on the joints and muscles and will retard your recovery.

One of the byproducts of physical activity is lactic acid, which builds up in the muscles during vigorous exercise. When you feel a burning sensation in your calf muscles and thighs, that's lactic acid. Some of it will be removed naturally, but it can build up. An active rest session, especially an easy swim, helps remove lactic acid that has accumulated.

As you train, you will increase what is known as your *lactate threshold*, the point at which your body can no longer remove lactic acid on its own. The higher the threshold, the more you can work at high intensity without feeling the effects of lactic acid in your system.

A great way to conduct an active rest day is to go to a yoga class. The stretching will be great for the muscles you have been working so hard, and it also will help with lactic acid removal. Even better, the relaxing setting will do wonders for your mood and your outlook. You will leave refreshed and ready for more training.

No training schedule is inviolable. If you don't feel good before heading out the door for a run or bike ride, just skip it. If a training session starts poorly and gets worse from there, bag it. Go home, rest, and get ready for your next workout. Write it off as just one of those days.

One final caution for older athletes: be careful about choosing your training partners. If that person is considerably younger, you could find yourself straining to keep up and moving into the danger zone, where injuries lurk.

The Effective Use of Massage Therapy

Massage therapy can be effective for an athlete of any age. It can be a lifesaver for the athlete in training at age forty or older.

The muscles and tendons that are less flexible in older athletes can be made more pliable by a good massage practitioner. Regular massages can help prevent injury and aid recovery from workouts and injuries.

As you train in any of the three sports, your muscles tighten up from the work you are making them do. It's normal. On occasion, perhaps even on a regular basis, you will need help to get them loose again. That's where massage comes in.

Sports massage can alleviate muscle strains and spasms and help flush toxins, primarily lactic acid, from your system. A massage can target a certain area or cover the whole body according to the client's needs. A good massage practitioner gets to know each client's body and can focus efforts where they are needed most.

Many elite athletes are firm believers in the value of massage therapy. During his last run at the Tour de France, Lance Armstrong had a massage every day to loosen his tight calf muscles and quadriceps. Massage helps shorten the recovery time so you can get back to your good workouts in better shape and ready for more work.

FACT

If you have never had a sports massage, you will probably be surprised by what you experience in your first. It's nothing like the gentle kneading you might undergo at a hotel or day spa. Sports massage involves deep strokes that can be intense at times. You will feel more relaxed at the end, but you might be gritting your teeth a bit while it's going on.

Different Strokes

There are two kinds of massage techniques that can be very effective for athletes. First, there is the traditional sports massage that focuses on the muscles and tendons you use in your sport. Another is called Structural Integration (SI), sometimes called Rolfing, after the creator of the technique, Ida P. Rolf.

The basic SI principle is that many problems in the body are caused by misalignment of the muscles and joints. Undergoing SI can be very intense, but many athletes swear by the process and the results of SI therapy.

It could well be worth your while to investigate both disciplines, but it would be a mistake to expect miracles from either, certainly not in one or two sessions. If you train a lot for any sport, it would behoove you to find a good massage therapist and schedule sessions at least once a month. Your body will thank you for it.

In Hot Water

A third way to relax your muscles, especially after a hard workout, is to take an Epsom salts bath. That can be very therapeutic and doesn't entail the expense of massage therapy.

Fill your bathtub with water as hot as you can stand it, then pour in two cups of Epsom salts. Swish it around before you step in to make sure the salts have diluted, then sit with your legs under the water for about twenty minutes.

ALERT!

If you decide sports massage is for you, ask around. The best practitioners will be known to the triathlon community. Some of the masseurs and masseuses will be athletes themselves. Who better to deal with your training-induced aches and pains?

Nutritional Supplements for Older Triathletes

As you age, your nutritional needs change as your body changes. As already pointed out, your body does not do as good a job of policing free radicals, which you will be producing more of as you train. That means more inflammation in your tissues and joints.

There are several supplements that can help you cope with your body's reaction to the stress of training.

The first is omega-3 fatty acid, commonly found in fish oil and flax oil. Omega-3 fatty acid is an excellent natural anti-inflammatory supplement that can be of significant benefit to older athletes.

One caution if you are considering taking fish oil capsules: if you are on blood thinners, consult your physician before using omega-3 supplements.

Cramping Your Style

Many new athletes experience problems with leg cramps, particularly in warm weather when they lose a lot of fluid. Electrolyte depletion is one of the causes of cramping. You can help prevent the onset of cramps in your workouts with supplements of calcium and magnesium, two electrolyte minerals (the others are sodium and potassium). It is a good policy to take these supplements together because magnesium helps your body absorb calcium more efficiently than if you take calcium by itself. Calcium-magnesium supplements can also help you sleep better.

The best source for omega-3 fatty acid is fish oil, but not all omega-3s are created equal. It is not unusual for fish oil to contain high levels of mercury. If the product you are considering does not specify that it is mercury free, look elsewhere for your supplement.

Fighting Back

Physical exertion produces free radicals, the bad molecules that can damage tissue and increase inflammation, the body's natural reaction to injury. The damage caused by the free radicals is known as oxidation. Any substance that combats this process is known as an antioxidant.

There are a variety of antioxidant supplements you can take that will combat free radicals. The list includes vitamins A, C, E, and B, and there are many fruits that contain antioxidant properties, blueberries being one of the stars in this area.

Nutritional supplements can be very beneficial to you as an older athlete, and it's a good idea to take them. Even better is to plan your daily meals to include plenty of fruits and vegetables, which naturally provide the vitamins and minerals you need. Eat healthy so you can swim, bike, and run hard.

Another way to combat inflammation is through proteolytic enzyme supplementation. Your body produces these enzymes naturally, but production slows down as you age. Some of the food you eat—cooked or processed meat, for example—causes the enzymes to be diverted from their main role of regulating protein function in the body. Instead, they are used to help the body digest the food.

Proteolytic enzymes work against inflammation by neutralizing biochemicals associated with the problem. Between the body's natural slow-down of enzyme production and the diversion of the enzymes for food digestion, you are losing a soldier, so to speak, in the battle against inflammation caused by free radical damage. Supplements work well in replacing those lost enzymes. You can find proteolytic enzyme supplements at any health food store.

CHAPTER 6

Strength Training

You may have seen people in your area wearing the yellow bracelets marketed by Lance Armstrong, seven-time Tour de France winner and cancer survivor. If you take a close look at one of the bracelets, you will see the motto LiveStrong. It would not be a bad idea to adopt that as your motto for your triathlon training. A stronger athlete is a better athlete—with a better chance of success.

Why Strength Training Is Important

You may think that all the swimming, riding, and running training will naturally make your muscles stronger. That's true to an extent, but much of your training will be aimed at improving your form and your endurance rather than increasing muscle strength. However, how strong you are going into your triathlon training will have a significant bearing on your success.

Stronger muscles and tendons are less likely to incur injury. They hold up better to the stresses of training and are more pliable. With stronger muscles, you can go faster or longer with the same effort. Increase the effort and the results improve even more.

Seasonal Issues

It is worth noting, by the way, that the recommendations that follow are more important for the triathlon off-season than for in season. In other words, you should do some strength training in the weeks leading up to your race, but the time to focus heavily on strength training is after the triathlon season is over. If you weight train right before triathlon season, you won't have a lot of strength issues to deal with when you start your serious race training.

FACT

Tired muscles are much more susceptible to injury. Muscles improved through strength training fatigue less easily and are less prone to injury.

Many injuries result from muscle imbalance. For example, a shin splint—a painful lower-leg injury—is often the result of an imbalance between the calf and shin muscles (tibialis anterior). Plantar fasciitis, a common malady among runners, is often caused by tight calf muscles, which also can cause Achilles tendon problems. Strength training and stretching (see Chapter 7) will correct those imbalances. The result will be more effective workouts and fewer injuries.

Joint Responsibility

All the training you have on your schedule, especially the running, will put stress on your joints, especially the hips and knees. When your muscles and tendons have been strengthened through specific workouts, your joints will be more stable. Your training will be easier and you will be much less likely to have to take time off because of injury.

Understand that even a minor injury can upset your training schedule. A more serious injury might force you to postpone your triathlon. There is no question that avoiding layoffs caused by injury will result in a more effective training schedule. Strength training will not prevent injury from trauma—a twisted ankle or wrenched knee, for example—but a stronger athlete will recover from these injuries more quickly.

Strength training includes working with weights, but it is not body building. The objective is not to have massive biceps or washboard abs. You are not aiming for the Arnold Schwarzenegger look. In fact, if you strength train properly, you will probably look leaner than before you started.

Most amateur recreational athletes neglect strength training until they get hurt. Many find out what they should have been doing all along when they end up in physical therapy and are given a set of strength-training exercises. The smart ones keep it up even after the problem is corrected.

Functional Strength Training

Functional strength training is an important part of your preparation for your triathlon. It may sound esoteric, but it is just a series of exercises that involve more than one muscle or joint and often are designed to replicate the movements you use in one or more of the three triathlon sports.

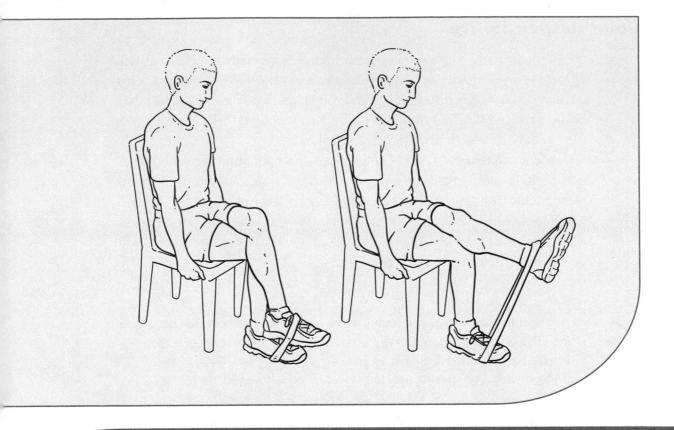

Knee Extend: Sit in a chair with your legs crossed so that your left knee is resting on your right leg. Loop an elastic band over your left ankle and under your right foot. Straighten your left knee. Return to starting position. Do two sets of twelve reps.

Your primary aim as you complete the exercises is to improve your flexibility and stability. While there may still be some weight training involved, most of the exercises recommended in this book do not require dumbbells or machines. Rather, they involve pushups, sit-ups, and squats, which provide the strength training you need without weights or machines.

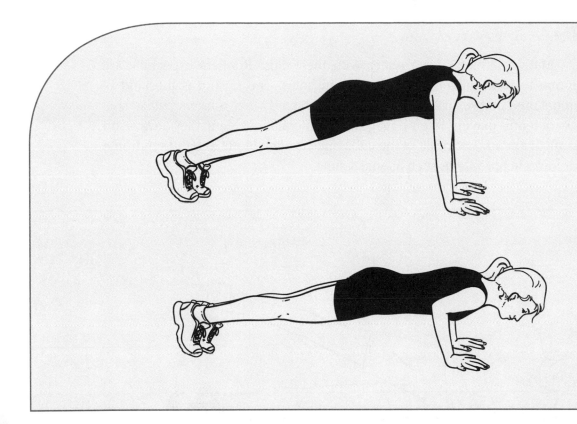

Pushups: Kneel on the floor on all fours; your hands should be directly under your shoulders. Straighten your legs, supporting your lower body weight on your toes. Engage your abdominal muscles and lower your body using your arms. Push back up through your palms. Do as many as comfort permits, building up to three sets.

QUESTION?

Can yoga help with my strength training?
Yes it can. Yoga trains the entire body and is ideal because it is a low-impact activity with great benefits. Regular participation in a yoga class can vastly improve your balance, and you will definitely reap strength benefits.

Not Hip

Many triathletes have issues with their hips. Runners especially are prone to weak gluteus medius (hip) muscles. The upshot is the kind of imbalance that results in injuries. The problem is that runners, unlike soccer or tennis players, rarely engage in any lateral movement; they always run straight ahead. The result of the imbalance is often iliotibial band syndrome or lower-leg problems such as shin splints.

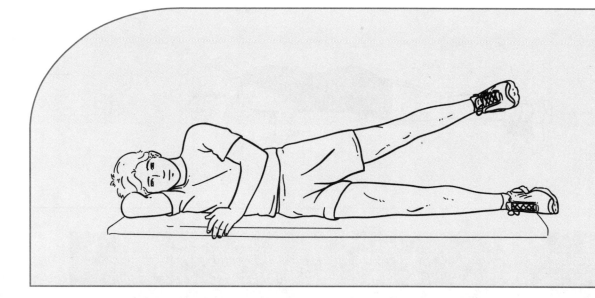

Hips: Lie on your side on the floor, legs straight and stacked on top of one another. Tighten the muscles on the front of your leg and then lift your leg eight to ten inches off the ground. Hold for two seconds and then slowly return to the start position. Repeat ten times, two sets.

Swimmers often experience problems with their rotator cuffs (shoulders) because of an imbalance between pectoral and upper back muscles. Functional strength training will address these imbalance issues and help avoid the injuries that will have you on the sidelines instead of in your race.

You can strengthen your rotator cuff by using the seated rowing machine. In the absence of a rowing machine, you can lie on each side and pull your arm up and across your body with a weight of three to five pounds. You can do the same drill standing up with a stretch band that you pull across your torso. Also, take three to five pound weights in each hand and let your arms hang at your sides. Slowly lift the weights outward from your body so that your arms are parallel to the floor.

For all exercises, do two sets of twelve repetitions three times a week.

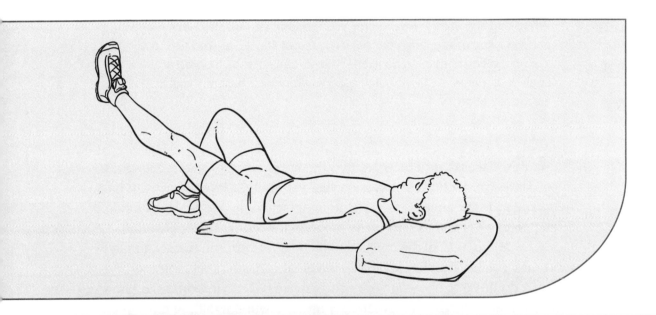

Leg Raise: Lie on your back on the floor. Bend one leg and place your foot on the floor; keep your other leg straight and locked. Tighten abdominal muscles, slowly raise locked leg eight to twelve inches, and hold for two seconds. Repeat ten times, two sets.

The Importance of a Strong Core

You may have seen ads for books or DVDs about strengthening your "core." It sounds like marketing hype, but don't be misled by your natural skepticism. The core is very important to your athletic career.

Your body's core is essentially made up of the muscles of your trunk—the area between the shoulder "girdle" and the legs. This includes, of course, your abdominal muscles.

You probably don't know it, but all body movement is initiated by the core. Everything you do comes from that core. If your core is weak, some of the force you use, especially in running, is dissipated. Exercise performed inefficiently promotes fatigue and will result in frequent injury.

When you run with a weak core, your abdominal muscles, which support your spine, sag, and your pelvis does not stay level. You tilt forward into an inefficient running position. Your stride becomes labored and you begin to struggle. A strong core keeps you running efficiently with little or no wasted effort.

All this discussion of the core and the importance of making it strong might leave you with the impression that yet another layer of activity has been added to an already-crowded training schedule. Please don't panic. Strengthening the core is part of the program for getting stronger overall. In fact, you can do most of the core-strengthening exercises in twenty minutes two times a week. The simple pushup is a great core-strengthening exercise. You can do those at home at your convenience. What's important to know is that time invested in strengthening your core will pay off big time when race day arrives.

What Muscles to Strengthen

As you embark on your strength-training program, turn your attention at the outset to the part of your body that probably needs it most—your hips. It doesn't come naturally to people to exercise muscles they rarely think about, so this part of your body is most likely to be neglected. Here is a list of muscle groups to work on:

- The glutes—the gluteus maximus (buttocks), medius (pelvis), and minimus (hips)
- Hamstrings, quadriceps, and calf muscles
- Pectorals (minor and major) and rhomboids (the two sets of muscles balance each other)
- Biceps, triceps, and deltoids

Single-Leg Step-Up for Quads: Place one foot on a five-inch step, with the knee bent. The other foot should remain on the floor. Straighten the leg on the step, lifting your body up. Repeat twenty times, one set.

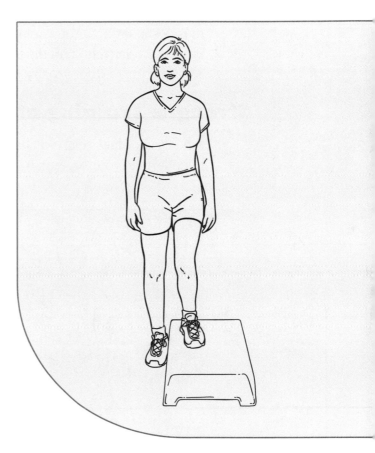

If you don't want to use weights or other exercises to strengthen your quadriceps (thigh muscles), there is an alternative. Running and riding hills is a great way to get stronger quads, and there is a side benefit to doing so. Strong quads help stabilize the knees.

These are all outside your core, but they are very important to your strengthening program. One of the best exercises you can do is the leg press. For that, you do need a machine. The leg press strengthens your quadriceps, hamstrings, and gluteus maximus—all important to your balance and stability.

That list of muscles to train might make it seem as though you will be spending hours getting stronger. Don't forget that many of the exercises train muscles in groups. You can actually get the job done with four or five exercises in a relatively short time span.

Strength Training at Home

A health or fitness club will have most or all of the equipment you will need to undertake your strength-training program, but not everyone can afford to

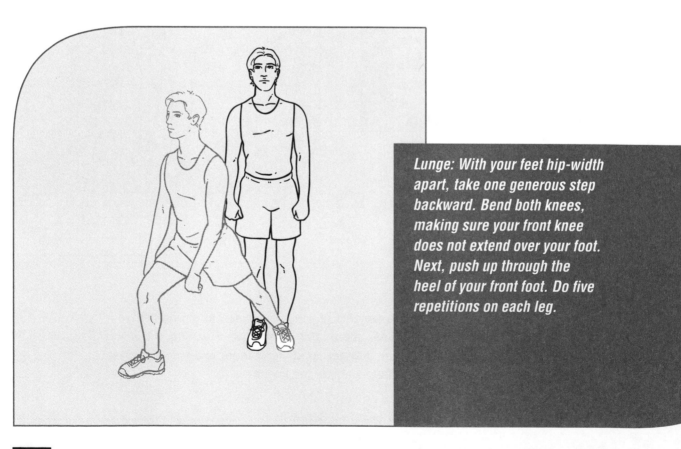

Lunge: With your feet hip-width apart, take one generous step backward. Bend both knees, making sure your front knee does not extend over your foot. Next, push up through the heel of your front foot. Do five repetitions on each leg.

pay the dues for a club. For others, there won't be a club that is convenient, and when you are trying to deal with an already hectic training schedule, inconvenient will translate to nonexistent.

That leaves you the choice of not trying to increase your strength or doing it at home. The latter option is highly recommended, so you should consider a couple of pieces of equipment that will help you accomplish your strength goals in the comfort of your home.

The first is a fitness ball. It is a very simple tool, but it can greatly assist you in achieving your strength-training objectives of increasing your stability, balance, and core strength. You can get one at your local sporting goods store for $20 to $25. The other is a stretch band, which you can acquire for about $15.

Ball Pushups: While kneeling on the floor, place the ball under your stomach. Roll forward on the ball, placing your hands on the ground for support, until the ball is under your shins. Your body should look like a straight plank. Raise buttocks to form an inverted V. Slowly lower back to the plank position. Do twelve reps, build to three sets.

Having a Ball

You will find that your fitness ball will help you with several different workouts that provide important strength benefits. One of the best uses of your fitness ball will be to assist you with pushups.

Put your ball in the middle of the floor and assume the pushup position with your legs atop the ball. Pushups are much more difficult in this position, so don't plan on doing your usual number the first time you try this. With your legs up on the ball, you are working your abdominal muscles a lot more than with standard pushups, and you are also working the lower half of your body as you fight to maintain balance in that position.

Fitness ball pushups are among the best exercises you can do for your strength training.

Over and Back

Another good workout with your fitness ball is to lie on your back on the floor, putting the ball between your feet. Raise the ball up to the point that you can take it with your hands. Take the ball from between your feet and lower it to the floor behind your head. Then take the ball and raise it up again and take hold of it with your feet, lowering it to the floor. Start slowly with this exercise, perhaps four repetitions initially. Strive to be able to complete three sets of twelve repetitions. This will strengthen your abs and your shoulders.

FACT

A typical fitness ball is made of elastic rubber and comes in different sizes, from fourteen inches to thirty-four inches in diameter when fully inflated. Unless you are very large or very small, you will probably choose a ball twenty-six inches in diameter. These should not be confused with medicine balls, which are smaller but considerably heavier (up to twenty-five pounds).

Here's another fitness ball workout. Assume pushup position, with your feet up on the ball behind you. Instead of doing a pushup, however, elevate your buttocks to form an inverted or upside-down V with your body. Return

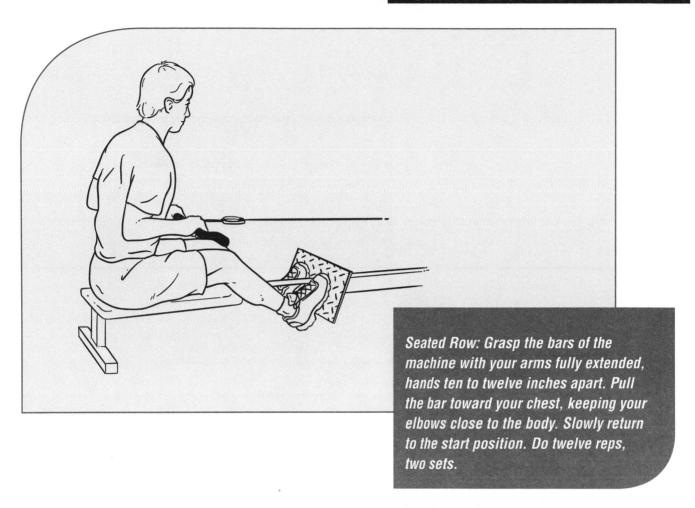

Seated Row: Grasp the bars of the machine with your arms fully extended, hands ten to twelve inches apart. Pull the bar toward your chest, keeping your elbows close to the body. Slowly return to the start position. Do twelve reps, two sets.

to pushup position. Start slowly with this exercise and try to work up to being able to do three sets of twelve repetitions.

Finally, try the hamstring curl. Lie on your back on the floor with your feet on top of the ball. Bend your knees and move the ball back toward your buttocks. Rest a second, and, using your legs, return the ball to its original position. Start slowly with this exercise and work up to two sets of twelve repetitions. This is a very good exercise for strengthening the hamstrings.

Stretching It

The stretch band can also help you with your workouts. One of the best exercises is to hook the band over your feet as you sit on the floor, then pull

Lat Pull: Open a door and stand facing the edge of it so you can have one hand on either side. Place the band over the top of the door so that equal sections hang down on both sides. Grasp both ends of the band and pull down. Do twelve reps, two sets.

straight back on the band as though you are rowing. In fact, the exercise is meant to replicate the seated rowing machine you find at health clubs. Be sure to keep your back straight, and when you pull back, make sure your elbows go behind your back.

QUESTION?

What is a stretch band?
Stretch bands come in different styles, some with handles and some without. The bands with handles are the easiest to use. The bands are typically rubber tubing that offer resistance, with handles on each end of the band for ease of use.

You can also hang the stretch bands over a door and do "chops," or lat pulls pulling the band downward at an angle. Another option is to attach the band to something on the floor and do your chops in an upward direction. With each stretch band exercise, work up to two sets of twelve repetitions.

Just Plain

You don't always need a prop to accomplish good strength training at home. You can do some workouts without any aids or tools.

One of the best is the squat. Start without any weights, then later add a couple of fifteen-pound hand weights to increase the effort required. Start in a standing position and squat to the position you usually see sumo wrestlers

Leg Squat: Stand near a wall and place one hand on it for support. Bend one leg up and hold it, supporting your weight on the other leg. Bend the support leg to lower yourself until your knee is in a ninety-degree angle. Stand back up. Do ten reps each leg, two sets.

assume. You should not lower yourself to the position of a baseball catcher. This is not good for the knees.

At the point where you are using weights, you may squat to a position that allows you to touch the weights on the floor. Work up to two sets of ten repetitions.

Another effective exercise you can do without equipment is the one-legged squat. That sounds very difficult, but you are not actually squatting. Do it this way: Balance on one leg. As you hold the other leg just slightly above the ground, reach to the other leg with the opposite arm—left arm to the right leg, and vice versa—and touch the foot that is on the ground. Do not extend the leg. Keep it parallel to the leg that is on the ground.

This exercise is very good for promoting stability and strength. Start with one set of ten repetitions on each leg and work up to two or three sets.

How Often to Strength Train

As mentioned previously, your really serious strength training should take place when you are not actively training for a triathlon. In the off-season, especially when the weather makes outdoor training difficult or impossible, strength training will help keep you occupied and maintain your fitness so that you don't start from ground zero when the new triathlon season arrives.

It's normal to want to do more than twenty or thirty minutes of strength training because you feel that you "didn't really do that much" for only a short period. The fact that you went through your workout without getting your heart rate way up can fool you into thinking you didn't do much. Have faith that the short strength workout did its job. Don't overdo it.

During triathlon season, you should limit your workouts to no more than twenty to thirty minutes, twice a week at most. It's okay to go to the gym for an hour or more, so long as a good part of that is socializing with your workout buddies and not passing the limit in pumping iron or whatever strength training you might have scheduled.

As the triathlon nears, cut back on your strength training. If you are on a twelve-week training schedule, cut your strength training in half in week eleven and skip it altogether in the week leading up to your race. Your strength workouts should follow your other triathlon training and should be the last or only workout of the day.

Strength training breaks down your muscles so that when they rebuild they come back stronger. In essence, your body is saying, "Hey, what we did today was hard. We need more strength to deal with this stress next time." The bottom line is that your body then adapts so that it can meet the challenge next time. After a hard strength workout, this process takes about two days.

That means that if you do a strength workout before you go running, you haven't given your muscles time to recover, and your run will suffer as a result. The same applies, of course, to swims and rides. Further, there is a tendency after a poor training session to push it in the next one to make up. This can result in a spiral of bad workouts that results in burnout or, worse, serious injury.

Using a Personal Trainer

It's not uncommon in the world of athletics for an aspiring competitor to look for professional help. For example, there are legions of golf and tennis pros out there trying to help their clients stay in the fairway or win that club tennis championship.

ALERT!

Most health clubs have personal trainers on staff or as contractors. If you are a member of the club, you may get a break on the price. If not, it is often up to you and the trainer to figure out a cost based on your goal and the time it will take to help you achieve it.

A personal trainer (PT) is a pro who trains all types of people, from aspiring athletes to fifty-year-old grandmothers. Some specialize while others are jacks of all sports, so to speak. What they all have in common, or should have, is the ability to tailor a fitness or training regimen specifically to the individual being trained.

A good personal trainer will first assess your fitness level and test you to see where your weak spots are. The PT will then design a training program to correct any deficiencies and prepare you for your specific goal.

Most personal trainers are athletes, so it is likely your PT will know what you need to achieve what you want in at least a couple of the triathlon sports. If you are really lucky, your trainer will be a triathlete.

The benefits of having a personal trainer include the one-on-one attention and instant feedback as you learn proper techniques for your sports. Your PT will be able to assess your limits and design a program that keeps you from overtraining. Most PTs will design workouts with some variety to keep you from being bored with your training while you work the same muscles with different workouts.

Finally, a personal trainer can be your motivator. The PT will take pride in your progress and will naturally want to cheer you on. After all, your success reflects well on your personal trainer.

CHAPTER 7

Stretching

Every new experience involves some learning, and there are different ways of finding out what you need to know. You can get help from experts, or you can learn by making mistakes. Try not to let the practice of stretching fall into the learn-by-error category. Stretching is a vital part of your training, and acquiring the habit early will make the road to your triathlon smoother.

Why Stretching Is Key to Success

The human body has more than 600 muscles, and you will use a significant number of them in your triathlon training. You have learned about how important it is for your muscles to be strong, but there's more to successful performance than just strength. You must keep your muscles loose or they will fight against you in your training and in the race.

Tight leg muscles keep you from achieving the proper running form. Tight arm and shoulder muscles hamper your swimming stroke. In both cases, you have to use more energy to get from point to point, and you tire more quickly.

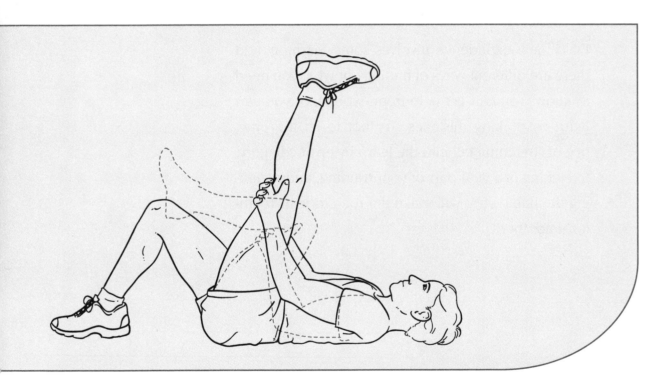

Hamstring Stretch: Lie on your back on the floor with both knees bent and feet flat on the floor. Grasp your hands on the thigh of one leg behind the knee. Starting with a bent knee, attempt to straighten the knee until a comfortable stretch is felt in the back of the thigh. Hold for twenty seconds, three reps, twice a day.

Gastroc Stretch: Place both hands on a wall for support. Take one step back so that your back leg is straight and your front knee is slightly bent. Keeping your back heel on the floor, lean into the wall gently until the stretch is felt in the calf. Hold for twenty seconds, three reps, twice a day.

Even worse, tight, inflexible muscles are more prone to injury, and the fact that your body is an interconnected set of muscles and tissue means that a defect in one area can mean trouble in another. For example, tight hamstrings can cause back pain. Tight calf muscles are one of the main causes of plantar fasciitis, a nagging foot problem that can affect your training and racing for months.

Swimming, biking, and running are challenging to your muscles, and it is normal for them to tighten under the strain. As the muscles tighten, they work less efficiently. The looser you can keep your muscles, the better they will work.

Learning how to stretch is important. Even more important is learning when *not* to stretch. Make it your practice to warm up for at least five minutes before stretching—every time. Stretching cold muscles is asking for injury.

Naturally Flexible

Everyone knows someone who seems to be made of rubber, who can twist and contort into all sorts of positions with no difficulty at all. People with that kind of ability are born with muscles that contain more than normal amounts of a protein called elastin. That substance gives their muscles the pliability others envy.

One way to loosen up the entire body is to go for a light swim. The water is naturally relaxing and will help lessen the tension in all of your muscles. A yoga class can also promote flexibility and relaxation.

In truth, however, too much flexibility can put extra stress on your joints. Former tennis star Kim Clijsters retired at an early age in part because her extremely loose muscles did not support her joints well, leading to a series of injuries.

The bottom line is that anyone, even the most flexible of individuals, will experience tight muscles after athletic activity. You can even tighten up just sitting at your desk at work or on a long airplane flight. Stretching is the best way to relieve the tension and relax the muscles. Once you acquire the habit of stretching, you will find yourself wanting to do it apart from training. As life's habits go, this is one you don't want to fight.

However you decide to do your stretching, just make sure you do it. You might get away with no stretching for a period, but eventually it will catch up to you in the form of an injury or increasingly poor performance. For example, if you never stretch your calf muscles, they will become tighter and tighter and you will have an excellent chance of developing, among other things, Achilles tendon problems.

How Often to Stretch

No set routine is right for everyone; some experimentation is reasonable. You might find that stretching works best for you after your workout, which means you don't stretch at all before you start. You might find it effective to do a short stretch before you start your workout with a longer series of stretches when the workout is complete. Whatever you decide, always warm up before that first stretch, perhaps with a light jog or easy five minutes on a stationary cycle. Your cold muscles are much more susceptible to injury in the first ten minutes of your workout. At a minimum, you should stretch after each workout, including your swim sessions. The upper body has the same needs as the legs and trunk.

A good place to stretch is in the shower or immediately afterward. By the time you have cleaned up, the warm water will have the blood flowing to your muscles, and they will be in an ideal state for stretching. It's a great way to start the day. If you shower at night, a good stretch will leave you relaxed and ready for bed.

If you can find the time, set aside ten to fifteen minutes per day just for stretching, always keeping in mind that you should warm up before doing so. The warm-up doesn't have to be elaborate. If you have a dog, take your

Soleus Stretch: Place both hands on a wall for support. Take a small step back with one foot. Both knees should be bent. Keeping your back heel on the ground, gently lean into the wall until the stretch is felt in the lower calf. Hold for twenty seconds, three reps, twice a day.

pet for a walk around the block before stretching. That will warm your muscles sufficiently.

If you find yourself tightening up at work, take a break and walk around for a few minutes to warm up, then lightly stretch your lower and upper body. You will feel fresher and more alert—ready to dive back into work.

What Muscles to Stretch

It's best to do your stretches in groups of muscles. For example, after a run, concentrate on the glutes (buttocks and hips), the hamstrings, calf muscles, and the plantar fascia (tissues in the foot). You can do them in a circuit— glutes, then hamstrings, and so on, in turn one by one—or simply do the requisite reps for each muscle before moving on to the next. Do what feels best to you.

For the gluteus muscles (minimus, medius, and maximus), sit on the floor or ground and cross your legs. Lean forward and feel the stretches. Hold for twenty to thirty seconds. Repeat one or two times more.

For the hamstrings, if you are at home, put your foot on a chair, keeping your leg straight, and lean forward. Hold for twenty to thirty seconds, then do the other leg. Do both legs two or three times. If you are outside, put your foot on your car bumper or a park bench.

For the calf muscles, put both hands on a wall or a tree and extend one leg back, keeping the sole of your foot completely on the ground. Lean in to create some tension in the calf and hold for twenty to thirty seconds. Do two or three repetitions on both legs.

To stretch the plantar fascia in your foot, stand on a step with the ball of your foot and let your heel down.

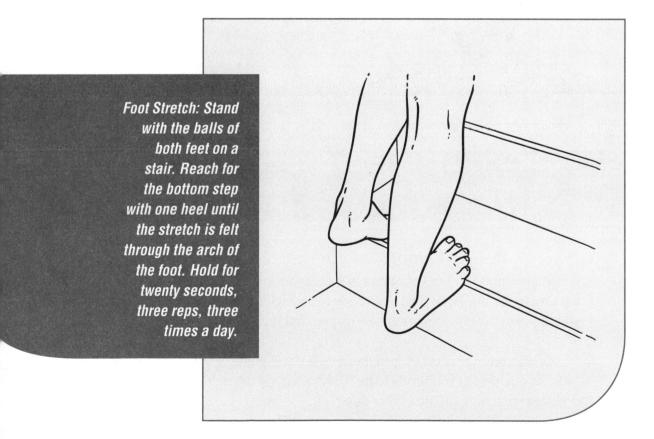

Foot Stretch: Stand with the balls of both feet on a stair. Reach for the bottom step with one heel until the stretch is felt through the arch of the foot. Hold for twenty seconds, three reps, three times a day.

A great postrun stretch can be accomplished by using a yoga pose known as Downward Facing Dog. Make an inverted V with your body, hands and feet planted on the ground or floor and your head down. This accomplishes most of the stretches you need for your backside in one step: glutes, hamstrings, calf muscles, Achilles tendon, lower back, lats (latissimus dorsi), and shoulder muscles.

Downward Dog: Hold for one minute, two to three reps.

After swimming, put your hand in a doorway and hold onto it. With your left arm in the doorway, turn your body to the right. With the right arm, turn your body to the left. This stretches the pectoral muscles and the front of the arm.

As with other aspects of your training, feel will guide you. It's not uncommon for one side of your body to be tighter than the other. If that is the case, do more stretching on the tighter side.

How to Stretch

There are two kinds of stretches: static and dynamic. In a static stretch, you reach a position and hold it, usually for twenty to thirty seconds. Release and wait a few seconds, then repeat the stretch.

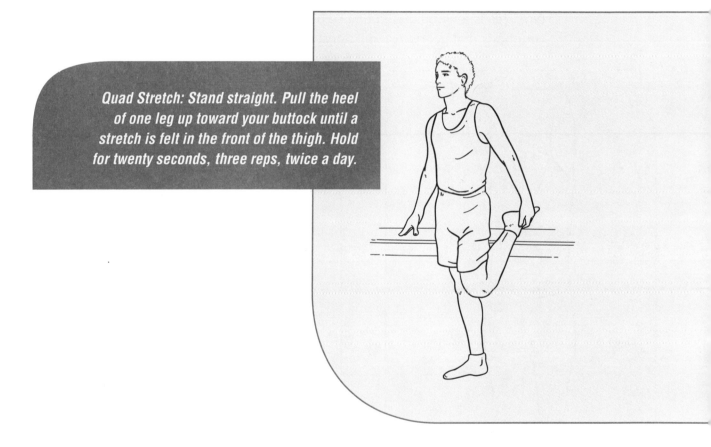

Quad Stretch: Stand straight. Pull the heel of one leg up toward your buttock until a stretch is felt in the front of the thigh. Hold for twenty seconds, three reps, twice a day.

When you are doing a dynamic stretch, you are going through a range of motion. For example, standing and twisting is a way of stretching the obliques, the muscles around the spine and the core muscle group.

A lunge—stepping forward in an exaggerated motion, low to the ground—is another type of dynamic stretch for the hip flexors, quadriceps, and glutes. Different varieties of static stretches will take up most of your stretching time, especially after your workouts. Dynamic stretches are most effective in preparation for a workout or a race.

Stay Still

When you are working on a static stretch, the muscle you are stretching should feel some tension, but the stretch should not be painful. If a muscle hurts when you start your stretch, stop. Work on another area, assuming it is pain free, then return to the stretch that hurt. If it still hurts, give up for the day. This is a warning sign that something may be going on in that part of your body that needs rest or extra attention.

Shoulder Stretch 1: Raise your arm next to your ear, bend your arm back behind your head. Gently pull on the elbow of the bent arm with the other hand until a stretch is felt in the shoulder. Hold for twenty seconds and do three reps, twice a day.

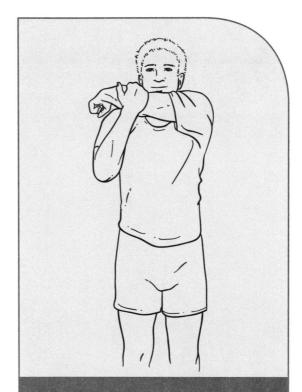

Shoulder Stretch 2: Reach one arm across your body to the opposite shoulder, keeping your elbow at chest height. Gently pull on the elbow of the bent arm with the other hand until a stretch is felt in the shoulder. Hold for twenty seconds and do three reps, twice a day.

Once you have achieved some tension on the muscle you are stretching, hold it gently for twenty to thirty seconds. You could hold the stretch longer, but it's not necessary. You actually get more benefit from two or three thirty-second stretches with small breaks in between than you would with one long stretch for the same amount of time.

Do It Right

You can do more harm than good if you do your stretching the wrong way, but it's best to start with a list of recommended activities. Here are stretch principles that will be of benefit to you.

Do:

- Warm up before stretching. This cannot be overemphasized.
- Hold most stretches for at least twenty seconds.
- Stretch daily. If necessary, take ten minutes off one of your workouts to make time for stretching. It's that important.
- Be careful about stretching outside in very cold weather. For example, when there's snow on the ground, take extra time to warm up before you try to stretch.
- Take a deep breath before you begin the stretch.
- Exhale as you stretch the muscle. This practice allows the spine to increase flexion, which enhances the effectiveness of the stretch.
- Focus on problem areas and stretch the tighter side more if there is an imbalance.

Stretching Taboos

Done properly and regularly, stretching is very beneficial for an athlete. Poor technique can do a lot of harm. Here are some stretching practices to avoid.

Don't:

- Bounce when stretching. You should maintain a constant tension on the muscle. Bouncing can cause injury.
- Push to keep stretching when it hurts to do so. At most, the tension in the muscle should be mild discomfort. It should never hurt.

- Stretch injured muscles.
- Stretch cold muscles. Always warm up before stretching. This can be done with as little as a ten-minute walk or five-minute jog. You risk injury when you try to stretch cold muscles.
- Forget to stretch opposing muscle groups. Stretching one side but not the other can lead to imbalances that cause injuries.
- Forget to stretch the upper body as well as the legs.

Act Your Age

Taking the time to stretch may try your patience, but if you are an aspiring triathlete who is over age forty, it's even more important for you. As you age, you lose range of motion, and your muscles lose flexibility. Failing to stretch is inviting disaster. Your triathlon career will end prematurely if you can't get to the starting line because of injury.

Tips for Good Stretches

If you were a runner or cyclist prior to starting your triathlon training, you probably already know the benefits of stretching and how to do it right. If you are entering the world of triathlons without much experience in competitive athletics, you will definitely want to start slowly. The advice you received about starting your running program applies equally to the stretching drills.

Invest the time necessary to do your stretches properly. An adequate stretching routine should take ten to fifteen minutes.

Be very gentle with your muscles the first time you stretch them. You will be in new territory, and it will behoove you to be cautious. That said, you will notice the benefits of stretching almost immediately, and as you grow more flexible—and as your muscles become stronger through training—you can increase the intensity.

There is no need for you to be competitive as a stretcher. There are no medals for longest or most intense stretch. Fortunately, your body will always tell you when you're overdoing it. When it hurts, back off.

Piriformis Stretch: Lie on your back on the floor. Cross the right leg over the left leg at the knees and bend both. Gently pull the left knee toward the chest until a comfortable stretch is felt in the right buttock/ hip area. Hold for twenty seconds, three reps, twice a day.

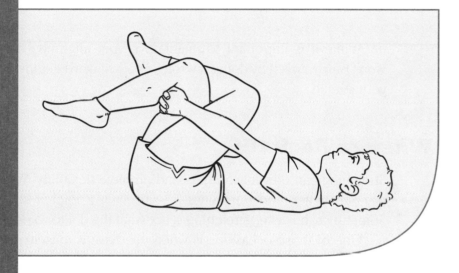

Line Up

When you are stretching, it is important to maintain proper alignment. What that means is that when you are stretching your calf muscles, for example, your feet should be aligned with your knees and hips as you lean against the wall or the car. In other words, your foot should be straight and in alignment with your knee. If your foot is turned outward or if your leg is at an angle to your body, you're doing it wrong.

If you are out of alignment, you might actually be stretching muscles you don't intend to stretch. Put another way, you won't be stretching the target muscles.

FACT

The Achilles tendon, which benefits from leg stretches, is the largest tendon in the body. When injured, the Achilles tendon takes longer to heal because, like all other tendons in the body, it does not have a good blood supply from the body.

While it is important to maintain proper alignment in stretches, you won't hurt yourself by doing it wrong. You just won't get the full benefit from your stretch.

When to Back Off

Stretching can prevent soreness and promote flexibility. You will swim better, ride better, and run better if you follow a regular stretching routine. Sometimes, however, stretching is not what the doctor ordered.

One of those occasions is when you have a muscle cramp or spasm. These typically occur during long training sessions, mostly rides or runs, and often arise from a deficiency in the body of one or more electrolytes (sodium, potassium, magnesium, and calcium).

When your muscles are cramping, stretching can exacerbate the problem. Often it will hurt too much to stretch a cramping muscle. A better strategy is to massage the locked-up muscle until it loosens.

Injury Alert

One of the stretching Don'ts noted earlier in this chapter involved stretching injured muscles. In addition to being pretty painful in most cases, stretching an injured muscle is simply a bad idea. There may be microtears in an injured muscle that will be made worse with attempts at stretching. An injured muscle needs time to heal.

My quads are sore, I have a cold, and I'm feeling burnt out. Am I a bad person if I take a day off?
Not at all. You will improve your chances for success if you put your training experience in perspective and cut back a bit. One or two days off won't matter at all.

As with a cramping muscle, massage may be a better solution in case of an injury. If you can't afford regular massage, there are relatively inexpensive devices that can assist you with self-massage. Any running or cycling store will have numerous massage aids available, and local massage schools usually offer inexpensive sessions to give students practice. An added benefit of some of the massage aids is that they can help you warm up your muscles for safe stretching before a workout.

CHAPTER 8

In the Swim of Things

You may have taken swimming lessons as a child, and
no doubt you benefited from that experience. Bear in
mind, however, that the main goal of mixing young
people with water in a formal class is to keep them
from drowning in the pool or ocean when they go
out for a swim. Competitive swimming is an entirely
different matter, as you will discover when you hit the
pool for your first set of laps.

Swimming Essentials

If you are a veteran competitive swimmer, you can skip the first part of this chapter. However, if you are new to this part of the triathlon experience, prepare yourself for a major surprise and a significant challenge, at least initially.

Get it into your mind that the swimming you will do in your practice and in the competition is all about form and technique. Sounds great, you say, but what does that mean? It means that you will probably have to relearn all you thought you knew about how to swim.

Stroke

The essential element of the swim is your stroke. You want to move through the water smoothly. Think of yourself as a torpedo, moving swiftly and silently. Your strokes should be compact and straight. Every movement is designed to propel you through the water. You do not want to be flailing or splashing about. That wastes energy.

Your objective is to cut down on frontal resistance. Whereas on the bicycle you want to reduce wind resistance through aerodynamics, in the water you practice hydrodynamics to reduce drag.

An ideal swim stroke is accomplished as the body turns slightly sideways in the water. At the beginning of the stroke, your hand is extended straight forward as far as you can reach. Entry into the water should be about a foot in front of the head. As one hand enters the water and pulls back, the other hand is moving forward to duplicate the first motion. In the "pull," the hand goes along your side close to the midline.

The two hands should be slightly less far apart than your shoulders are wide. Your hands should not cross. In the recovery—the motion of the pulling hand as it prepares for the next stroke—the elbow leaves the water first and should remain high as the hand hangs down toward the water to prepare for the next stroke. The trailing arm comes up—not out—from the back to start another stroke.

A swim coach can help you perfect your technique by pointing out the flaws in your stroke.

As essential element of the swim is integrating your breathing with your swim strokes. When you first start swimming, you will instinctively keep your head up in front of you and out of the water so that you can see where you are going. That is inefficient, awkward, and uncomfortable.

Learn to keep your head down, turning it briefly between strokes as you swim to get air and see where you are. Smart learners will practice breathing on both sides, alternating as they go. That balances the stroke and improves efficiency.

FACT

The use of the feet in swimming is often misunderstood. You probably have seen competitive swimmers kicking their feet as they go through the water, and it may seem they are using their feet like flippers to propel them forward. In reality, they use their feet to stay level in the water. Without the kick, the lower part of the body would sink.

Meeting the Challenge

If you are like most new triathletes, you probably dread the swim more than the other two sports. Many consider themselves poor swimmers, mainly because they haven't had or taken many opportunities to learn how to do it properly. They haven't had instruction in the proper techniques, and their experience with swimming has been strictly recreational.

One of your biggest challenges will be learning to swim for distances longer than you ever have. When you get into your race, you will have to sustain that swim without a break. Yes, it will be difficult at first, but if you find a competent swim coach, take it in baby steps, and stay with it, you can do it. Your body will get used to the swim and you will improve. You don't need to become an Olympic-caliber swimmer to get through your triathlon, just good enough to complete the distance. If you get serious about the sport, then you can work to become a good competitive swimmer.

Swimming Equipment

Swimming doesn't have a lot of high-tech gadgets like running and biking, but you do need some gear, probably more than you would think. The swimsuit won't be difficult because they are pretty much the same. You need something that is just enough to cover you without interfering with your goal of smooth movement through the water. You are definitely not trying to make a fashion statement. Your best bet for the right kind of swimwear is a specialty shop or sporting goods store.

Seeing Straight

You will also need a good pair of goggles. Remember, you will be keeping your head down as you swim, turning to breathe and orient yourself in the pool. That means your eyes will have to be open. Swimming pool water always contains chlorine, and it will irritate your eyes if you don't have some protection.

Fit is very important for your swim goggles. If they don't fit right, water will seep in as you swim and you will be continually pulling off your goggles to get the water out. If the goggles fit properly, there will be suction that holds them on your face with a seal to keep the water out.

You may have to experiment with different styles of goggles to get the right fit, so try them on before you buy. If you go to a swim shop for your goggles, a knowledgeable staff member can help you pick out the best type for your needs.

You should probably also look for a swim cap. This is not necessary for your swim training, but you will be required to wear a swim cap in your triathlon, so you might as well get used to wearing one.

One option for swimwear for your training and for your race is a pair of bike shorts. They hug your body closely, and if you get used to swimming in your bike shorts, you will be ready to hop on your machine right out of the water without having to change.

Also consider purchasing a set of hand paddles. The primary use is helping you learn proper hand entry and the "catch and pull" part of the swim stroke. A key part of the stroke is "catching" the water and pulling backward to propel you forward.

Paddles also help strengthen the arms and shoulders because of the increased resistance. One caution: if you have a rotator cuff or shoulder problem, lay off the paddles until the injury heals. Using paddles could make either problem worse.

Next on your shopping list should be a set of fins. Proper use of them will help strengthen your legs and promote ankle flexibility.

Most pools have a pace clock you can watch while you swim, but you will probably be happier with a waterproof watch that you can wear to time your workouts. Look for a watch with lap and split-time functions so you can track and store your workout times.

A kick board is useful for your kick drills. You hold it out front for support as you do your kick drills.

Also useful is a pull buoy, a large piece of foam that you put between your legs to keep your back end afloat—and keep you from kicking—as you do drills to improve your stroke. Using a pull buoy, you propel yourself through the water exclusively with your arms.

If you find the water in your ears at the end of the swim annoying, consider earplugs to keep the water out. If you don't want to wear earplugs, there are alcohol solutions that work very well in ridding your ears of water after a swim. Finally, with all this gear you are buying, you will need a mesh bag to carry it.

One note: If you sign up for a swim class at a health or fitness club, check with the club to see if they have some of the equipment listed in this chapter. It might save you the expense of buying it and the bother of lugging it around.

Swim Training

If you are planning your first triathlon, your goal for your swim training should be relatively simple: get to the point where you can swim the required distance in your race without stopping. You should be able to estimate from your workouts how long it will take to swim the distance. Once you determine the time, you can focus your training on gaining confidence that you can make it. Only experienced swimmers should consider trying for a certain time in the swim.

Planning Time

There are a couple of ways to start your swim training. You could just make regular trips to the pool and swim back and forth to build endurance. If you don't already know proper technique, this might reinforce bad habits.

The other, smarter way is to get with a group and a coach and learn the right way to swim. The next section of this book describes the role of a coach in your triathlon success.

If you are not already an experienced swimmer, you will be surprised to find out how little you know about the proper form, the right drills to do, and many other aspects of the sport. Proper swimming technique is not intuitive. You need guidance to prevent aimless and counterproductive efforts. Whatever you do, have a plan, even if it is no more than training yourself to get from one end of the pool to the other faster each week.

Drills

Most of swim training is about drills—repetitions that train you in the most efficient ways to move through the water—but there are other workouts as well. For example, your program might include some intervals, which require you to swim a certain distance in a specified time. A coach might also have you do a bit of speed work to improve your ability to sustain a hard pace.

Why You Need a Coach

Fortunately for aspiring triathletes who are dreading the swim, most communities have at least one masters swim program. That's where you will find the swim coach to help you get through this scary part of the triathlon. What you don't know about proper swimming technique could probably fill an Olympic-size pool, and the coach is there to show you the way.

Look for swim classes that take place in the early morning. It may be a pain to have to get up at 5 A.M. or earlier, but think of the benefit: one of your key triathlon workouts will be done before you get to work. This will partly relieve some of the stress of finding time for all the workouts.

Even if you are part of a group, you will receive one-on-one attention from the coach, who watches all the swimmers and separates them by experience and skill. Whatever you do wrong will be noticed and corrected by your coach.

Tips to Improve

The coach will spot your weaknesses and come up with drills to help you improve in those areas. You will learn proper technique more quickly with the assistance of a coach.

The coach might even design a program of workouts specifically for your triathlon goal.

A coach can also serve as a motivator, cheering you and encouraging you as you progress, and if you know the coach is watching during your workouts, you will be more focused on doing everything right and fulfilling each assignment. You might end up thinking of your coach as a slave driver, but you will be glad for the push on race day when you approach the water with confidence, knowing you can handle the distance.

Establishing a Base

For new swimmers, here is the first assignment: just get in the water. Before you get into the complicated stuff—drills, techniques, and equipment—just go to the pool and start swimming. A typical health club pool has lanes that are 25 yards long. One lap is a trip from one end to the other and back—that is, 50 yards.

The first time you swim from one end to the other, you will be surprised at how difficult it is, but don't be discouraged. If you are a runner, perhaps you remember how tough it was the first time you tried it. It took a monumental effort to get to the end of the block, yet you survived that start and gradually built your strength and stamina. Swimming is no different. It's tough but you will adapt and grow stronger in your new discipline.

Get Comfortable

What you are aiming for is comfort in the venue. Just swim back and forth in the lane, resting for five to ten seconds when you reach an end.

Your goal right at first is to be able to swim ten to fifteen minutes without stopping, or with only a five- to ten-second rest between laps (from one end of the pool to the other and back).

Being able to swim for that long will give you the confidence to begin your serious swim training program. Swimming two to three times a week, it should take you one to two weeks to reach that comfort level.

Wake Up, Muscles

As with any new exercise, you will be using muscles in your introduction to swimming that you haven't used before. It is normal to experience some soreness in the arms and shoulders. You will also take this base-establishing period to get used to swimming with your face in the water, most likely the first time you have done so. Always remember to warm up with five to ten minutes of light swimming before you start your laps.

Different Drills

If you have enlisted the services of a coach and are part of a masters swim program, you will have drills as part of the weekly or biweekly classes. On the occasions when you are working out on your own, or if the swim coach isn't there for your session, you can do one or more of the following drills that help you learn proper swimming technique.

The first drill is called the "catch-up." In this exercise, you swim with one arm. Take a kick board and hold onto it with one hand. Use the other arm to go through a complete swim stroke, from entry into the water in front of you to the push through to the back.

All the while you are stroking with your free arm, keep the other arm on the kick board without moving the arm. This is a tough drill that teaches you to keep your hands in the proper position through each stroke. Do four laps (50 yards each) for this drill.

When your arm goes forward for a swim stroke, it should stay in a straight line, not crossing to the other side of your body. There is a natural tendency to do this in swimming, but it is inefficient movement that wastes energy.

Going Sideways

For a sideways swim, you use fins but no arm movement. Enter the pool, turn on your side, and extend one arm straight out. Put the other arm at your side or on your hip. Now kick to the other end of the pool. Turn onto the other side on the way back.

This drill helps you keep going straight when you swim. It may seem strange to create a drill for this purpose, but it won't take many swim classes for you to see how easy it is to stray from one lane to another. Even if you don't veer off course yourself, you will see others doing so. Do two laps (100 yards total) in this drill.

During your triathlon, you will be aiming for a target off in the distance—probably a buoy around which you will turn—and it will be of great benefit to you if you have trained yourself to swim straight.

Kick It Up

You will use your kick board and fins for this drill. Your aim is to practice fast turnover of your feet. Aim for quick, short kicks rather than long slow ones, and do two laps (100 yards total) in this drill.

Here's another drill that involves kicking: start your swim (using fins) and do three strokes (left arm, right arm, left arm), then turn onto your side and kick, counting to six slowly as you go. Turn onto the other side, do three more strokes, and then kick for a count of six. Do this drill for two laps (100 yards total).

QUESTION?

Why are fins involved in so many workouts?
Fins help you get a better feel for the particular drill you are doing. For example, if you are practicing keeping your arms straight in your swim stroke, it will take away from the exercise if you are continually fighting to keep the lower half of your body from sinking. The fins take care of that for you.

For the fist drill, you will use a pull buoy instead of fins. Using the buoy, swim one lap with your hands closed and a second lap with your hands open in the normal position. This drill helps you get a feel for the role your forearms play in propelling you forward. Your hands act like scoops, grabbing the water for traction and pulling you forward as they go back, but the swim stroke is more than hands.

Heads Up

If you are a new swimmer, you will have learned that most of your workouts will be done with your face in the water and your head down. One important drill that seems to contradict that practice is designed to help you stay on course in your triathlon.

When you start your race, you will be swimming for a target some distance away. To keep that target in your sights, it may be necessary for you to pull your head out of the water for two or three seconds. It will often not be possible to see what you are swimming toward without looking up.

It would be a good idea to practice taking these peeks during your swim training so that sighting the buoy or boat where you will turn is not completely new to you on race day. Once or twice during your workout, simply look up from your swim and check on the other end of the pool. The better you prepare for race day, the more confident you will be when the starting gun goes off.

Keeping a Swim Log

You have gone to the trouble of making a plan for your swim training, so it makes sense to keep track of how it's going. Are you meeting your objectives? Are there some areas of the training that need extra work? You won't be able to answers these questions if you don't keep track of your activities.

That's where the swim log comes in. After each session, you should record the workouts you undertook, how long it took to do them, and how you felt overall. You did buy that watch that tracks your laps and splits, didn't you? You will gain confidence if your log reflects that you are swimming your laps at a faster pace.

QUESTION?

It's tough keeping separate training logs for swimming, biking, and running. Does anyone sell an all-in-one triathlon training log?
Yes, there is such a thing as a triathlon training log, with spaces for each daily workout in each of the three sports. It's a lot easier managing one log. You should be able to find one at your local running store, bike shop, or swim shop.

Using your training log, you can keep track of your workouts, with notes about your progress or lack thereof. With proper notes, you can even discover the source of an injury. For example, you might not know why shoulder pain keeps cropping up on certain days of your swim workouts. You might be able to correlate that pain with a specific drill and discontinue it until you recover.

Tips for Success

Before you jump into the water in your triathlon, you will have spent a lot of time in the pool, on the bicycle, and on the road as a runner. That is good preparation, to be sure, but you can do better.

If you are a triathlon newbie, your swims have probably been restricted to the pool where you have had your swim sessions. It will be a completely different experience when you hit that lake or dive into the ocean for the first time. Why not get a preview?

If the triathlon you plan to take part in is nearby, take a friend out to the lake. With your friend in a boat, experience an open-water swim so that you get a feel for what's coming. If your triathlon is too far away, try to find some other open water for your "test drive."

A good way to see how well you stay on course as a swimmer is to close your eyes while swimming in the pool. Most lap pools are separated into lanes that are roped off, so if you veer off course you will find out quickly enough when you hit the rope. That will give you a good idea of whether you need more practice swimming straight.

No Bottom

You will see how much different it is from the pool. For one thing, you probably won't be able to touch bottom once you move away from shore. For another, you probably won't be able to see the bottom of the lake, and there will be no black line present, as you see in each lane of the swimming pool, to keep you going straight.

It is imperative that you have a friend along with a boat or canoe to help you if you find yourself in trouble. Never do this alone. Try to sight something in the distance and swim for it. That will be practice for race day.

If the water temperature on race day is lower than 78°F, you will be allowed to wear a wetsuit, a rubber outer shell that improves buoyancy and protects from the cold water temperature. Some wetsuits are designed specifically for triathlons.

If you plan to wear a wetsuit, it would be a mistake not to give it a whirl beforehand. Some trial and error may be involved, particularly in selecting the correct size. A wetsuit that feels just fine in the store might be overly restrictive when you start swimming in it.

Do yourself a favor. Practice swimming in your wetsuit before race day.

Don't Pick Sides

Earlier in this chapter you were advised to learn to breathe on both sides because it promotes the efficiency of your stroke. There's another good reason for doing so: the orientation of the buoys on the swim course of your race. Sometimes the buoys used to mark the course on the swim are on the right. Sometimes they are on the left. If you have trained yourself to alternate breathing sides, the orientation of the buoys won't matter to you. If you have to keep looking to your nonbreathing side, your swim efficiency will suffer.

Here's one final tip involving equipment. Your triathlon will start in the morning, and you may find yourself swimming into the rising sun. There are goggles with darker lenses to help you cope with this problem. Check your race for details, and look at the course if you can. Anything you can do to deal with problems before they arise will help you succeed.

CHAPTER 9

Biking Toward Success

No one said it was easy to get ready for a triathlon. Perhaps the most complicated part of the process is selecting the bicycle you will use in the race. Your mind will boggle at the range of options, but it will be worth your time and effort to sort through it all to make sure the machine you take to the triathlon is right for you. The wrong choice will do more than hamper your effort: it could ruin your race.

9

Biking 101

Here is the disclaimer for aspiring triathletes about to start the process of picking out a bicycle for their training and the race: do not attempt on your own. Unless you are already familiar with road bikes, you don't know enough to begin to make an intelligent choice. Get professional help at your local bike shop.

Start with this principle: the cycle you will ride in the race is nothing like the old bike you got as a kid—the lumbering, clunky machine that you braked by pushing back on the pedals. Race cycles are light and sleek with hand brakes and gears that you actually use.

On Loan

For triathlon newbies, the best choice might be to borrow a road bike for the training and the race. A new entry-level road bike will cost about $700, and you can spend many thousands for state-of-the-art machines. It would be smart to delay investing in a fancy road bike until you are sure you want to continue doing triathlons.

FACT

You could ride an old-fashioned bicycle in a triathlon. It would be within the rules. Without gears to help you up and down hills, however, you would finish the ride with dead legs and nothing left for the run. Don't even think about taking a "lead sled" to a triathlon.

If you have a friend with a road bike, ask if you can borrow it. If the bike is available, it would be worth your while to take it to a bike shop and have the staff check out the cycle to make sure it will be functional for your training and the race.

If you do not have access to a loaner bike, consider purchasing a used one. Your local bike shop might have some on hand, or they might know where you could find a good used machine.

You could probably find a used bike at a reasonable price on eBay, but there is a potentially major downside to doing so. It is very important that your bicycle fits you, which requires in-person inspection with the assistance of an expert. You can't get that if your bike has to be shipped to you. There is more about how to make your bike fit later in this chapter.

Biking Equipment

Face it, triathlon training is a gear-intensive pursuit, so just head on over to the bike shop with your credit card handy. Number one on your list is the helmet, and chisel the following in stone if you have to, but don't forget it: *never, ever, ride without your helmet.*

If you head out for a ride and find you left your helmet at home, turn around and go back for it or cancel the ride. Obviously, the key issue is safety, but your triathlon will require you to wear a helmet during the race, so you might as well get used to it. Always ride with a helmet.

The triathlon rules about helmet wear are so strict that you will be disqualified if an official sees you with so much as a loose chin strap. Triathlon organizers take safety very seriously. So should you.

An adequate helmet will set you back about $50. Used helmets are available, but be careful. Before you buy, check inside to make sure the foam isn't cracked. If it is, the helmet will not provide protection in the event of a spill.

Next on your shopping list is a good pair of bike shorts. They come with padding in just the right place to stave off major discomfort that you would inevitably feel from the pressure on the sit-bones of your backside. Don't skimp on this item.

Also consider a good riding jersey. Most come in very bright colors and wild designs, no doubt in part to make it easier for drivers of cars and trucks to see cyclists, but jerseys have another important function. Bike shorts don't have pockets, so where are you supposed to keep your identification (always take that), a bit of cash, or whatever else you might want to carry? Most riding jerseys have a zippered pocket in the back with plenty of room for your driver's license, some folding money, and a cell phone.

Hand in Glove

Riding gloves are also important. They, too, are padded. Remember that you will be leaning forward on your bicycle as you ride, and there will be a lot of pressure on the palms of your hands. The padding in the gloves can help with that.

The gloves will also come in handy should you crash. If you topple over, your natural tendency as you hit the ground will be to put out your hands to take the fall. The gloves will protect your hands from cuts and scrapes.

If you ride enough, and you will be doing lots of it in your triathlon training, you will eventually get a flat. Spend about $30 for a flat change kit. You will also need oil for your bike's chain, and don't forget the lights for riding at dusk, dawn, or even in the dark. Some states require lights for bicycle use after the sun has gone down. Lights in the rear should be red, and they should flash. In front, the light is used to help you see where you are going.

The Importance of Bike Shoes

Bike shoes are one of the truly specialized items of gear you should consider before you start triathlon training. Bike shoes are useful only for riding. They are not good for anything else, and they are not cheap. A pair will cost $75 to $200, so you might want to hold off on the purchase until you can judge how committed you are to the triathlon.

Bike shoes come in different varieties. For the ease of getting into and out of them during your competition, look for bike shoes with the fewest straps.

Most bike shoes have a hard sole made of carbon fiber. They have straps instead of laces, and they are not flexible. The reason for this is that if you ride with, say, a pair of running shoes, the flexibility of the shoes will dissipate the force of your pedal stroke, making you work harder. With the hard bike shoes on, the full force of your pedal stroke goes into making the wheels turn, and you get a better result for the same effort.

Keep in mind also that riding in sneakers or running shoes can promote foot cramps because of all the extra effort involved in the pedal strokes.

Once you know that there are more triathlons in your future, look into a combination of clipless pedals and bike shoes to fit them. The clipless pedals have a cleat that connects to the pedal in much the same way that ski shoes connect to skis. They also disconnect in the same way that ski shoes do in case of a fall. If you plan to use the clipless pedals in your race, practice getting in and out of them to avoid problems during the triathlon.

Do You Need a Bike Computer?

It's called a computer, but it's really just a fancy speedometer/odometer with a few added features—or a lot of them if you want to pay the price. A bike computer adequate for your purposes will cost about $25. A typical model hooks by wire to your bike's front wheel. Mounted on the handle bars, the computer provides useful information once you get started such as the amount of time you have been riding, your speed, the distance traveled, and the current revolutions per minute. When the ride is over, the computer will tell you your average speed and how far you went.

All of this information is important because as you enter the date in your logbook, you will be able to tell if you are improving or regressing. Knowing your revolutions per minute (rpm), or cadence, is important because you normally want to stay at about 90, but some drills will call for you to go faster. With your bike computer, you will meet the target goal but not exceed it. Your workouts will be better.

Bells and Whistles

As you might imagine, bike computers can do a lot more than the basics. Some are wireless, and some provide altitude, barometric pressure, temperature, or even GPS information. In fact, there are GPS devices designed for the bicycle that can convert to run mode for triathlon training. Hop off the bike, push a button on the GPS device on your wrist, and start running.

What could be simpler? You can also find bike computers that will monitor your heart rate and count the calories burned.

Even a basic computer will keep track of total miles to help you know when your bike needs some maintenance. After 5,000 to 6,000 miles, the gears on your bike will have worn down, and you will need to replace them. The information you need is always right there on your bike computer.

QUESTION?

Do I really need a computer for bike training?
Without a bike computer, your workouts will be time based. That's okay for nonserious competitors, but if you don't know how far you have ridden week to week, you won't know if you are improving or going in the opposite direction.

Finding the Right Bicycle

Bicycles come in different styles and are made with different materials. Do not try to make a decision about your first triathlon bicycle without help from someone with knowledge and experience.

Basic road bikes are similar to what you see in bike races such as the Tour de France. The handles curl down and allow you to get lower as you ride to lessen wind resistance. The tires are thin. An entry-level cycle will usually be made of aluminum and cost $600 to $700.

There are also bicycles made specifically for triathlon competition. The handlebars form an arrow shape to allow you to put your hands together as you ride. This further decreases drag for faster speeds. Because you end up in a lower position than on a regular road bike, you give up some comfort, but all things being equal, you will go faster than on a road bike. Many have armrests to add to the comfort. An entry-level triathlon bicycle will cost about $700.

Mountain bikes are meant for off-road riding, and there are off-road triathlons. If that's what you have signed up for, check into mountain bikes. This style machine has wider tires with knobs to help with traction in the dirt and mud. A mountain bike is heavier, and the gearing is usually lower to cope with the hills typically found in a mountain bike course.

Material Issues

Not all bicycles are created equal, and the material used can make a significant difference in the ride. Most road bicycle frames are made of aluminum. Those machines are stiff and provide a comparatively rough ride.

Frames made of titanium are lighter and ride better than bikes with aluminum frames, but they don't measure up to the best—bikes with frames made of carbon fiber. They are the most comfortable of all, and usually the fastest. Naturally, they are also the most expensive. A high-tech, state-of-the-art bicycle can cost $7,000 or more.

Think 3 o'clock when you are being fitted for your bicycle. If the fit is right, when the pedal is at 3 o'clock, your knee should be directly over the crank. If it's not, adjustments are in order.

Fit to Be Tried

Whatever you decide on for the style and material of your bicycle, the key issue for you will be the fit. For this, you need help. You wouldn't walk into a department store, pick a jacket off the rack, and buy it without trying it on. Purchasing a bike for your triathlon is no different. In fact, it's even more important to try it on before buying. For this chore, you need the expert help of the bike store staff, and this factor argues strongly for making your bicycle purchase locally.

Every body is different, so it's imperative that you adjust your new bicycle to fit you. If you don't, you won't enjoy riding and your training will suffer.

Start with the seat. Get it too low and you will kill your knees. Put it too high and you will rock your hips too much as you pedal. It will hurt; not the sensation you want with your bike rides. The tilt of the seat is also important. Get it wrong and you'll feel it in your rear end long after the ride.

Another important measure in fitting you to your bicycle is the distance from the seat to the handlebars. If it's too long or too short, your back will hurt and you won't be using your legs efficiently. You don't want to be cramped or too stretched out as you lean forward during the ride. As you can see, this is a complicated process, but the experts at your bike shop are very good at putting you on the type of bike that fits your needs—and fits you.

If you purchased your bike from the shop helping you with the fit, they probably won't charge for the service. In fact, a good bike shop probably would not sell you a bicycle that didn't fit you. Expect to spend about $100 getting fit with a bike you bought elsewhere, perhaps online.

The bottom line is that, although you will push yourself at times to the point of discomfort because of the effort, the ride itself should not hurt. An easy ride should be pain free. If it's not, head back to the bike shop for a fit adjustment.

QUESTION?

Do men and women need different styles of seats?
Indeed they do. The anatomical differences between the genders are significant. Female cyclists should spend the extra money for a women's seat.

Keeping a Biking Log

All logs in your triathlon training are meant to help you keep track of your progress and to help you identify aspects of your program that need improving. Good log keeping includes more than simply entering data. It is very useful to include information about the weather and other external factors (a cold perhaps, or an injury). Your log should also include notes about how you felt during each workout.

Your bike computer will provide the raw data. You should make the extra notes. If, for example, you frequently note that a beginner-type workout was very hard for you, it might be because you are doing too many hard workouts. Ease up for a week in all three sports to see if that makes a difference.

Keeping a biking log will also help you keep from overdoing your training. You should be riding no more than sixty miles a week. That's three respectable rides, more than enough for your triathlon training.

ALERT!

Perceived effort is a phrase often used in sports training to indicate how hard a session felt. You can quantify this using what is known as the Borg Scale, which originally ran from zero to twenty-one, later revised to range from six to twenty. Six indicates no effort, eleven is a light level of exertion, and twenty is maximal effort.

Training on Your Bike

The primary objective of your bicycle training is to build enough endurance to complete the distance in your triathlon with enough energy left to complete the run.

Your bike training should include some hill workouts to strengthen your legs, and this is very important if your race has a hilly course. Don't wait until race day to get that hill training.

You also want your training to get you used to pushing during the race. This is less important for first-time triathletes whose main goal is just to finish, but it has great relevance for anyone who wants to be competitive. The design of the course will dictate some of the features of your bike training. Translation: does the course feature a lot of hills, or is it mostly flat?

No Junk

Your training will include using your bike computer to learn about the gears and how to use them. You should keep your cadence at about 90 revolutions per minute. If you find yourself at 120 rpms, you know you need to shift gears. After you have been riding for a while, you will be able to feel when to shift gears.

What you want to avoid is simply logging miles on your bicycle without some purpose to the movement. In running, these are called "junk miles," not completely useless but largely ineffective and aimed mostly at adding to statistics. Don't be a slave to your training log, and don't pile on miles just for the sake of logging them. Always have a plan, and follow the plan.

Indoor Training

There will be occasions when the weather prevents you from a scheduled ride. That's inevitable. Should you just scrap the ride that day, or is there an alternative?

There are a couple of ways you can go if a scheduled ride is canceled. One option would be to head for your health club to see if there is a spin class you can join. A spin session can be a very good workout.

Out for a Spin

In a spin class, you pedal a stationary bicycle that works with a big flywheel instead of a chain. Once you get the flywheel going, there is no stopping it except with a brake. On a regular bike or stationary cycle, you can coast. You just stop pedaling and let the bicycle roll on its own. With a spin machine, you have to keep pedaling.

One positive feature of a spin class is that it will be led by an instructor who will vary the routine from slow to fast, spicing up the session with increased resistance or having you stand as you pedal. A spin class is a quality workout, usually lasting forty-five minutes to an hour.

It would be good practice during the triathlon off-season to sign up for a regular spin class. It will help keep you in shape if the winter weather where you live is not good for outside training.

Rack It Up

Another useful piece of biking gear is a bike trainer. It is a device that allows you to use your own bicycle indoors by putting the rear wheel on a stand with a flywheel so that you can pedal without moving. You can increase and decrease the resistance to simulate hills and other conditions. It's a fine second choice if you can't get to your scheduled ride.

To stave off the boredom of a solitary ride, you can set up the device, which is not very big, near a television. There are DVDs you can buy that have bicycle training programs to guide you through a workout and keep your attention. Some of the bike trainers are fancy, changing resistance through magnetics and with other bells and whistles, but you can get a good one for about $100.

Apart from the at-home trainer and spin class, there is the good, old-fashioned stationary bicycle. They don't cost that much, and they don't take up a lot of space. If you set the resistance high, you can get a decent work-out. It won't have the social aspect of riding outdoors with your friends, and it won't be quite as good as riding your own bike on the trainer, but any workout is better than none. Sometimes you just have to be creative.

ALERT!

At-home bicycle trainers are very handy for bad weather days or for saving time, but they are hard on the tires. If you are doing a lot of training on this device indoors, invest in a set of training tires.

Different Drills

A lot of your riding will be designed to develop endurance for your triathlon, but there are specific drills that can improve your technique and strength while preparing you for what lies ahead. Here are a few useful drills to consider.

First is the one-legged drill. On a stationary cycle with stirrups to keep your feet in place, pedal with one leg for about thirty seconds, then shift to the other leg and do the same. If one of your legs is weaker than the other, not an uncommon circumstance, pedal a bit extra on that side. Repeat this drill three to five times.

The next drill is called the spinup, typically done outside, although you can do it indoors. During your ride, hunker down in the seat so that you don't bounce and quickly increase your revolutions per minute to 110. Hold that pace for one minute, then cool down for as long as you need to before starting the next. Do this five times during one ride, once a week.

Gear Shifts

This drill should be outside too, but you could do it on an indoor trainer. While riding, shift to a harder gear—one that makes you drop from 90 rpm to between 70 and 80—and stay with it for one or two minutes. Repeat five or six times.

This drill simulates hills, so if you regularly ride in a hilly area, you don't need this drill. What you should do once a week, however, is push hard when you come to those hills to help strengthen your legs. You can also simulate hill climbing by changing to a harder gear and standing up to pedal for about thirty seconds at a time.

Right on Time

Another good workout is called the time trial. Find yourself a long stretch of road, one without traffic issues, and push your workout for approximately 10 miles (roughly thirty minutes). This will get you used to sustained effort in your coming race.

Do this drill once every couple of weeks. Do the time trials on the same course so that you can see how you are progressing.

Bricks

As previously mentioned, in triathlon-speak, a brick is a bike ride followed by a run. One explanation for the term is that a brick is what your legs feel like after one of the workouts.

No matter why it's called that, a brick can be a very effective triathlon training drill. For one thing, it simulates race day, when you will be starting the third phase of your triathlon, the run, immediately after racking up your bike. Bricks will train you to do something you probably have never done, as not many athletes would follow bike rides with runs without a reason. Plan to do a brick once a week.

Different Brick Workouts

There are two kinds of brick workouts, each emphasizing a different aspect of the training. In the first, you follow a ride of about seventy-five minutes with a run of fifteen minutes. Your ride will include some intervals—short periods of ramping up the pace followed by cooldowns. The run will not be just a jog, but you will not push it.

Another brick workout consists of equal parts riding and running—forty-five minutes for each, for example—but the run is harder with interval workouts or at tempo pace (slightly faster than usual for the entire run).

No matter which brick workout you do, don't wait a long time before you start running. You should be running within five minutes of dismounting.

As you ride, your pedal stroke should be similar to the motion of your foot when scraping mud off the bottom of your shoe. You should push the foot all the way through the stroke. Practice this technique for more efficient riding.

Your brick workouts will give you a chance to practice your transition between biking and running. Beginning triathletes will not be that concerned about potentially wasted time in the transition phase, but it will behoove anyone to work on this aspect of racing.

As you get nearer to your race, include the gear you will use during the triathlon as part of your brick. You will get good transition practice and make sure the gear you plan to use during the race will work for you.

Tips for More Effective Training

A triathlete in training has a lot to think about and many irons in the fire. Eliminating even small irritations can produce big benefits for the harried triathlete-to-be. Here are a few tips to ease the way:

- Before you ride, always check your tire pressure. Low pressure causes extra wear and makes the ride harder.
- Buy a tire change kit and learn how to use it.
- Make a list of what you need for each workout and set out the requisite gear well in advance.

- Carry an energy bar and sports drink on your rides. If you bonk on your bike ride, it's pretty close to a disaster.
- Don't eat a heavy lunch on a day when you have a bike ride on the schedule. You don't need stomach issues in your workouts.
- Check the weather the day of your ride to make sure you don't get miles away from home and have to return in a thunderstorm or worse.
- Try to find group rides. They are more fun while increasing motivation.
- Get adequate sleep.
- Don't make it a practice to skip workouts, but if you get into one and find it's just not your day, bag it and plan to come back strong tomorrow. And forget about the bad workout. Negative energy saps you.

CHAPTER 10

Running for the Finish Line

In many ways, running is the simplest of the triathlon disciplines. You don't need a machine or a manmade hole filled with water. You just throw on your shoes and your shorts, and it's out the door for a run. It really is that easy if you are running just for recreation or fitness. Training for races is more complicated, but it can still be fun. Train hard, but always strive to enjoy the experience.

Running Basics

Most aspiring triathletes come to the sport with some running under their belts. If you are an exception—a person with no running experience—add four weeks to your projected triathlon training schedule and plan on a sixteen-week buildup to your race. The first month will be spent getting your body used to running. Chapter 11 has a training schedule for brand-new runners.

The primary goal of the schedule for new runners will be to get the body used to the stresses of the sport. It is designed to ease you into your new activity with a program of running and walking. By the end of the four weeks, you will be ready to start training in all three sports for your triathlon.

Good Form

Even veteran runners need help with their running form. It's easy to get into bad habits, reinforcing them in each workout. It is far easier to start correctly so that you don't have to unlearn anything later on.

One of the most important elements of your form is how your foot strikes the ground. Heel striking is a common flaw. When you run with your heel hitting the ground first, your strides become long and inefficient. You have to work harder to get where you are going, and you can't go as fast.

Your goal should be to strike the ground with the middle of your foot, not the heel.

QUESTION?

I heard someone say you should always "run tall." What does that mean?
Running tall means you should always keep your body erect when you run. That posture keeps your weight balanced and your diaphragm open fully so that breathing is easier.

What you should aim for is short, quick steps with rapid turnover rather than long, slow strides. Practice running so that when your foot hits the ground, it is always under your knee.

Running is a full-body experience, so make sure all of your parts are involved, especially the arms. If you don't think arm movement is important, trying running with your arms at your sides for a few minutes. You will be surprised how difficult it is.

Swing your arms as you run so that when the left arm is out in front, so is the right leg, and when the right arm is out, the left is leg is in front. March in place, swinging your arms, to see how this works. Moving your arms and legs in this combination creates momentum that helps propel you forward.

Over All

Aim for a smooth running style, and think of yourself as running *over* the ground rather than on it. Try to avoid a herky-jerky motion as you run. It wastes energy and eventually could lead to injury. Don't bob up and down as you stride. Spend your energy going forward, not up and down.

It is also important to stay relaxed as you run. Tension drains your energy and makes everything more difficult. If you find yourself clenching your fists, you are tensing up. Drop your arms briefly and just shake them to ease the tension in your shoulders. Stop and walk if necessary.

Running Equipment

You will purchase nothing more important to your running than the shoes that will accompany you as you log mile after mile on your way to a successful triathlon. The right choice will enhance your running and help you improve as you train. The wrong choice could put you on the sidelines with an injury.

Nonrunners tend to think of all athletic footwear as "tennis shoes" or "sneakers." Don't even think about anything for your run training except actual running shoes. You can find them in many places, but your best bet for getting what you need is a store that specializes in running gear. You can buy running shoes from a mall retailer, but it is less likely that the person who sells you the shoes will have the kind of knowledge you need to assure a good fit.

Not Cheap

Expect to spend $80 to $100 or more for a good pair of running shoes, but don't make your decision based on price. You should not skimp in this area. The type of shoe you need will depend on your size, gait, and what you intend to do with the shoes. Most running shoes are designed for training, but there are lighter shoes available for racing.

ALERT!

Pronation is the inward motion of the leg during running that provides a natural cushioning function. Some runners, especially those with flat feet, pronate too much, which usually results in knee problems. These runners need shoes that provide stability. Severe overpronators need motion-control shoes or specially made orthotics.

Most shoes generally fit into one of three categories: neutral, stability, and motion control. Runners with naturally good biomechanics go for neutral shoes. Others need varying degrees of correction in their gaits. There are even models made just for heavier runners, who tend to wear out shoes more quickly.

FACT

Many experts believe that two pairs of shoes alternated in training will last as long as three pairs used consecutively. If you buy two pairs, pick different brands of the same style. The subtle differences will give your leg muscles some needed variety.

If you visit a store that specializes in running, the staff will take the time to evaluate your running style and will offer choices among shoes that meet your needs. If you run off-road more than just occasionally, you probably should invest in a pair of trail shoes. The soles are usually equipped with lugs for better traction on trails.

Shoe manufacturers often change their models with updates and redesigns. If you find a running shoe that really works well for you, consider buying more than one pair at a time. That will save some time if the next incarnation of your favorite running shoe no longer works for you. In any case, finding the right shoe might take some experimentation.

Dress for Success

You need more than good running shoes for your regular workouts, and you should look for apparel specifically designed for the sport. A key issue is the fabric, and your choice should never be cotton. Look for material that wicks perspiration away from your body, which is the standard now.

When you dress for your run, especially if the weather is warm, use light-colored, loose-fitting T-shirts and singlets (which look like tank tops). Shorts made for running almost always have key pockets, and some come with mesh pockets in the back for storing energy bars or gels.

Look for socks designed for running. Again, avoid cotton, which holds perspiration. Good running socks, some with double layers, can help prevent blisters.

If you will be training during cold weather, be sure you have a good pair of gloves, and wear a hat. You lose a lot of heat through your head, so covering it will help keep you comfortable.

Show Yourself

Good running shoes come with reflective material to help keep you visible as you run in the dark. You can also find vests with reflective strips, or you could consider wearing a belt with a flashing light. Whatever you do, make it easy for drivers to spot you when the sun isn't shining.

For your long training runs in warm weather, you will need plenty of fluids, so you should invest in a belt with a pouch to carry your water bottle. Many have pockets to hold your car keys and gels.

Monitoring Shoe Wear

Running shoes are usually pretty sturdy, especially those made for heavier runners, but they don't last forever. The midsole of a typical running shoe is made of a foamy substance called EVA, ethylene vinyl acetate. With each stride, the EVA is flattened. It then rebounds to provide the cushioning you need.

As you run, the cushioning properties of the EVA diminish, and the foam is also affected by the perspiration from your feet. Eventually, the EVA just stays compacted. At that point, your running shoes have become a liability, and this happens long before the shoes show outward signs of wear.

A good pair of running shoes should last 300 to 500 miles. If your shoes start giving you problems before you get to 300 miles with them, seriously consider changing brands or styles. To keep track of the miles, make sure that your logbook indicates which shoes you were wearing during each run.

Running in worn-out shoes is asking for trouble. If you try to extend the use of running shoes that have lost their protective properties, you will end up injured. Shin splints and Achilles tendonitis are common problems associated with running in shoes past their prime.

How a running shoe feels is a good gauge of whether it's time to get a new pair, but there are other indicators. Look at the shoe from the back. If the heel is worn down or compressed on one side, it's probably time to change.

Such wear might also be a sign that it's time for you to visit a podiatrist, who can evaluate you for a pair of orthotics. These are inserts designed to correct flaws in your gait. If you show excessive wear on one part of your shoes, that may be indicative of a problem that can be solved with the inserts.

Monitoring Your Heart Rate

One of the most popular training gadgets is the heart rate monitor, which is very useful in what is known as effort-based training. Time spent during a run is not always the best indicator of successful training. In fact, depending on conditions, you might feel that you had a bad run because you slowed down at some points and seemed to struggle at others. With a heart-rate monitor, you might discover that your "bad" run was actually pretty good.

Most heart rate monitors work with a strap that goes around the chest. The strap has sensors that detect the heartbeat and send a radio signal to a watch on your wrist. You can monitor your heart rate continually as you work out, increasing the intensity or cutting back according to your training plan.

If you don't like the idea of figuring your maximum heart rate on paper, you can pay $150 or more to a health club or a physician to put you through a test to designed to give you a definitive answer. Here's a more practical alternative: wear a heart rate monitor in a 5K and go all out in the race. That's about as good as anything, and the entry fee won't be more than about $15.

Number Crunching

There are different ways to determine your maximum heart rate. Here are three:

- Subtract your age from 220. The sum is your maximum heart rate.
- Subtract half your age from 205.
- Subtract 80 percent of your age from 214.

The latter two formulas are more appropriate for people who are active and fit. The formulas aren't completely accurate, but they are close enough for you to use in designing your workouts.

Bad to Good

Now, back to how a "bad" workout can turn out to have been good. Say your run took you over some difficult trails or hilly terrain. You slowed noticeably because of the impediments, so you thought you weren't doing very well on your run. With a heart rate monitor, you would be able to see that although your pace slowed, your effort remained constant, as reflected in your heart rate. You had a useful workout, not a poor one.

As you might expect, heart rate monitors come with a wide variety of features beyond the basics of showing the heart rate and keeping time. You can find heart rate monitors that allow you to set a minimum heart rate for your workout, with an alarm to tell you if you drop below the minimum. Similarly, you can set a maximum heart rate.

There are heart rate monitors so advanced that they record virtually every aspect of the run and then download the data to your computer. You can get the fancy heart rate monitors to do just about everything except run.

On the Alert

Besides improving your workouts, a heart rate monitor can help you avoid overtraining or undertraining. Signs of overtraining include a sluggish feeling, an elevated heart rate, and an inability to get the heart rate up. The best way to check is to put on your heart rate monitor when you first wake up in the morning. If your heart rate is higher than the normal resting level, you should scale back your workouts for a week or two. Don't stop working out, just lower the intensity.

Wearing your heart rate monitor during a race can help you keep from overdoing it early. It is a common error for new runners to start their races at breakneck speed. Keeping an eye on your monitor early in the race will help you maintain the kind of pace that lets you finish strong instead of just barely making it.

Most specialty running stores sell heart rate monitors. Let the staff help you determine which model is best for you.

Tracking Mileage

It's not always necessary to know how far you ran during a workout. Sometimes the time spent on your feet is more important than the distance traveled. Mostly, however, you will want to know your mileage so you can enter it in your logbook. You also need the information to monitor your shoe wear. There are several ways to keep track.

If you often run a particular course, perhaps in your neighborhood or on a trail nearby, you can measure it once and always know how far you went. That keeps you from having to do anything special to measure each time.

There are also fancy pedometers that keep up with your mileage. Some can be calibrated for your gait and will measure distance traveled whether you are walking, running, or doing something in between. Some will also time your run and, based on information about your age and weight, will calculate the calories burned during your run.

Then there are the GPS devices, which are just the ticket for the triathlete who likes toys. Each year, although the devices seem to grow smaller, they continue to add features. The unit you wear on your wrist when you run works like the device in your car that gives you directions.

The principal drawback of GPS devices is that they sometimes lose touch with the satellites in wooded areas or where there are tall buildings. As the devices improve, however, lost signals are less of an issue. Most are very reliable, and some "catch up" by guessing your route while the signal was weak or lost.

The device, which looks like an oversized watch, is in touch with a global positioning system—a series of satellites orbiting the earth—and it knows where you are and tracks you as you go. As with other high-tech devices, the available features are impressive. Some of the GPS devices keep track of your entire run and can even help you find your way back to the start if you become disoriented or get lost. Some of the more sophisticated models are made for biking and running, allowing you to toggle between modes.

Whatever you use, make it a habit to log your mileage and time. You keep the log, after all, in part to compare similar workouts from week to week. How else will you know if you have progressed?

Useful Drills

There are ways to improve your running form that don't take a lot of time. Consider the following simple drills to make you a better runner. First, at a track or on the grass, measure off 20 to 30 yards. Warm up with an easy run of ten to fifteen minutes, then start:

- **High knee kicks.** Moving at a moderate pace, cover the distance with your arms swinging high and your knees going as high as you can get them. Jog back to the start and do a second repetition.
- **Butt kicks.** As you cover the 30 yards, bring your legs up in the back, trying to touch your buttocks with your feet. Swing your arms. Do two reps.
- **Skipping.** Just like you did when you were a kid. Go as high as you can. Do two reps.
- **Walking lunges.** Put your leg out as far as it will go with the knee directly over the ankle. Cover 15 yards. Repeat twice.
- **Single-leg hops.** Hop 20 to 30 yards on one leg, then hop back to the start on the other. Start with one rep and build up to two. Hopping backward is a great workout for your hamstrings.

QUESTION?

I heard someone talking about doing fartlek workouts. What is a fartlek?
Fartlek is a Swedish word that translates to "speed play." During a run, usually by yourself, you pick up the pace significantly for very short periods, usually twenty seconds. During a forty-five-minute run, you might do ten to twelve fartlek bursts to improve your aerobic capacity.

If you have access to a track, that is an ideal surface for speed workouts. Tracks are usually made of rubber or similar material and are very easy on the legs. A typical track is 400 meters around (roughly a quarter mile), so it's easy to know your distances. You can add variety to your workouts with speed sessions, tempo runs, and fartleks, among others.

The length of your tempo run in training will depend on the distance you will cover in your race. If your triathlon features a 5K for the run, your tempo sessions should be no more than fifteen to twenty minutes. Never do more than one hard session per week.

Hill workouts are tough, but they provide very effective training. Find a hill that takes one to two minutes to climb and run it at a hard (but not all-out) pace. Jog back to the start as a recovery period. Start with two to three repeats on the hill and build up to eight reps.

Outdoor Training

Most of your training will be outdoors, as it should be. With rare exceptions, your triathlon will be outside. That means that, on occasion, weather will be a major factor in your workout.

The most threatening will be hot weather. You don't want to avoid warm-weather training altogether because you will almost certainly need to become acclimated to the heat for your race. Common sense is in order, however.

You have already been told to stock up with light-colored, loose-fitting apparel for your training. Now wear it.

If you live in a warm climate, avoid training in the middle of the day, when the sun is high in the sky and temperatures are at their worst. Get out of bed early or wait until the sun is down or going down and conditions are more favorable.

Always take lots of fluids and have them at hand when you are running in hot weather. Dehydration can be a very serious problem. If you can, train with at least one or two other runners so that assistance will be at hand if you get into trouble.

It's okay to brave the elements for a training run in the heat, but don't let bravado put you in danger. If it's just plain baking outside—temperatures in the nineties or a heat index approaching triple digits—do your run on a treadmill at the health club or at home, or just let it go for the day.

Rain is a separate issue. Except in cold weather, rain can be refreshing as it cools you off while you exert yourself. Face it, if you have a workout of more than fifteen or twenty minutes, you will probably be soaking wet from perspiration anyway. The main caution about rainy weather is lightning. If lightning is present, go home. Plan to run another day.

When running at night, always wear gear with reflective strips, and avoid running in the dark on streets or roads with heavy traffic. No matter how easy it is to see you, drivers who aren't paying attention won't notice, and you know there are plenty of them driving the streets. Stay away from traffic. Even if you aren't struck by a car, you will still be breathing fumes that can irritate your airways.

Layer Up

Running in cold weather can be invigorating, and it doesn't sap you like the heat and humidity. But there are dangers in extreme cold, and you should always wear layers and a head cover when temperatures are freezing or lower.

If wind chill is a factor, make your outer shell a windbreaker, and always wear gloves. Remember, too, that cold weather doesn't mean you don't perspire. You don't notice because it's not pouring off of you as it does in the heat. You are still losing fluid, however, and it's just as important to stay hydrated when you are running in the cold. It will take you longer to warm up in cold weather, so add a bit of extra time in slow mode before you start pushing hard in your run.

FACT

A key advantage to treadmill training is that once you set the speed, you have to keep up or you will go flying off the end. It's a good way to do a tempo run, the goal of which is to sustain a speed for a set length of time.

Treadmill Workouts

On the days when you can't run outside or you don't have time, the treadmill is a viable option, and the quality of the training is right there with a run on the road. One great benefit of the treadmill is that it has a soft surface. Your legs take a pounding on asphalt, the most common running surface, so you might even schedule a treadmill run once every week or two just to give your legs a break.

Bear in mind that there may be an adjustment period at the outset of your treadmill training. For starters, there's the speed factor. What seems to be a very quick pace on a treadmill may be a lot slower than you think it is. It is also a different feel from the road.

You can adjust the incline of your treadmill to make your session more like a hill workout, and you can preset some treadmills to vary the speed and incline to simulate realistic, outdoor conditions. To combat boredom, you can set up a television near your machine or wear earphones to listen to the radio or recorded music. Podcasts and audio books are also possibilities. The treadmill is one venue where it is safe to wear headphones.

CHAPTER 11

Putting It All Together

It's not enough just to know the correct workouts for
your triathlon training. You must also combine them
in a way that gives you the best chance to progress
toward readiness for the challenge of the triathlon
while minimizing the risk of overtraining and injury.
The training schedules in this chapter are designed
to get you to the starting line feeling confident, fit,
and with all parts working.

Why You Need a Training Schedule

Training for a triathlon is much more involved than training for a single sport. If you are trying to get ready for a 5K, for example, you will do a weekly long run, speed work once a week, plus at least one other run of moderate distance or intensity, perhaps mixed in with some cross-training or strength training.

As simple as that might appear to be, a training program for a road race should have structure. You aren't just randomly running around, hoping that the activity will result in enough fitness to compete.

Multiply that concept by three when considering what you will need to do to get ready for your triathlon. The training for each sport must have structure, but you must also keep in mind that the workouts are vastly different from each other. They should be integrated in a way that keeps you from the common mistake of overtraining.

For example, you wouldn't want to have a workout with weights, a run, and a cycling session all in the same day, especially if the run and the ride were at high intensity. Chances are you wouldn't be able to move for a couple of days after that.

Through the first eight weeks of training, every fourth week is a recovery week. Workouts are shorter and lighter to give your body the chance to benefit from the hard workouts that were aimed at building your strength and endurance.

Lighten Up

The training schedules in this chapter include rest periods. No matter how strong you feel as you advance in your training, stick to the schedule and cut back as directed. Piling hard workouts on top of each other will only cause burnout or injury. Overdoing it could even jeopardize your race.

You should also remember, of course, that the training schedules do not represent unbreakable rules. Missing one or more workouts will not ruin your training. Further, if you start to feel burnout or unusual fatigue, it would be wise to add an extra day of rest.

The Training Schedule and How to Read It

Of necessity, the charts that contain the training schedules include some abbreviations and other language that might seem cryptic. Following is a guide to reading and understanding the charts.

The most common abbreviations are WU (warm-up) and CD (cool down). Previous chapters have detailed the importance of the warm-up. In each of the three disciplines, the warm-up session is usually five to ten minutes of light activity, be it swimming, biking, or running. You want to warm up the muscles and get your blood flowing before you start any heavy activity.

At the end of your workout, a five- to ten-minute period of light activity is advisable before stretching or heading for home. The cool-down period helps your tense muscles relax while your heart rate returns to normal.

The training charts in this book focus on time spent in the different sports, not miles run or covered on a bicycle. Nevertheless, it is a good idea to chart your mileage in running and cycling in order to gauge your progress from week to week. You can do similar calculations if you record the number of laps you swim in the pool.

Numbers

On the charts, when you see a number next to an activity—swim, cycle, run—the number in almost all cases indicates how many minutes you are supposed to do that activity. For example, if you see "Swim 20" on the chart, that means your swim workout should last twenty minutes. "Run 30" means you are going to have a run workout that lasts half an hour. "Drills 10" means do ten minutes of drills.

As your training progresses, the times will lengthen and you will see notations such as "Bike 1:10." The means your bike session will last an hour and ten minutes.

When you see something like "4 × 100" in the swim column, that means you will be swimming 100 yards or meters (depending on which your pool uses) without stopping, completing the distance four times. Rest in between is permitted. Similarly, "6 × 50" means six swims of 50 yards each.

The training charts have many references to drills. All of them were described in the respective chapters on swimming, biking, and running. In the chapter on running, for example, drills include butt kicks, high knee kicks, and single leg hops.

When your chart calls for drills, pick two or three of these drills and do them for a minute or two each. You will do these along with your warm-up to get into the swing of your activity. If one of the drills is harder for you to do than others, be sure you include it each time your training chart calls for drills.

Defining Moments

Here is a rundown of other terms on the charts that require an explanation:

- **Easy.** When your chart recommends an activity to be done "easy," that means more than a jog (for running) and with some effort but not to the point of discomfort.
- **Hard.** When this appears on your training chart next to an activity, you will push yourself to the point that you are straining. "Hard" does not, however, mean all out. The training programs in this book only rarely call for all-out effort.
- **Cadence.** This is revolutions per minute (rpm) on your bike. High cadence is higher than 90 rpm.
- **Push hills.** This means that when you are biking and you come to a hill, give it some extra effort for one to two minutes. Coast if you need to for recovery. If your riding course does not have many hills, change to a harder gear to accomplish this part of the workout.
- **Time trial (TT).** A workout of set duration after which distance is measured. Good for comparing progress week to week. Used mostly with the bicycle workouts.

- **Tempo.** A tempo run is done between a comfortable pace and race pace. If your goal for your race is nine minutes per mile, your tempo run should be 9:30 to 9:45. For a race pace of ten minutes, do your tempo runs at 10:30. You do not stop during your tempo run.

- **Strides.** A drill in which you run on a soft surface for approximately 100 yards, building your speed as you go. You should finish at a hard pace. Strides are listed in the charts by the number to be done: "4 Strides" means do the drill four times. Focus on your form whenever you do strides.

- **Spin and aerobic spin (cycling).** Usually includes a minimum rpm for spin, with gears adjusted so it's not a hard effort. Aerobic spin is done at an easier pace, much like the long run for runners.

- **Spin-ups (cycling).** Short-duration increases in rpm, usually to 100 to 110 rpm for thirty to sixty seconds.

- **Build and descend (swimming).** If the chart says "6 × 75 Build," that means you should swim 75 yards six times (with rest between segments) and push in the last 25 yards of each segment. For descend, make each full segment faster than the previous one.

- **Intervals.** Structured workouts that call for increased effort during a run, bike, or swim, almost always calculated in time rather than distance. Interval duration varies from one minute to five or more.

- **Fartlek (running).** Unstructured increases in speed—pickups of twenty to thirty seconds—usually at random, as in running fast from one telephone pole to another.

- **Stretch, strength, core.** Details on these exercises can be found in Chapters 6 and 7. When one or more of them is listed as an alternative to a complete day off, spend about thirty minutes on the workout.

Prep for Absolute

	Sunday	Monday	Tuesday
Week 1	Day off or stretch	Swim 15 minutes: rest at each end as needed	Run 10: jog 1, walk 1, repeat 5 times
Week 2	Day off or stretch	Swim 20 minutes: rest after every 2 lengths	Run 12: jog 2, walk 1, repeat 4 times
Week 3	Day off or stretch	Swim 25 minutes: rest after 3 lengths	Run 15: jog 3, walk 2, repeat 3 times
Week 4	Day off or stretch	Swim 30 minutes: warm up with 5-min. continuous swim, rest on each end	Run 20: walk 1, run 7, walk 2, repeat

Beginners

Wednesday	Thursday	Friday	Saturday
Bike 20: easy gear, coast and rest as needed	Swim 15: attempt two lengths before rest	Bike 20: easy gear, coast and rest as needed	Run 12: jog 1, walk 1, repeat 6 times
Bike 25: easy gear, spin, rest less	Swim 20: rest after every 2 lengths	Bike 25: focus on cadence (keep above 90)	Run 14: increase jog time from Wed.
Bike 25: experiment with harder gears on flats	Swim 25: swim 4 lengths before rest	Bike 30: high cadence	Run 18: walk 2, run 5, walk 2, repeat
Bike 30: spin, push harder gear 5, spin	Swim 30: WU, swim until rest needed, count laps	Bike 30: high cadence	Run 20: walk 2, run as long as possible, jog remainder

Beginner   Triathlon

	Sunday	Monday	Tuesday
Week 1	Day off or strength/core	Swim 20 minutes: WU 5, drills, 6x25, CD	Run 20: aerobic walk/jog, stretch
Week 2	Day off or strength/core	Swim 25 minutes: WU 5, kick/pull 8x25, CD	Run 25: drills 3, stretch
Week 3	Day off or strength/core	Swim 30 minutes: WU, 6x50, drills, CD	Run 30: WU 5, continuous 15, drills 5, CD
Week 4	Day off, stretch	Swim 20 minutes: WU, drills, CD	Run 20: easy pace, drills, CD
Week 5	Day off or strength/core	Swim 30 minutes: WU, 8x75 build, drills, CD	Run 30: WU, drills, 4 strides, CD, stretch
Week 6	Day off or strength/core	Swim 35 minutes: WU, 10x50 descend, CD	Run 35: WU, drills, 6 strides, CD, stretch

Training

Wednesday	Thursday	Friday	Saturday
Bike 30: WU 10, drills 10, CD 10	Swim 20: core/strength	Bike 45: continuous, optional swim	Run 25: walk/jog
Bike 40: WU 10, drills 10, spin 10, CD 10	Swim 25: 4x50, drills, core/strength	Bike 50: continuous; optional swim	Run 30: easy, no walking
Bike 45: WU 10, drills 10, medium hard 20, CD	Swim 30: WU, 5x100, drills, CD, core/strength	Bike 60: continuous, cadence at 90+	Run 30: pick up speed last 10
Bike 40: high cadence, easy gears	Swim 20: easy, stretch	Bike 50: easy, optional swim	Run 25: slow, keep heart rate down
Bike 50: WU 5, drills 5–10, 4x1 hard, CD	Swim 35: WU, 6x100, drills, CD	Bike 1:15: 4x2 hard, run 10 easy	Run 40: 6x1 fast, CD
Bike 55: WU 5, drills 5–10, 6x1 hard, CD	Swim 35: WU, 3x200 descend, CD	Bike 1:15: 4x2 hard, run 10 easy	Run 40: WU, 6x1 fast, CD

Beginner Triathlon

	Sunday	Monday	Tuesday
Week 7	Day off or strength/core	Swim 40: WU, 6x50, 8x25 all out, CD	Run 35: WU, drills, 8 strides, CD, stretch
Week 8	Day off, stretch	Swim 30: WU, drills, CD	Run 25: WU, 1 or 2 drills, 2 strides, CD
Week 9	Day off or strength/core	Swim 40: WU, drills, 4x150, CD	Run 40: WU, drills, 8 strides, CD
Week 10	Day off or strength/core	Swim 45: WU, drills, 1x150, 2x100, 4x50, 6x25, CD	Run 45: WU, drills, tempo 10, CD
Week 11	Day off or strength/core	Swim 45: WU, drills, swim 20 continuous, CD	Run 45: WU, drills, 6x90 sec. hard, CD
Week 12	Day off	Swim 25: WU, drills, 4x50 fast, CD	Run 20: WU, 6 strides, CD

Wednesday	Thursday	Friday	Saturday
Bike 60: tempo 20, otherwise easy	Swim 35: WU, 2x300, drills, CD	Bike 1:20: 6x2 hard, run 10 easy	Run 45: increase pace last 10
Bike 45: easy, cadence 90+	Swim 25: WU, 3x100, CD	Bike 1:10: easy, cadence 90+	Run 35: easy pace, optional swim
Bike 60: WU, 4x3 hard, CD	Swim 40: WU, drills, TT 15, CD	Bike 1:25: WU, tempo 20; Run 15 easy	Run 45: WU, 4x2 pickup, CD, optional swim
Bike 1:10: WU, drills, 4x4 hard, CD	Swim 45: WU, drills, 1x500 hard, CD	Bike 1:30: WU, tempo 30; Run 10	Run 50: steady pace, push hills
Bike 1:15: WU, drills, 4x5 intervals, CD	Swim 45: WU, drills, 4x200, CD	Bike 1:30: WU, tempo 30, run 10	Run 45: easy pace
Bike 35: easy with 4x1 pickups, CD	Day off/stretch	Bike 15; Run 5	**Race Day**

Intermediate Triathlon

	Sunday	Monday	Tuesday
Week 1	Day off or strength/core	Swim 25 minutes: WU, drills, 8x25, CD; Bike 25: easy	Run 30: WU, drills, CD, core/stretch 15
Week 2	Day off or strength/core	Swim 30 minutes: WU, drills, 6x50, CD; Bike 25: easy	Run 35: WU, drills, 2 strides, CD, stretch 15
Week 3	Day off or strength/core	Swim 35 minutes: WU, drills, 8x50, CD; Bike 30: easy	Run 40: WU, drills, 4 strides, CD, stretch 15
Week 4	Day off, stretch	Swim 25 minutes: WU, drills, 4x50, CD, stretch 15	Run 30: WU, drills, 2 strides, CD, stretch 15
Week 5	Day off or strength/core	Swim 35 minutes: WU, drills, 10x50 descend, 4x25 sprint, CD; Bike 30: easy	Run 40: WU, drills, 6 strides, CD, stretch 15
Week 6	Day off or strength/core	Swim 40 minutes: WU, drills, 10x75 (50 easy, 25 hard), CD; Bike 30: spin	Run 45: WU, drills, 8 strides, CD, stretch 15

Training

Wednesday	Thursday	Friday	Saturday
Bike 45: WU, drills, 90 rpm spin	Swim 25: WU, drills, 4x100, CD, strength/core	Bike 60: aerobic spin; optional swim or run	Run 35: slow, maintain pace
Bike 50: WU, drills, pickup 10, spin, CD	Swim 30: WU, drills, 8x100, CD, strength/core	Bike 1:10: aerobic spin; optional swim or run	Run 40: aerobic, push any hills
Bike 55: WU, drills, tempo 20, CD	Swim 35: WU, drills, 4x100, CD, strength/core	Bike 1:15: aerobic, push hills; optional swim or run	Run 45: aerobic, push hills
Bike 45: WU, drills, tempo 5, CD	Swim 25: WU, drills, 4x100, CD, core	Bike 60: easy; optional swim	Run 35: low heart rate
Bike 60: WU, drills, 6x2 hard spin, CD	Swim 35: WU, drills, 4x200, CD, strength/core	Bike 1:20: WU, tempo 20, CD; Run 10: easy	Run 45: middle 10 run hard
Bike 1:10: WU, drills, 6x3 hard, CD	Swim 40: WU, drills, 3x300, CD, strength/core	Bike 1:25: WU, tempo 30, CD; Run 15: easy	Run 50: last 15 hard

Intermediate Triathlon

	Sunday	Monday	Tuesday
Week 7	Day off or strength/core	Swim 45: WU, drills, 8x100 descend, CD; Bike 35: moderate	Run 50: WU, drills, 8x1 hard, CD, stretch 15
Week 8	Day off, stretch	Swim 35: WU, drills, 8x50; Bike 20: spin	Run 40: WU, drills, 4 strides; stretch 15
Week 9	Day off or strength/core	Swim 45: WU, drills, 6x75, 5x100 all out, CD; Bike 35: high cadence	Run 50: WU, drills, 4 hills, 6 strides, CD, stretch
Week 10	Day off or strength/core	Swim 50: WU, drills, 8x50, 6x100 all out, CD; Bike 40: tempo 10	Run 55: WU, drills, 6 hills, 6 strides, CD, stretch
Week 11	Day off or strength/core	Swim 55: WU, drills, 6x100 fast, 10x25 sprint, CD; Bike 40: tempo 15	Run 60: WU, drills, 6 hills, 6x1 hard, CD; stretch
Week 12	Day off, stretch	Swim 40: WU, drills, 4x100 fast, CD; Bike 20	Run 30: WU, 6 strides, CD; stretch

Wednesday	Thursday	Friday	Saturday
Bike 1:15: WU, drills, 6x3 hard, CD	Swim 45: WU, drills, 2x (1x300, 2x100), CD; strength/core	Bike 1:30: WU, 6x5 hard; Run 15: easy	Run 55: push every hill
Bike 60: WU, drills, 4x2 hard spin, CD	Swim 35: WU, drills, 2x200, CD; strength/core	Bike 1:20: WU, tempo 10, CD; Run 10: easy	Run 45: WU, easy with 4x1 push, CD
Bike 1:15: WU, drills, 30 min. alt. 1 hard, 1 easy, CD	Swim 45: WU, drills, 4x200, 8x25 sprint, CD; strength/core	Bike 1:30: WU, 3x10 at race pace, CD; Run 20	Run 60: last 15 hard
Bike 1:15: WU, drills, race pace 20, CD	Swim 50: WU, drills, swim 15 race pace; strength/core	Bike 1:30: 6x5 at race pace; Run 20	Run 60: last 15 hard
Bike 1:20: WU, drills, 30 min. 2 hard, 1 easy, CD	Swim 55: WU, drills, continuous swim race pace 20; strength/core	Bike 1:30: tempo 30; Run 20	Run 60: WU, last 20 hard
Bike 30: WU, 6x1 hard, CD	Day off, stretch	Bike 20; Run 10: 4 strides	**Race day**

When Your Job Is Physical

For most aspiring triathletes, the training schedule will represent nearly all of their physical activity, mainly because there won't be time for much else after work and family obligations are met. Prospective triathletes whose jobs involve a lot of physical activity will face different challenges from those who work in offices or are still in school.

If your regular job involves a lot of lifting or other physical activity, you could be more prone to injury from your triathlon training. If you are in, say, construction and are picking up heavy objects all day, that can count as part, or even all, of your strength training, depending on the types and frequency of the exertion.

If you come home physically exhausted from your job, cut back on the intensity of the workout you planned for that day, especially if it's a run. You can still do your workout, but you risk injury if you are already physically spent and you try to get through a hard run. If you are especially tired, just skip the run for that day.

If the physical demands of your job come in cycles, you can maintain your training schedule without significant change while in a light period at work. When the work demands on your body are heavy, you will have to make adjustments in the training schedule, perhaps adding an extra day off or eliminating one or more of the high-intensity workouts.

Hurt at Work

If you are injured on the job, you must treat it just as though you hurt yourself in training. That doesn't mean all training goes out the window, but if you hurt your shoulder on the job, you will probably have to skip your swim training until the shoulder heals. In the meantime, you can replace a swim session with a bike ride or run to maintain your fitness and keep your head in the game.

Avoid trying to train through an on-the-job injury. It will almost certainly get worse, and you could end up having to postpone the race altogether.

Inside Versus Outside

If you do a lot of your work outdoors, you will have an advantage over the athletes who sit at desks in air-conditioned buildings most of the day. Because you work outdoors, it will take little or no time for you to become acclimated to outside conditions, especially the heat.

That does not exempt you, however, from the sport-specific training you will need for your triathlon. It just means you won't suffer as much getting used to the heat and humidity if your training occurs in the late spring and summer.

Mental or Psychological Preparation

This chapter contains a formula, so to speak, for getting your body ready to compete in a triathlon. It's all about putting in the work, increasing the difficulty as you get your body to adapt, eating the right foods, and getting adequate rest. The schedule has the numbers, the times and distances, for you to follow.

It's a completely different matter to prepare yourself mentally for your first venture into the world of triathlons. For many, the whole idea can seem pretty daunting. You're planning to jump into the water to swim farther than you ever have before—in a crowd—followed by a bike ride with people zooming around, then a run—possibly in the heat of the day on tired, wobbly legs. Wow! How do you approach that without being scared to death?

High Anxiety

It's normal to be anxious about doing something you've never done, particularly if you do not have a strong background in athletics. Just keep in mind that there are dozens, perhaps hundreds, of people signed up for the race you are doing who are in that same boat. If they can do it, so can you.

You must approach the training and the race with a positive attitude. Fight to maintain it if you must, but if you give up before you start, you won't enjoy a truly unique experience.

It has been proven in clinical studies that your muscles are stronger when your attitude is positive rather than negative. Believe in yourself and trust that your training will carry you through the triathlon challenge.

Don't Overreach

An essential element to keeping the right frame of mind is setting realistic goals. Most beginners should forget about time goals for the triathlon. Instead, concentrate on getting to the finish line. The confidence you gain from knowing you can do it will allow you to focus on improvement in your next one. Set your time goals in triathlon number two, not number one.

One of the best psychological tools you can use to prepare for your race is visualization. See yourself completing a strong swim, a swift bike ride, and a good run to the finish line. What you have seen yourself do a hundred times will be easy when crunch time comes.

It is also useless to compare yourself to others, although if you did some or a lot of your training in a group setting, it will be normal for you to silently view one or two others as competitors. It is much better to compete against yourself. You can't control what others do, but you can control your own effort and the outlook you take to the training and the race.

There will be times when you have a difficult workout. Instead of bemoaning the circumstance, focus on the positive aspect, such as finishing the session even though it was hard. Tell yourself the next workout will be better. Ask yourself if you learned anything from your last training session.

Keep all thoughts positive. Block out the negative. If you're having a tough run, don't say to yourself, "I'm not going to stop." Rather, say, "I'm going to finish." Keep it positive. If you practice a positive mantra during your training, you can carry it over to your race. Say it: "I'm fast. I'm strong. I can do this."

Don't let a bad training day or two get you down. After all, if you never had a bad day, how would you recognize the good ones?

Dealing with the Unexpected

You have your workouts all set and have arranged your job schedule just so. Everything is lined up for that long ride this weekend. Then the in-laws come to town, and, if you don't want a divorce, you have to entertain them. Drat! Two training days shot.

It's annoying, to be sure, but it's not the end of the world. How you handle the small detour in your training can mean a lot to the bottom line of your program. The key is not to let stress take over when life interrupts your training plans. Stress is your enemy. In a stressful state, you are more prone to injury.

In a twelve-week training program, you will be lucky if your plans are not messed up several times. Plan for interruptions and be creative when they occur. For example, if your long weekend ride is canceled by the weather, try to make it up during the week, perhaps riding instead of swimming one day, or just shorten the swim to give you more time for riding. If you find that your bike has a flat and you don't have a tube to fix it, do a run instead.

Just remember that your training doesn't have to follow the schedules in this book to the letter. Small deviations will not screw up your training.

CHAPTER 12

Nutrition Issues

Once you start triathlon training, your nutritional needs will change dramatically. For starters, you will be burning more calories, and your near-daily training routines will increase your metabolism. You will need to eat more to sustain the new activity, but you must monitor what you put in your body. Your workouts are integrated to produce maximum gains, and the fuel you take in is just as important.

How to Eat for a Better Race

The first rule of training for any endurance sport is simple: you need lots of carbohydrates. Your muscles run on a fuel called glycogen, which is stored in the liver and in the muscles. It is converted from glucose (sugar), a common carbohydrate.

When you are exercising a lot, your body is burning glycogen, which must be replenished. When a person "hits the wall," a common problem for marathon runners, that means the body is out, or nearly out, of glycogen and the energy is gone. Extreme fatigue sets in and it becomes almost impossible to move.

FACT

One reason you feel extreme fatigue when glycogen supplies run low is that your brain runs on glucose, which is converted to glycogen for the muscles. When glucose supplies get low, the brain tells the body it's tired. That is the brain's way of saving for itself what glucose is left.

Hitting the wall, or "bonking," should not be a problem in your daily training in any workout that lasts up to an hour long, although hot weather training will speed the onset of glycogen depletion and shorten that window. It will behoove you to get used to a high-carb diet because of all the calories you will be expending as you train.

At a certain point in your training sessions, your body will begin to burn fat as a fuel, but it won't do so without carbohydrates, a kind of starter to the process. An axiom of endurance training is that "fat burns in a carbohydrate flame."

Don't Keep It Simple

When it comes to carbohydrates, complex is much better than simple. Simple carbs, such as sucrose (table sugar), break down quickly in the body and can cause a spike in your blood sugar level. These are the famous "empty calories" you may have heard about. Consuming simple sugar may result in a burst of energy, but just as quickly there will be a "crash" in your blood sugar level, leaving you fatigued and craving more sugar. Further, because the sugar is broken down so quickly, it is immediately stored as glycogen, but cells have a limit to the amount that can be stored. The excess is converted to fat.

It takes the body a lot longer to break down complex carbohydrates, so you have a steady stream of energy rather than a series of spikes and crashes. Good sources of complex carbohydrates are whole grains such as oatmeal and brown rice, pasta, bagels, potatoes, and fresh or canned fruit. Simple sugars to avoid are in candy, cakes, table sugar, soft drinks, jellies, jams, and canned fruit in heavy syrup.

The difference in carbs accounts for the fact that many energy gels— what you would use during a race, especially a long one—are rich in carbohydrates and low in simple sugars. Simple sugar is good as a readily available carbohydrate source. When you are working out or racing, a small amount of simple sugar will not cause a crash because it is used quickly.

The recommended diet for athletes includes lots of fruits and vegetables, which might seem to be a contradiction because many fruits contain fructose, a simple sugar. These are natural sources of carbohydrates, and are low in simple sugar, and they contain fiber, which slows down the absorption of the sugar. Foods with added sugar are the ones to avoid.

Protein

Lest you think that your diet during your triathlon training will be nothing but bagels, lentils, and brown rice, there is one very important ingredient in your nutrition needs not mentioned so far: protein. As mentioned previously, building stronger muscles involves breaking them down through training, with the muscles growing stronger as they rebuild. A key component of that process is available protein. High-quality protein breaks down into amino acids, which support muscle repair and growth. Carbs are good for energy, but they don't help build your muscles.

Good sources of protein are lean meat, fish, poultry, eggs, milk, tofu, and yogurt. The best sources of protein for your purposes are those without a lot of fat. Yes, there is protein available in a double cheeseburger or pepperoni pizza, but those foods are high in the kind of fat that will slow you down and threaten your health.

FACT

Fat is an important component to your diet. Many vitamins are "fat soluble," that is, they need fat to be absorbed by your body. Fat also provides long-lasting energy and helps your body produce hormones. Take in fat, but make sure it's the right kind: monounsatured or polyunsaturated, the kind you get from olive oil, canola oil, and omega-3 fatty acids in fish and leafy green vegetables. Stay away from saturated fat and trans fats.

What Vegetarian Athletes Should Know

The most significant challenge for an athlete who does not eat meat is getting adequate protein, the building block for muscles. There are many sources of protein for vegetarians, even vegans, who eat only plant products (no dairy foods).

A good plan is to combine plant foods. For example, a peanut butter sandwich on whole-wheat bread is a good source of protein. Another good combination is brown rice and lentils.

Good sources of protein for nonvegan vegetarians are tofu, milk, cheese, yogurt, soy milk, beans, and lentils. You can take in protein with supplements as well, perhaps with a soy- or whey-based protein shake or smoothie. Make the shake or smoothie with the protein powder mixed with skim milk and perhaps a bit of fresh fruit (strawberries or blueberries). It tastes good and helps your body handle the rigors of triathlon training. You can find these protein supplements at any health food store or nutrition center, but before you take that leap, if you believe your diet is protein-deficient, consult a licensed dietician to be sure.

Bar Shopping

If your normal vegetarian diet does not provide adequate protein for your needs as a triathlete in training, consider supplementation in bar form. There are many good energy bars on the market with increased levels of protein designed to meet the needs of active people. They are more useful after your exercise than before. That's when you need extra protein to aid recovery and the building of muscle. Most contain some sugar, but it's usually a negligible amount.

Nutrition Just for Training

It's not difficult to define a healthy diet: stay away from saturated and trans fats, eat healthy carbohydrates and adequate protein, and take in lots of fruit and vegetables. That's great for the general population, but what about the triathlete in training? Are there specific foods that should be on the list?

It has already been stated that you should increase your intake of carbs once your training starts. You need them for energy to get through your workouts. Good carbohydrate sources include:

- Potatoes, preferably sweet potatoes
- Fresh fruit or canned if it's not in heavy syrup
- Fresh, frozen, and canned vegetables (but watch out for the sodium in some canned foods)
- Cereal, bread, and pasta made from whole grains
- Brown rice

Good protein sources for triathletes in training inlcude:

- Lean meat
- Tofu
- Beans, nuts, and seeds
- Eggs
- Cheese
- Yogurt (nonfat provides the same protein benefits)

Remember to limit the fat you include with these nutrition sources. Excess fat will slow you down in your training and may cause gastric problems.

Foods to Avoid

The training schedule you are following is designed to integrate the three sports in a way that will get you to the starting line fully prepared. Your plan for nutrition as you train should have a similar design.

The good components of your nutrition plan have been laid out, bringing on the natural question as to whether there are foods that should be avoided. A good starting place is junk food. Yes, most people, even athletes, love it, and you can indulge occasionally. If you feel completely deprived during your training, you won't enjoy it as much. But try to limit the potato chips, donuts, and candy bars. These treats contain lots of calories but virtually no nutrition, certainly nothing that will assist you in your quest to become a fit, fast triathlete.

QUESTION?

I've heard a lot about the glycemic index. Is it relevant for an athlete in training?

As popularly cited, the glycemic index (GI) is an oversimplification of a complex issue. The GI is a way of rating foods based on their effect on blood glucose levels when only that food is eaten. A high-GI food eaten with protein will not affect the blood glucose level in the same way as if eaten alone. Further, some high-GI foods are beneficial during exercise.

Not So Sweet

As you become more familiar with triathlons and what goes into participating, you will discover many sources of information and products designed to help you compete at a higher level, including many involving nutrition. Nowadays, even your grocery store will have shelves of energy bars, drinks, and other supplements touted as just what you need to excel at your sport.

The best way to evaluate various bars, gels, and drinks is to check the nutrition information on the package. If it contains a high percentage of simple sugar, see if there is something with a smaller amount. You are aiming for the most carbohydrates you can get in the smallest package.

Always look at the ingredients in anything you plan to eat. The ingredients are listed in order of predominance, that is, the first thing listed is what the product contains the most of. If high fructose corn syrup is the first ingredient, look for something else. While there is debate about whether high fructose corn syrup is worse for you than other sweeteners, the fact is that it's simple sugar, which should be limited in your diet.

Not So Fat

If your diet includes a lot of greasy, fried, and fat-laden foods, you are going to have to change your habits or your triathlon training will crash before takeoff. Think of a change in diet as yet another positive result of your decision to become a triathlete. As with junk food, you can indulge occasionally in heavier foods such as hamburgers or pizza, but be careful about doing so immediately prior to a scheduled workout. Saturated fat sitting on your stomach from last night's meal will slow you to a crawl on your morning run or ride. It can also upset your stomach.

Remember, too, that any problems brought on by your diet will be exacerbated if your training takes place in the heat. Be very careful about what you eat the night before training if it's going to be warm outside.

Not all fats are bad. In fact, athletes need fat in their diets, preferably two servings a day from fat-rich plant foods. There are many good fats that you should include in your diet. Leading the list is olive oil, a great source of monounsaturated fat, as well as avocados. And don't forget about the good fats in certain nuts (almonds, walnuts, pecans). Certain fish, notably salmon, contain high levels of omega-3 fatty acids, considered very good for the heart. Even butter, a source of saturated fat, has beneficial lauric acid and is believed by many to be superior to margarine, which contains trans fats.

Trans fats, which come from partially hydrogenated oils, is present even in products whose labels declare them to be trans fat free because federal regulations allow that statement if the amount is negligible. Tend to view a product with partially hydrogenated oil as the tenth listed ingredient differently than one with it listed second. There is evidence that no amount of trans fat is healthy in your diet.

Alcohol and Training

When it comes to alcohol and sports training, conventional wisdom is simple: take it easy. That doesn't mean you have to give up beer, wine, or your favorite Scotch on the rocks. Keep in mind, however, that alcohol can dehydrate you, so you should be careful about consumption the night before an important training session and especially the night before your big race.

Your goal leading up to the race, especially if it will be warm that day, is to hydrate as well as possible. Drinking alcohol will hinder that process. Alcohol consumption can lower heat tolerance as well.

FACT

Before you chug down that beer (or three) the night before your training run, here's something you should know: alcohol is metabolized by the liver. While that process is going on, the liver is not making as much glycogen, which you need for fuel to swim, bike, or run. That can have an effect on your endurance.

Alcohol affects different people different ways and to different degrees. If you have a high tolerance for it, this may not be an issue for you. If you don't know, don't take chances.

Eating Before, During, and After Training

Just as training regimens are different for the three sports of the triathlon, your nutritional needs are different before, during, and after each discipline. The first thing to know is that you should eat something, especially if your activity is taking place in the morning. When you arise after a night's sleep, your blood sugar is low. If you engage in vigorous exercise on an empty stomach, you will suffer. You will feel weak, possibly dizzy, perhaps sick to your stomach. Certainly your workout will be a poor one and most likely will have to be cut short.

In all three sports, postworkout nutrition should take place within about thirty minutes of stopping. It is during that period that your body is most receptive to the replacement of the glycogen you lost during the workout. Ingest carbohydrates for glycogen replacement and protein for your muscles.

Swim Bites

Of the three sports, the least demanding in terms of preactivity nutrition is the swim workout. You can get by on a piece of toast or fruit—just something to elevate your blood sugar level a bit. A sports drink would also work for that purpose. Of course, the more time you have before your workout, the more you can eat without feeling bogged down.

After your swim workout, you should have a good meal that includes protein. Consider oatmeal, for carbohydrates to replenish glycogen stores, and eggs or a smoothie to supply protein for muscle recovery. Do not get your protein from something like sausage and biscuits. Don't ingest greasy food after your swim. Keep it healthy.

Swims rarely last longer than forty-five minutes, so it is highly unlikely you will run out of energy from lack of fuel in your body. Heat won't be an issue because of your surroundings, so hydration won't be much of a problem.

In fact, even if you awake pretty hungry, don't get into the pool with a big meal on your stomach. You will feel sluggish, and cramps are an issue when you combine a full stomach and swimming.

Don't plan on eating during the swim, but you might take a few sips of water or a sports drink. Keep the bottle at hand near one end of the pool so you don't have to get in and out.

Bike Snacks

Of the three sports, cycling requires the highest caloric intake because most rides are longer than swims or run. It is recommended that you take in 400 to 500 calories in carborhydrates, protein, and fat before any ride lasting an hour or longer. You burn a lot of calories on your bicycle, so you need a good store of fuel to start out.

Also, although eating that many calories may make you feel a bit full, you will manage that fullness much better on the bike than you would out running on the road or the trails.

Foods to consider as a preride meal include oatmeal or cold cereal, fruit, and eggs (but not fried or otherwise greasy). Don't eat a lot of fat, but take in enough calories to see you through the workout.

Be sure you take some additional fluid and fuel (a gel, energy bar, banana, or some fig cookies) along on your ride. You expend a lot of energy on the bicycle, and you don't want to hit the wall half way through your ride, 10 miles from your car. That is a miserable experience you don't need.

You can conveniently carry a gel pack with you on your bike by taping it to one of the bars. If you carry gel, make sure you have water to take with it. If you wash an energy gel down with a sports drink, both will sit on your stomach too long to do you any good.

Run for It

Nutritional preparation for your run is similar to what you need for the bike workout, but it is best to eat less than you would for your ride. A full feeling will hamper you more when you're on foot than when you're riding.

A small bowl of oatmeal would work, but you could probably get by with just one energy gel or half of an energy bar followed by water to aid digestion. Save your sports drinks for when you're actually running, or at least water it down if you're going to drink it before you start.

Most of the training runs for your first triathlon will be of relatively short duration, so you will not be in danger of running out of energy, but it can't hurt to take a gel with you (or the other half of that energy bar) just in case. Bonking is no fun no matter where it occurs.

ALERT!

If you carry a bottle for fluid replacement, a sports drink will serve you better than plain water, especially if it's hot. Pick a drink with a high content of electrolytes, which are essential to prevent cramping and other problems associated with intense activity in the heat.

It will serve you well to purchase a waist pack with a holder for a water bottle. Even on relatively short runs, if the temperature is elevated and it's humid, you will need to replace fluids as you go.

Ergogenic Aids and Legal Supplements

An ergogenic aid can be as simple as a bottle of water, and it can be as complex and sinister as injected steroids. There are businesses out there selling a wide variety of products that they claim will turn you into a super athlete. Know this: your success will not come out of a bottle, from a pill, or from some drink.

If you train well, you increase your chances of having a good race. If you train haphazardly and rely on a magic elixir, you will be disappointed. That said, there are some aids beyond water that can help you succeed.

Joltin' Joe

One of the most common and widely used ergogenic aids is plain old caffeine. Not everyone agrees that taking in caffeine helps with training and racing, but it is a widely held opinion that a cup of coffee an hour before a workout or race will have beneficial effects.

For one thing, the caffeine, a central nervous system stimulant, wakes you up. There is also evidence, not universally accepted, that the presence of caffeine aids in the release of free fatty acids into the blood stream, making them available for energy production. This spares the glycogen stores and aids in endurance. Use of caffeine also helps reduce the perception of fatigue, and you feel more alert.

QUESTION?

If one cup of coffee can help with my workout, will more be better?
Don't overdo it. Caffeine can also act as a diuretic and lead to dehydration (another concept about which there is dispute). Too much will leave you nervous and cause tightness in the muscles, not to mention headaches and stomach upsets. One or two cups should do it, but most people know their limits.

If you don't like coffee, you can get caffeine from a pill, and some energy gels include it as part of the formula. In any case, caffeine is a legal aid. It is possible to test positive for excess caffeine, but the amount of coffee you would have to drink to flunk a postrace test—40 ounces in two to three hours—is beyond the tolerance level of most people.

Squeeze It Out

Another popular aid is the energy gel. These come in an amazing variety, each striving to separate itself from the others with some feature like added protein or all-fruit ingredients.

Gels are just about essential for any endurance event, certainly for anything lasting longer than an hour. Your body uses up its stored energy in about that amount of time, and if you don't supplement with something, you will surely hit the wall.

Because of the variety and the different features, it is probably best to just try them to see what works. Most feature complex carbohydrates, but look at the total carbohydrate content for guidance.

Taste will be a big factor, and that's entirely your decision. Look for gels that have a bit of added protein, which can be helpful in long runs or rides.

Bars and Drinks

The energy bar is similar to the gel in that there are so many it's impossible to keep track, and it all boils down to taste. Be sure to read the labels closely. Some of the energy bars on the market are little more than candy packaged to look like they are something healthy.

Most gels come in a small packet that contains an ounce of a sticky substance that contains about 100 calories, most of them from complex carbs. Bars are larger and have a much higher caloric content and lots more sugar.

ALERT!

If you don't mind an extra expense, there are companies that will formulate energy and recovery drinks just for you, your needs, and the event you plan to enter. This service is pricey, but anything custom made usually is.

Also be wary of the widely popular energy drinks you see advertised everywhere. One look at the label will probably tell you all you need to know. If the "total carbohydrates" indicates 39 grams and the "sugar" also totals 39 grams, that means you could do just as well by going to the kitchen table with a spoon.

These drinks, of course, have a lot of fancy-sounding additives, but the calories—the energy—come from pure sugar. Further, these drinks are not regulated by the U.S. Food and Drug Administration, and it's worth noting that products with some of these ingredients are banned in other countries. Give these a wide berth.

Sweat Factor

If you are training or racing in hot weather, it is essential to maintain adequate levels of electrolytes. These are sodium, potassium, calcium, and magnesium. When you train or race in the heat, you lose electrolytes as you perspire. Deficiency in these minerals can cause severe problems, not the least of which is muscle cramps. Bad cramps can shut you down in a race.

A good diet is usually adequate to maintain proper electrolyte levels, but training or racing in hot and humid conditions, especially if you perspire heavily, can rob you of the electrolytes you need. There are supplements, capsules for example, you can take during exercise to restore lost electrolytes and fend off cramps or other serious conditions that are worth your consideration.

As you examine the vast array of supplements, bars, gels, drinks, and other aids, just remember that there are no magic pills for success. Don't get caught up in the hype. Hard work and determination are your keys to success.

CHAPTER 13

Injury Prevention and Treatment

In any twelve-week training program, there will be snags—events you didn't expect or circumstances beyond your control. There will be missed workouts, bad weather, and family matters that demand your time. One factor that you can influence, at least to an extent, is downtime because of injury. Smart training and discipline will help you avoid most injury-related problems, but be ready to deal with them if they crop up.

Play It Safe

Your knees, ankles, hamstrings, and other worrisome parts of your body are just waiting to give you trouble from poor technique, overtraining, or other factors related to the newness of your activity. Don't compound the risk of downtime by putting yourself in harm's way unnecessarily. It would be tragic for you to get through most of the twelve-week training program without a training-related injury only to be sidelined by a broken leg because you were careless on your bicycle. Always take precautions when you train. Be aware of your surroundings.

Fun Run

When running, avoid dimly lit, narrow streets or busy highways. Always wear reflective gear if you run before sunrise or after sundown.

If it's raining, stay off the streets altogether. The roads are slippery, and drivers can't see as well. You can still run when it's raining (so long as lightning is not present), but find a park or a trail if you just can't stand to put off that workout. If you live in an area where ice is common in the cold months, stick to the treadmill indoors unless you have special spikes for your running shoes.

A relatively inexpensive way to retrofit your running shoes for icy terrain is to use sheet metal screws to provide traction. Simply take several one-quarter-inch or three-eighths-inch sheet metal screws and screw them into the bottoms of your shoes. The heads of the screws provide a good grip. Voila! Homemade spikes!

Also consider wearing a strap with a flashing light on your back to make sure drivers can see you in poor conditions, and look into purchasing a headlamp to help find your way in the dark. Never run trails in the dark without something to light your way.

If you run on city streets with any automobile traffic, do not wear headphones. That is just asking for trouble.

Dirty Water

Most public swimming pools have a strong odor of chlorine. The chemical is necessary to kill waterborne bacteria and other microscopic pests. If the smell of chlorine at your pool is overwhelming, that's a sign that someone didn't mix the chemicals properly. You can become ill from swimming in a pool with a chlorine mix that's too heavy. Ask someone to check it to see if the mix is normal. If it's not, put that swim off to another day.

Other signs of troubled waters include a cloudy appearance or simply a bad smell not related to chlorine. If you notice either of those, bag your swim workout for that day, but tell someone at the club and hope it can be fixed in time for your next workout.

When planning your bicycle workouts, remember that there is safety in numbers. Group rides are better because ten riders are easier to spot than one or two. It's also more fun, and you will find yourself motivated to work harder to keep up, both of which are better for your training.

Easy Rider

Many of the top triathletes do 25 to 35 miles per hour on their bikes during competition and training. When you're used to cruising at 60 or 70 mph in your car, 25 to 30 doesn't sound so fast.

You will discover that when you and your bike are on the road, 20 mph will seem like you are flying. On some downhill stretches, even beginning bikers might hit 30 mph. If you crash into something doing even 20 mph, it's going to be bad, and if you and your bicycle get into a fight with a 3,000-pound car, who do you think will win?

If a runner takes a spill on the road or a trail, chances are the result will be no more than a bruise or a scrape. If you hit the pavement off your bicycle doing 20 mph, you will be lucky not to have something broken. Being safe while doing your bike training is an absolute must.

Wet Streets

When streets are wet, your chances of an accident are increased. The streets are slippery, making curves very dangerous. Similarly, descents down steep hills become more treacherous because your brakes do not work as efficiently in wet conditions. The brake pads just don't grip as well.

The bottom line is that when conditions are wet, slow down. If it's really bad, head for the health club and do your workout on a stationary bike. One final caution: Never wear headphones while you ride outdoors.

First-Aid Needs

No matter how careful you are, there will be accidents that require some kind of treatment, especially in your training on the bicycle. Most bikes have a kind of saddlebag or pack that can be mounted under the seat to carry things, including a flat repair kit. Here is the checklist of other items for your bike pack. Consider these essentials:

- First-aid kit
- Cell phone
- Identification (driver's license)
- Medical insurance card

If you have a serious accident on your bicycle, you may need all of those items. Don't leave home without them.

ALERT!

It's a good idea to carry something that tells who you are. There are companies that inscribe items with your vital information, such as your name, blood type, phone contact in event of an emergency, and anything else you want to include. The information is etched into a plate that can be mounted on your shoe or on a bracelet for your wrist or ankle. It's money well spent.

Most bike stores carry first-aid kits made just for bicycles, and you should consider having a first-aid kit in your car as well in case of an accident during a run. Most swimming pools have lifeguards and first-aid kits on hand.

Plantar Fasciitis and IT Band Syndrome

Once you start working your muscles, tendons, and joints, sooner or later you will experience problems with them. Among the most common ailments for athletes are plantar fasciitis and iliotibial band syndrome (ITBS).

Plantar fasciitis is an inflammation of the plantar fascia, the thick connective tissue on the bottom of your foot that runs from the toes to the heel, supporting the arch. The primary symptom of plantar fasciitis is pain in the heel, usually most intense when you first get out of bed in the morning.

There are many causes of plantar fasciitis, including flat feet and abnormally high arches. Tight calf muscles can also contribute. Training errors such as increasing running mileage too quickly, too much running on steep hills, bad running shoes, and poor running technique can also bring on plantar fasciitis. Heel strikers are more prone to plantar fasciitis than mid-foot strikers.

ALERT!

Take action immediately at the first sign of plantar fasciitis. Untreated, it can develop into a lingering problem. It is not unusual for a case of plantar fasciitis to go on for a year or more. This is one ailment you want to nip in the bud.

Feet Treatment

If you feel pain in your heel on your first step out of bed, see a physical therapist if you have access to one. If you are treating the problem yourself, learn how to stretch the plantar fascia and certain leg muscles, in particular the gastrocnemius (calf) and the soleus, closely connected to the calf muscle. Custom orthotics and even over-the-counter arch supports can be effective treatments.

Many athletes find that using a night splint works well in ending a case of plantar fasciitis. When you sleep, the toes of your foot tend to be fixed in a flat plane under the covers. In this position, the plantar fascia can tighten, and the pain you feel in the morning comes from the tight fascia. A night splint keeps your foot perpendicular to the bed, stretching the fascia all night, often easing the pain immediately. If you don't have a night splint, keep the covers loose at the foot of the bed. If the covers are loose, your feet won't lock down in the wrong position.

There are other ways of trying to head off a case of plantar fasciitis before it gets too serious. Ice massage on the affected area can help. Take a 20-ounce water bottle, fill it and freeze it, then roll your foot back and forth over it for five to ten minutes a couple of times a day. This helps reduce inflammation. Taping your arch can also relieve some of the pain.

FACT

Unless you have a truly severe case of plantar fasciitis, you can usually continue to train through it, although you should reduce your mileage. Let the intensity of the pain be your guide.

IT Band Syndrome

The iliotibial band is thick, fibrous connective tissue that runs from the outside of the knee to the outside of the hip. The primary symptom of ITBS is pain on the outside of the knee. It is usually a very tight feeling in the tendon on the side of the knee.

Factors that contribute to ITBS are high arches, downhill running, running on a pitched surface, inadequately cushioned running shoes, too much running on hard surfaces, and weak hip muscles. Pain usually subsides if you stop running, but the problem can be exacerbated by running, walking down stairs, cycling, or skiing.

The first course of treatment is to rest until the pain goes away, then begin a regimen of stretching the IT band, the hamstrings, quadriceps, and hip muscles. You can also ice the IT band and make an effort to be certain the running shoes you are using are right for your stride and foot type. Also, make sure your shoes are not simply past their prime. Running in worn-out shoes can cause a variety of physical problems. The best way to stave off this annoying problem is to stretch, stretch, stretch.

Avoiding Knee Problems

Knee pain can come from different sources and is often detected in different parts of the joint. A common knee problem is patellar tendonitis, or inflammation of the tendon that connects to the kneecap (patella). Patellar tendonitis is felt as pain in the front of the joint, just below the kneecap. It can occur because of overtraining and usually is confined to one knee.

You can tell if you have tendonitis if you have less pain in the affected area once you warm up and get into your exercise. Treatment for tendonitis is usually relatively simple: rest, ice, and anti-inflammatory medicine.

Bad biomechanics can also contribute to knee pain. A person with flat feet, for example, is more likely to have knee pain without some measure to correct the gait. The foot has a natural cushioning action, an inward roll called pronation. People with flat feet overpronate, so when they run, each step wrenches the knee. Orthotics can quickly and easily correct this problem and eliminate knee pain that results from it. Orthotics can also correct problems with arches that are too high.

For cyclists, knee pain can result from improper seat adjustment. Usually the seat is too low or too far forward.

A good strategy in preventing knee pain is to be sure you have strong quadriceps and hamstrings, the muscles that help support the knee.

Supplements

Many athletes have found that taking supplements of glucosamine and chondroitin sulfate are helpful in alleviating knee pain. Both substances are found naturally in the body. Some experts believe glucosamine plays a role in cartilage formation and that chondroitin sulfate helps give cartilage elasticity. Some knee pain results from a degradation of the cartilage in the knee, and there is anecdotal evidence that glucosamine-chondroitin supplements help in this area.

Muscle Pulls

A torn muscle is a very serious injury. Pulled muscles are annoying but rarely a cause for grave concern. A pulled muscle is one that has been strained or stretched too far. It is usually sore but not incapacitating. An injury of this type can occur just about anywhere on the body and usually results from overdoing a workout.

The best strategy for preventing muscle pulls is to warm up adequately before you get into any intense workout, especially running speed work. Even after a good warm-up, be sure to build your intensity slowly. As muscles warm up they become more elastic, decreasing the chances of a pull.

FACT

You are more at risk for a muscle pull when you exercise in cold weather. It takes your muscles longer to warm up and become pliable. When you work out in the cold, take extra time to warm up.

Your triathlon training doesn't necessarily have to be interrupted by a pulled muscle, but be cautious. It's okay to start a workout with such a minor injury, but if the affected muscle hurts—and especially if it hurts more—don't continue. Wait until the pain is completely gone. You can ice the strained muscle and take anti-inflammatories to speed recovery.

Shin Splints

Shin splint is a general term that describes pain or tenderness in the front of the lower leg. Some experts say that shin splint is not a diagnosis but a symptom of an underlying problem.

As with other injuries, there can be different causes of shin splints, although the injury occurs mostly with runners. Chief among the causes is overtraining—running past the point of muscle fatigue—leading to increased stress on the bones and tendons. Other causes include falling or excessively high arches, weakness in anterior muscles, tightness in calf muscles, and changing from soft to hard running surfaces.

You can strengthen your lower leg muscles by swimming in a pool with fins. This exercise is helpful in treating a case of shin splints. Do not follow this strategy, however, if the activity hurts the affected leg.

A shin splint can be very painful, and it is not an injury to be trained through. If you develop a shin splint from running, it will only get worse if you continue in that sport. You can, however, cross-train on a bicycle or elliptical machine, or hit the swimming pool to maintain your aerobic base while your leg heals.

Although a shin splint is a painful and potentially serious injury, it is easier to treat, and quicker to be cured, than plantar fasciitis. Here are some strategies:

- Active rest with alternative training (bicycle, swimming)
- Arch supports or physician-prescribed orthotics
- Ice cup on the tender area five to ten minutes a couple of times a day
- Stretching calf muscles before and after activity (especially after)
- The "alphabet" exercise. Sit down and extend your leg to the floor. Using only your ankle and foot, trace each letter of the alphabet on the floor. Do this twice a day to strengthen the lower leg muscles.
- Tape the ankle to take pressure off the lower leg muscles

If the condition persists despite rest and self-treatment, it may be necessary to consult a physician or physical therapist.

Swimming Injuries

The most common injuries in the swimming pool involve the shoulder (primarily the deltoid muscle) and the rotator cuff. The rotator cuff is the set of muscles and tendons that stabilize the humerus, the long arm bone that runs from the shoulder to the elbow, in the shoulder joint. The rotator cuff also stabilizes the scapula (shoulder blade). Most people have heard the term from rotator cuff injuries suffered by baseball pitchers. Whereas the injury in baseball usually involves a torn rotator cuff, fortunately in swimming it's usually just a strain. Injuries to the shoulder and rotator cuff almost always originate with one of two mistakes: improper form or overuse of paddles.

Don't Cross Over

When you swim, you are supposed to keep your arms going straight ahead, then back through in a straight line. A common error is swimming with your arms crossing over in front of your body. This is an inefficient stroke, and it puts strain on the joint that often results in soreness and discomfort during swimming.

Another mistake that can cause shoulder strain is swinging the arms too wide in the swim stroke. If you swim all out in your workouts too often, the result can be shoulder strain.

Paddle Protocol

Swimming paddles are large plastic devices that fit on the hands. When you swim with paddles, the extra surface increases resistance, making each stroke harder. Using paddles helps strengthen your arms and improves your stroke. As with any training device, too much of a good thing can turn bad. Paddle workouts can be an effective part of your swim training, but keep the sessions to once a week to avoid shoulder problems.

Swim Injury Treatment

If you hurt your shoulder or rotator cuff in the pool, you will have to take it easy or skip your workouts altogether until it no longer hurts to do the exercise. There are strengthening exercises you can do once the pain is gone or nearly gone, so long as a workout doesn't increase the discomfort.

For example, take a ten- to fifteen-pound weight, hold it at your side, then extend the arm to the side of the body to ninety degrees. Repeat ten times, do two sets. With the same weight, extend the arm to the front of the body to ninety degrees. Repeat ten times, do two sets. Pushups are also good shoulder-strengthening exercises.

Training When Injured

If you get through twelve weeks of swimming, biking, and running workouts without so much as a muscle tweak, don't tell your triathlon friends. It will only make them envious—if they believe you.

Chances are greater that you will face at least one injury that will cause some downtime. Be sure you are ready to deal with it. First, fight the urge to feel sorry for yourself. Don't panic about the lost training. If your goal is simply to finish a triathlon, a little time off won't hurt you much. Even if you have a higher goal than just to complete the triathlon, only an extended break will affect you in a major way.

QUESTION?

I'm substituting a bike ride for a forty-minute run because of injury. How long should I ride?
Whenever you substitute one workout for another, put in the same amount of time you were planning for the canceled workout. In the case in question, ride forty minutes.

Cross-Train

Say you develop a shin splint that keeps you from running for a week or more. Instead of bemoaning your tough luck, look into possible substitute workouts. A stationary bike will give you a good aerobic workout without making the shin splint worse. You could also substitute a swim for a run. If you're like most triathlon newbies, you probably need more work in the pool anyway.

You could also consider pool running. Most health clubs have waist belts that will keep your feet from touching the bottom of the pool, allowing you to work your legs and arms in the running motion. You get a reasonable workout without the pounding. Your shin splint has time to heal while you're working out.

Some injuries require only that you scale back a bit in your workout. For example, if you strain a hamstring, you can keep the next running appointment on your calendar, but not if it involves speed work or hills. You can run, but go slower, and plan to stop if the pain increases during the workout.

Mind Over Matter

Injuries happen. Life sometimes gets in the way of training, even racing. Weather is unpredictable. Lots of things can happen to screw up your plans. How you handle these disappointments says a lot about you and your future success.

Don't get down if you're hurt. Find an alternative workout, get treatment, stay positive, and recognize that if you don't get to compete in the triathlon you planned for, it's not the end of the world.

You will have gained from the experience of training. Perhaps you learned something from the circumstances of your injury that will help you avoid a similar problem in the future. Just don't give up.

CHAPTER 14

Countdown to the Race

You have put in the time and worked hard. You feel that you have made progress. That first step you took on your triathlon training was only a few weeks ago, but it seems more like years. There are more laps in the pool and miles on the road to go, but the hour is approaching. The challenge awaits you. Will you be ready to accept it?

14

Entries, Hotel, Logistics

Once you decide to make the commitment to complete a triathlon, your next step is to decide which one you will enter. The distance you will have to swim, bike, and run will influence your training, and triathlons are not created in cookie-cutter fashion.

You should buy an entry in your chosen triathlon right away. There are a host of reasons why this is a good idea. First, many races offer discounts for early registration. But perhaps more important, spending the money for the entry fee represents a commitment on your part. It's a psychological move that is likely to keep you motivated.

In most cases, once you have entered a triathlon, the money is committed. Races rarely offer refunds of entry fees. A few race organizers will, however, allow you to use a portion of your entry for the following year's race. If money is an issue for you, check the refund policy of the race you have targeted.

Signing up early can prevent disappointment. Most triathlons have strict limits for participants. If you wait around too long to buy your entry, the triathlon you really wanted to do might fill up. Also don't put off entering the race for fear of getting injured during training. That's the wrong mental attitude. Always think positive.

Sleepover

Just as you don't want to delay entering your triathlon, the same goes for booking your hotel if the race you have chosen is out of town. Most large races will have a list of recommended hotels that are close to the venue, and it's customary, but not required, for hotels to offer discounts for race participants. Make your reservation early to avoid the major headache of finding a place to stay at the last minute. That will only add stress to your experience.

Six Weeks to Go

With six weeks left, you will be half way through your training. Your program was set up to have three weeks of increases in intensity and duration, followed by week of slower, lighter workouts so that you could recover. At the halfway point, you are looking at week seven just ahead. It is supposed to be a tougher workout than in week six.

At this point, you should have more confidence. You should feel considerably stronger than you did when you started. All exercises should feel easier now. Here are some measuring sticks to help you decide if you're on target. You should be able to:

- Run forty minutes without stopping and with a few pickups—short, slightly faster bursts—thrown in.
- Ride an hour and fifteen minutes, followed by a run of ten minutes, without undue strain. You should be able to push a bit more during your bike rides without blowing up.
- Swim 500 to 600 yards without stopping. That's roughly the distance of your race swim if you are entered in a sprint triathlon. Even if you fall a little short of 500 yards without stopping, you should at least be feeling more comfortable in the water.

Time Trial

With six weeks of training under your belt, add a weekly time trial to your bicycle training. Plan to ride thirty minutes at a brisk pace, and check to see how far you went. Do the same time and intensity in the following week and again check the distance. You will gain a lot of confidence if you went farther the second week, even if it's just a small improvement.

Regarding the bike, by six weeks you should have your seat position dialed in for total comfort. All adjustments should have been made, and your rides should be completely free of back pain. If you have any issues with your bicycle, now is the time to take it to the shop and have adjustments made. You cannot afford to continue training on a bicycle that is not completely comfortable.

At the halfway point, it's a good idea to start practicing your transition from the bicycle to the run. On days when you have training rides, set your bicycle up in your garage to simulate as close as you can how it's going to be at the race.

On race day, your bike will be in a rack, with your helmet hanging on one of the bars. You will not be able to move the bike until you have your helmet on and the chinstrap tightened. It's a time penalty or disqualification if you break the rules about helmets, and that includes a loose chinstrap. You might as well get used to that routine. Practice it on training days to get used to the drill.

On days when you have a brick on the schedule, set your running shoes out as they will be on race day so that you can move smoothly from bicycle to running. If you have bike shoes, practice leaving them on the machine as you dismount to change into your running shoes.

Half way through your training, if you're feeling a bit burned out and stressed, take an extra day off the rest of the way. It might also be wise to adjust your goal from finishing in a certain time to just finishing. You will enjoy the rest of the training more if you feel less pressure.

Two Weeks to Go: Starting the Taper

In the two weeks leading up to the triathlon, you will face another challenge: the taper. You have to pull back enough to assure that you are fresh on race day without losing your edge. The ten weeks of training have given you confidence that you can succeed in your race, and now it's time to back off a bit. Without the taper, you will do no better in the triathlon than in your workouts. If you start your taper two weeks out, your swim, bike, and run times will be improvements from your training.

Bear in mind that the taper period doesn't mean a total lack of activity. You simply start pulling back gradually as you get closer to race day.

With two weeks to go, you should have sorted out your nutritional needs and preferences. All experimentation should be behind you. You should know by this point what fuel is going to work best for you before and during the competition. If you are entered in a sprint triathlon, you probably won't need a lot of fuel during the race, perhaps a gel during the ride, so your major concern will be the prerace meal. If your triathlon will be of longer duration, your fuel needs will be different. In either case, you will not be trying something new on race day.

Being in taper mode doesn't mean all workouts are at a slow pace. In fact, you should include some short, hard workouts to keep your edge and to make sure your muscles are ready for the intensity of the competition.

Semantics

At some point, you may hear an athlete comment about "racing" or "not racing" a certain event. That may sound odd to you. Isn't everyone in the race *racing*?

In the vernacular of sports, some people are racing and some are just training or participating. The racers are the ones who are dead serious about the whole thing and are pushing hard from the starting gun.

Experienced athletes have a method of rating their competitions: A, B, and C. An A race occurs only once or twice a year. Preparation is very intense and is designed so that the athlete peaks during the race in question. An A race is one that is truly *raced*. A race with a B rating is also important, but preparation is less rigorous. The taper is usually two to three days. The C category is for races that can be considered part of training for a more important competition.

The point of this discussion is that if you are entering your first triathlon, look upon it as a C race at best. Plan on a good effort, but don't give the outcome undeserved weight. After all, part of your motivation in undertaking this adventure is to see if you like it. If you turn it into a life or death struggle your first time out, the added stress will eliminate the fun. Relax and enjoy it.

You might be wondering how you will make it through the final two weeks if you are scaling back. You fear that you will be climbing the walls, and two weeks will seem like forever without the daily training to keep you occupied.

This is where your discipline comes into play. All that work you have done will go for nothing if you don't follow the program and you aren't totally shutting it down. Enjoy what workouts you can do, and hang out with fellow trainees if you need to do something to pass the time. They, too, are probably feeling restless.

ALERT!

If the idea of shopping for all your triathlon gear is daunting, you should look into purchasing a package that includes everything you need except for your shoes and socks. From one source, you get can it all: bicycle, aerobars, water bottle and cage to hold it, wetsuit, tri shorts, tri top, helmet, goggles, swim cap, and a duffle bag to hold it all.

One Week to Go: Cutting Back Further

Now you are really feeling antsy, and you're starting to fear that you will lose your fitness with such a light workout schedule. Don't worry about that. You don't lose fitness in one week. Stay with the program.

Now is a good time to concentrate on visualizing your race. If your triathlon is taking place in or very near your hometown, take the time to visit the venue. Ride the bicycle course if you can, but go slow—it's not a workout. If your race is too far away for a quick visit, go over the course details again, especially elevation charts to remind yourself about where you will encounter hills during the race.

Practice your transition moves in the extra time provided by the light training schedule. At this point, the transition from bike to run should be automatic, something you can do correctly without thinking. This is not just for the elite racers. The more things you do well, the more confidence you will feel going into your first triathlon.

Checkups

The final week before your race is a good time to take your bicycle to your local shop for servicing and adjustments. Also, if you don't already have them, consider purchasing an extra pair of swim goggles. You never know when you might need a pair with darker lenses.

With a week to go, you should be able to find a reasonably accurate race-day weather forecast on the Internet. What you find out might not be entirely to your liking, but forewarned is forearmed. Now is the time to make your checklist (see the next chapter for what should be included) for the race.

Mind Games

With a week to go, you should be feeling like a caged animal. It's okay. Just try to harness that nervous energy, and work at relaxing and staying calm. Keep your thoughts positive, even if some weather issues are looming. Remember, everyone in the race will face the same challenge.

If you have a triathlon magazine handy, check for articles about the people in the sport. Someone's story might inspire you. But be careful if you read about some new technique, training regimen, energy bar, or drink. You don't want to try anything new so close to the race.

Getting to the Race

If your race is in your hometown, you won't have much to worry about when it comes to transporting your bicycle. You already know how to haul your bike around town. You've been doing it for nearly three months during your training.

Even at this point, it is worth stating that when you invest in a bike rack, pay a little extra to get a good one. A cheap rack won't work as well and might damage your car. Ask the bike shop staff to show you their best racks.

Have Bike, Will Travel

If you have to travel to your race and you aren't driving, getting your bicycle to the race is a bit more complicated. One option is to rent a bicycle from a local shop in the city where your race is taking place. This is not recommended. You have been training for weeks on your own bicycle and presumably have achieved the desirable level of comfort on that machine. You will not have that with a rented bicycle. Use this option only if you have no other choice.

You can rent a bike box from your local shop that will hold your machine and keep it from being damaged in transit. Packing your bicycle in the box requires removing the wheels, the pedals, and the seat, then loosening the handlebars and turning them sideways. Be sure that you know how to put your bike back together when you arrive at your destination, and don't forget the wrenches you will need for the job.

When packing your bicycle in a box for an airplane flight, remember to mark the seat post before removing the seat to make sure you put it back in the right position. If the seat is too high or too low, your triathlon ride will be miserable. You don't want to waste time adjusting the seat during your race.

The airline will charge for carrying your bike box. It's usually about $100 each way. After you get your bicycle taken care of for the flight, do something for yourself in preparation for the journey: make sure you take water on the plane. The hyper-dry conditions in the cabin can leave you dehydrated at just the time when you need extra fluid.

Also consider taking extra vitamin C in preparation for the trip. During the flight, the air filtration system in the plane circulates whatever germs are in the atmosphere, leaving you more vulnerable to coming down with some ailment. You definitely do not want to wake up on race day with a cold or a sore throat, or both.

Two Days to Go

Whether you are traveling to your triathlon or looking forward to competing in your own backyard, there is a key day coming up. If your race is on a Saturday, that day is Thursday; for a Sunday race, it's Friday.

Two days before your race, plan on complete rest. The only activity you should contemplate that day is stretching, but do only the stretches you have used during your training. Don't try anything new.

Add some carbs to your diet on the key day, perhaps an extra helping of rice or pasta. Doing so will help build up the glycogen stores you will need for fuel on race day.

No Grease

Avoid high-fat food from now through the end of the race. You want your system functioning at its best, not bogged down trying to digest a greasy meal. Stick to lean protein—chicken, lean beef, or fish. Forget about pizza, ribs, and French fries. You didn't come this far to blow it because of a bad eating decision.

Take in lots of fruit and vegetables, and it's okay two days out to take in some high-fiber foods. It's not recommended the day before as you could end up wasting precious time in the port-a-john during the race.

If the forecast for your race calls for warm temperatures, be sure to take in extra sodium prior to the event to fend off cramps. That does not mean you can go wild with potato chips or other salty junk food. Look for some electrolyte tablets, or just use a little extra table salt on your food.

Sweet Dreams

Conventional wisdom is that the key night for sleep is two days removed from your event, not the night before. It is normal to have restless sleep the night before a big race, and your first triathlon meets that standard.

If you are like many new triathletes, you may spend the night before your race waking up every hour, fearful you will oversleep. You can manage on less than adequate sleep for one night, but if you miss out two nights in a row, you will end up very tired during your race.

If your race is on a Sunday, get to bed early on Friday night, planning to sleep a full eight hours or whatever makes you feel good. If your race is out of town and you can go a day early, doing so will help you settle in and prepare for adequate sleep, perhaps even help you get used to a different climate. It will also give you time to lay out all your gear and double-check to be sure everything is there. If something is missing, you will have time to get to the expo or local bike or running store to pick up whatever you need.

The Day and Night Before

You followed your training schedule and did virtually nothing two days before your triathlon. With one day to go, you have permission to move about, but you still won't be doing very much. You are saving your energy for race day.

The day before the triathlon, do some light exercise. You can hop on your bicycle for a fifteen-minute ride with a couple of quick accelerations. Just spin a bit, but don't strain yourself. Likewise, hit the road for a short run at an easy pace, perhaps five minutes.

If you are already at the race site, do your light workouts at the venue if it's convenient. Your objective is to stay loose. If you do nothing, you could become sluggish.

If you are traveling to your triathlon the day before and leaving in the morning for the airport, fit in what exercising you can before you leave. If it's not convenient, plan on doing your light exercise once you arrive and after you have picked up your race packet and checked in at your hotel.

Don't Forget the Water

Maintaining adequate hydration is an ongoing need, and you should keep it up, even increase the effort the day before your triathlon. The day before, you should take in enough fluid to keep your urine clear.

If the idea of drinking so much water is a turnoff, mix in a sports drink for variety. Whatever you have to do, adequate hydration is a must, especially if race-day temperatures will be elevated.

Eat for Success

Lots of races have prerace meals for "carbo loading," frequently featuring mounds of pasta. Be careful. It's a mistake to take in a huge meal the night before your race. For one thing, your body has a limit to the amount of carbs that can be stored as glycogen. For another, remember that your first event will be a swim. Do you want to hit the water feeling weighed down by a massive dinner the night before? A big meal can also cause stomach upset and other gastric issues.

Take a couple of energy bars and eat small portions during the day before your race. At dinnertime, have a light meal as early as you can before turning in for the night.

ALERT!

If you can, it's best to do your light day-before workouts at about the same time your triathlon will start. If that doesn't work, do it when you can. Some light exercise is better than none, no matter when it happens.

Sleep Well

If you're on the road, try to get back to the hotel room early so that you can relax with a book or the television prior to turning out the lights early. You will have lots of pent-up energy and you will be nervous about the race, and that might interfere with your sleep. Don't fret if you don't sleep as well as you would like. If you got adequate rest the night before, you will be okay. Instead of counting sheep, picture yourself crossing the finish line feeling great and deservedly proud.

CHAPTER 15

Race-Day Preparations

The training is over. You have been swimming, cycling, and running for about three months now. The next workout you do, starting with the swim, is for real. A famous tennis player once said that the key to success is self-confidence, and the key to self-confidence is preparation. You are ready to take it from here. Good luck.

15

Equipment Checklist

When you arrive at the triathlon venue to pick up your packet, you may be amazed at the swirl of activity as people line up to get their essentials from the race organizers. There are race numbers (bibs) for you to wear and put on your bicycle, a swim cap with your race number on it, and a computer chip if your race will be timed that way. Your may also receive a goody bag with coupons, samples, and other giveaways.

A typical large race will also feature an expo, where myriad products are on display and for sale—from shoes to biking gear to energy bars and gels. Just about anything you might need for a triathlon, and plenty of stuff you don't need, will be available. The expo is usually very busy. You could find it overwhelming and confusing. You won't even be thinking about all the stuff you need for your race. That's why you did your homework before you left home for the race by going over your equipment checklist. That's the easy way to make sure you brought everything you need to compete. Here are your lists, separated by sports:

Swimming

- Swim trunks or swimsuit
- Triathlon suit if preferred. The tri suit is a one-piece outfit you can wear in all three sports without having to change. These things have zippers, so carry a backup tri suit or regular swimsuit in case the zipper breaks (it's been known to happen).
- Plastic garbage bag. Can have many uses.
- Waterproof sunscreen
- Two pairs of goggles (normal lens and dark lens)
- Wetsuit if needed (for water temperatures 78°F or lower)
- A lubricant (but not petroleum jelly) for the neck and underarms if a wetsuit is worn. You need this to prevent chafing. Spray-on cooking oil will work, but the expo will have wax-based lubricants that are easier to carry around.

- Swim cap. The race organizers will provide one, but you are permitted to wear your own underneath to keep out the cold if temperatures are unexpectedly low.

The plastic garbage bag is handy in case of rain. Put it over your running shoes and socks while you are riding so that you don't have to pour the water out of your shoes after the ride, then put on wet socks before you even get going.

Bicycle

- The bicycle
- Water bottle. Look for a specially designed bottle that attaches to your bicycle's aerobars and comes with a straw so that you can lean forward for a drink instead of having to grab a bottle from a holder.
- Cage to hold the bottle if you use a plain bottle
- Bike shoes
- Two helmets. You never know when you or another triathlete might need one.
- Sunglasses
- Energy source. Best is a gel that you can tape to the handlebars.
- Electrolyte tablets. These are very useful in warm weather.
- Pump for the bike tires
- Flat repair kit, including an extra tube
- A large towel for laying out and organizing your bicycle and run gear and for drying your feet after the swim

Take care in inflating your bicycle tires the morning of the race. If the temperature rises significantly that morning, the tire pressure will increase. It's not uncommon to hear several ominous pops on race morning as overinflated tires blow out while still in the racks.

Run

- Running shoes
- Socks
- Race number belt, best for displaying your race number in the run. You can grab it and put it around your waist as you go.
- Hat or visor in case of bright sunlight

Eating and Drinking the Morning of the Race

Eating something on the morning of the race is not optional. You must eat or you risk a debilitating crash shortly after the race starts. You might not even make it through the swim if you start on an empty stomach.

If you find yourself dizzy and disoriented from low blood sugar, you can toss down a gel or eat something—not during the swim, of course—but it won't take effect immediately. You will still be wobbly for a significant period before you come around. Don't borrow trouble. Eat before you swim.

You should take in some food two to three hours before you are scheduled to enter the water. That means, of course, that you will have to get up earlier than you might have planned to. It's a good thing, then, that a bit of sleep deprivation the night before the race won't affect your race negatively.

Eating Choices

What you eat will be determined in large measure by what you are used to. It's worth repeating that race day is not the time to experiment with something you bought at the expo because it was touted as the super-food that will turn you into an elite racer. Many of the professional triathletes reject solid food on race day, going for an energy drink instead.

Shoot for 200 to 300 calories for your prerace meal, depending on your size and needs. Bananas are a popular choice. They are easily digestible and provide an adequate supply of carbohydrates without a lot of bad sugar. You might also try a bagel with peanut butter. The protein in the peanut butter will give you a full feeling without being overly heavy. Avoid high-fiber foods that can have you making unscheduled pit stops, a problem that is made worse by warm weather.

Some competitors have been known to eat baby food because of the consistency and because it is very bland and therefore unlikely to cause stomach upset. If you think that might work for you, give it a try during training. Don't try strained peas for the first time on race day.

In Liquid Form

You spent a lot of time in countdown week making sure you are well hydrated for your race. Keep it up even as the race approaches. You should take in about a liter of water before the start.

A good way to tell if you are drinking enough is time spent in the port-a-john before the start of the swim. You should have to go at least once, preferably twice, before everything gets under way.

It's okay to have a cup of coffee, perhaps even two, the morning of the race, but don't try it for the caffeine unless you're used to it. If you want the caffeine but don't like coffee, green tea is a good substitute.

Some companies offer complete nutrition in liquid form for use on race day. It's easy to get down while providing what you need for a good race.

QUESTION?

I love orange juice. Is that a good way to take in fluid the morning of the race?
Skip the OJ, which has a lot of sugar. Because of the sugar content, it will take a long time to leave your stomach, and while it's sitting there, anything else in your stomach will also be hanging around.

Arriving at the Venue

Plan to arrive at the venue early, at least ninety minutes before the start of the race. Two hours would be even better.

There is a lot to do at the site of the race, including finding a place to park. The later you arrive, the farther you will have to trek with your bicycle and other gear, not to mention the effort to haul it back to your vehicle afterward. You won't enjoy that a lot when you are sweaty, hot, and tired from the exertion of the race, not to mention full of food and drink from the postrace feed.

Here is a list of things you will have to do after you find a parking place:

- Have your race number written in waterproof marker on your arms and legs. It's mandatory for everyone so that race officials can identify competitors. This can mean long lines and lots of waiting. By the way, the numbers disappear in a few days with normal bathing (or you can wash around them to retain proof that you are a triathlete for as long as possible).

- Find your transition spot. The earlier you arrive, the better spot you will find for racking your bicycle and laying out your other gear.
- Pin your race number to your bicycle and possibly also to your helmet.
- Hit the port-a-john line at least once.

Triathlon organizers are very strict about littering. In some races, disqualification is the penalty for that offense. If you carry a gel on your bicycle or during your run, be sure you have a place to put the empty packet.

Those are the certainties. You might also have to pick up your packet on race day, and you might need time to apply sunscreen and to oil your bike chain. There is a lot to do.

Getting Warmer

And, of course, you will have to do all of these aforementioned things before you warm up. All in all, it's much better to hurry up and wait. You will have time to check that everything is where it should be and socialize with your friends. You will be able to hydrate and fuel adequately and at leisure.

If you are tense at the start of the race because you had to rush through everything, it will affect your performance and enjoyment of the event. Do whatever is necessary to get to the race site well ahead of time.

Weather Issues

Thanks to the Internet, you can get a pretty good idea of what the weather will be like on race day in advance. Thanks to Mother Nature, the forecasts often miss the mark, and there can be freak events that take everyone by surprise. For example, at a race in South Dakota in 2005, high temperatures, as forecast, were in the seventies the day before the race and on the day after. On race day, temperatures soared to a high of ninety-seven. That can happen anywhere.

Hot to Trot

Dealing with unexpected and extreme heat will be your biggest challenge, primarily because if the mercury rises too high, it can be very dangerous for competitors. Here are some measures you can take in the event that heat and humidity become a major factor in your race:

- Stay in the shade as much as possible before the race starts.
- Forget about warming up.
- Drink extra fluid and take it with electrolytes.
- Go slower once the race starts. You want to live to race another, cooler day.

Water from Above

There's not much you can do in the case of rain, although in severe cases involving lightning, the race start might be postponed. It's not unheard of for race organizers to scrap the swim altogether, turning the event into a duathlon (run, bike, run).

ALERT!

Lightning isn't the only weather-related problem that will cause cancellation of a triathlon swim. Unrelenting fog will do the same because it's too difficult to keep track of swimmers, and it's a nightmare for swimmers trying to see where they're going. Ocean swims can be canceled if the waves are too high, posing serious danger to swimmers.

If the issue is rain and nothing else, the competition will start as planned and you will have to deal with it. Start by covering your shoes and socks with the garbage bag from your checklist. It's better to start your run with dry shoes even if they are going to be squishy from the rainwater in short order.

Rain will make for slippery roads, possibly poor visibility, so plan to slow down and take extra care in curves and on downhills. A crash can cause serious injury, even death. Running in wet shoes often causes blisters, but there are wool-based socks that perform very well in staving off the blisters in rain-soaked running.

Chills

When it's hot, there's a limit to what you can do, clothing wise, to cope. You can take off only so much, and even the ultimate won't help when it's really hot. On the other hand, you can bundle up when a northerly wind blows through.

Starting with the swim, you will be permitted to wear your wetsuit if the water temperature, measured twelve to eighteen inches below the surface, is 78°F or colder.

If it is really cold, a neoprene cap will come in handy. It is similar to a wetsuit and can be worn under your race cap to keep your head warm. Also, smearing your face with petroleum jelly can help protect the exposed skin from the cold.

Be careful about piling on too much clothing when temperatures drop. You will warm up a lot faster than you may realize, and you are not permitted to throw off clothing during the race. That's considered littering. It's okay to leave something at an aid station, but there's no guarantee it will be there later or that it will be returned to the staging area.

Riding will, of course, create a wind chill if it's cold, and gloves will keep your hands from feeling frozen, but they will be awkward in the transition from biking to running as you try to get your running shoes on.

What you must keep in mind about weather issues is that all competitors will experience the same problems. There's no point in freaking out or bemoaning your bad luck. Think of it as an adventure, and envision all the stories you will have to tell your friends when you get home.

Dealing with First-Race Anxiety

No one starts out in a triathlon as a grizzled veteran. There's a first time for everyone. Top runners who have never tried multisport events are getting their feet wet just as you are. Who's to say that person isn't just as nervous as you are, perhaps more so if the athlete feels a lot of pressure to perform at a high level.

You may be edgy and anxious, but you don't have grand expectations or goals. Your aim is to finish feeling good about your accomplishment, after which you will consider further participation. If you feel any pressure, it's coming from within.

Dismiss fear of failure. If something goes wrong and you don't finish, it's not the end of the world, and you certainly won't be the first person to drop out of a race. Learn from your experience and come back stronger the next time.

Tricks and Treats

There are some tricks that could help you deal with your anxiety. First, you will feel more relaxed and confident about the coming challenge if you take the time to orient yourself to the layout of the transition area. Walk from where the swim will end to where your bicycle is racked. Then go from there to the bicycle mount/dismount area, then back to the rack. Next walk to where you enter the course for the run. Do it again, looking for landmarks or other ways of helping you find your way in the heat of the competition.

Feeling confident about this aspect of the race will ease the tension and remove the feelings that your race is a series of accidents waiting to happen.

Beyond Compare

Don't compare yourself to the other athletes at your race. They and their goals are not relevant to what you are doing, and as a first-timer you are not competing with them or anyone, even other first-timers. Some, perhaps most, of the competitors are probably more accomplished than you, but you're just starting out. You're not supposed to be an elite athlete at this point.

If you find yourself feeling overwhelmed by everything, take a deep breath, do some stretches, then tell yourself that once the race starts all the nervousness will be gone. You will be surprised to find that it actually happens that way.

QUESTION?

Can I mark the rack in some way so that I can find my bike more easily?
Yes. You can tie a balloon to the rack near your bicycle or use chalk to draw an arrow on the asphalt or concrete pointing to your spot.

Above all, don't forget that you have just concluded three months of preparation for this race. You worked hard, you learned as you went along. You are ready. This is neither the time nor the place for doubts.

Stay in the moment and focus on what you are doing in each phase of the race. While you're swimming, don't be thinking about how hard it's going to be to ride in the biting wind or run in the brutal heat. Before you know it, you'll be off course and looking around frantically for the buoy you overshot. Concentrate on your strokes and where you are in the water.

FACT

If you know any of the competitors, especially veterans who have competed in your race before, ask them for advice. You will be surprised at how helpful better athletes can be when someone shows interest in their sport. They'll tell you things to watch out for and give you encouragement. It will boost your confidence to know they are rooting for you.

Adopt the same strategy for the cycling and running phases. If one of the sports didn't go as well as you had hoped it would, don't dwell on it. Fretting about a mistake while you were riding won't change what happened, but it could affect your run.

Should You Shave Your Body?

That may seem an odd question, but it's relevant for a lot of athletes. Swimmers in the Olympics routinely shave their bodies to facilitate movement through the water. A fraction of a second can mean the difference between earning a medal and going home with nothing.

Experienced triathletes are known to shave their bodies for a number of reasons. Some say it makes them feel faster, and a small psychological edge or boost in confidence, however it is gained, can pay a big dividend in the competition for prize money. There's also a practical aspect. In the event of a crash on a bicycle, it's easier to clean a scrape or cut if there's no hair in or around the wound. Finally, for some, shaving is akin to the rituals ancient warriors used to go through to prepare for battle. Shaving makes some triathletes feel more prepared.

It's a fact that many triathletes go to great lengths to improve their aerodynamics and hydrodynamics. Whether a hairless body represents an improvement in either of these areas is uncertain, but shaving definitely doesn't harm their prospects.

For those who are new to the world of triathlons, it's best to leave the ritual of body shaving to those who might, in one way or another, reap some benefit from it. Even if you knew for sure it could take a few seconds of your swim, bike, and run times, would it help that much?

Also, men should remember that if they're not used to shaving their legs, the whole enterprise could end up being pretty bloody and very embarrassing. Mere mortals should plan to enter the triathlon battle with hair and dignity intact.

CHAPTER 16

Important Race-Day Tips

If you followed the advice in the previous chapter—good move—you arrived at the race venue well ahead of time. You have checked in and are now sporting your race number in marker on the correct limbs. It's time to settle down, take a deep breath, and start thinking about how you're going to organize all your gear, warm up, and be ready for a fun adventure —emphasis on fun.

Managing Your Transition Area

The transition phase of the triathlon is often referred to as the fourth sport, one to be practiced just as you do swimming, biking, and running. In the triathlon, you have to make two transitions—from swimming to cycling, followed by cycling to running.

Veterans know that saving a few seconds in the transition can make a huge difference in how they finish in the standings, so they try to make sure that all changes go smoothly.

If you are a first-timer, those few seconds won't matter much, but you will feel better about the experience if you have a sense that you are doing things correctly. If you followed the suggestions from Chapter 14 and practiced your transitions, you'll feel even more confident. It's a good thing if you don't feel as though you are bumbling around as you make the changes.

Organize

Once you find a spot in the bike rack, it's time to lay out everything you will need for your transition in the order that you will need each item. If you brought all your stuff in a bag, put it to the side.

Your helmet might be the most important piece of equipment in the safety-conscious triathlon. Hang your helmet on the handlebars of your bicycle and buckle it with the chinstrap tight before you move the bike. To do otherwise can result in disqualification before you even start riding.

Put your towel near your bicycle and spread it out, then put your bike shoes and socks close to the edge. If you are putting on bike shorts, make sure you have easy access to them, too. If it's a bright day and you need sunglasses, put your eyewear in your helmet, which should be hanging on the bike handlebars.

When you return to the bike rack after your ride, you will be changing into your running gear, essentially your running shoes and the belt with your number on it. You must remember the number, so place the belt on the towel with your shoes where you won't overlook it in the heat of the battle.

If the day is particularly warm and you feel you might need extra fluid, you can carry a water bottle, but it's not recommended. You don't want to hand carry it during your race, and adding another belt to hold the water bottle would be cumbersome. A better plan for a hot day is to carry two bottles of fluid on your bicycle and hydrate as well as possible while you ride. There will be plenty of aid stations on the run course.

If you were listening to music on an iPod or similar device to relax while you waited, put it out of the way in your gear bag. Nothing with earphones is allowed in a triathlon.

Warming Up

After you have set up your transition area, it's important to warm up before the race starts—and not just yourself. Your bicycle also needs a warm up of sorts. Take the machine out for a short ride. You don't need to go fast, but it's a good way for you to get your heart rate up a bit and to loosen your muscles.

You can also check to make sure your bicycle's gears are shifting smoothly and properly. Your warm-up ride should be done, if possible, in the first part of the bicycle course. The objective is to make sure that you start your race in the right gear depending on whether the first part of the race is flat or hilly.

ALERT!

Most larger triathlons will have at least one bike shop representative on hand for last-minute tune-ups and to help with mechanical problems you might encounter on the morning of the race.

Ride your bicycle at an easy pace for about ten minutes, then put it back in the rack and go for a short run. As with the bicycle ride, you don't want to go tearing around, but you should put enough effort into it to break a sweat.

Remember your training: you were advised to warm up before every workout. Race day is no different.

You could probably skip the warm-up without significant harm, but the result would be a slower pace starting out as you did your warm-up, even if you didn't call it that, in the first part of the race. Putting stress on cold muscles, of course, risks injury.

> If you do your warm-ups too early, you will have a lot of time to kill before the race, and the effects of the effort will wear off. Try to time your warm-ups to be finished about five to ten minutes before the swim starts. Allow time to visit the restroom or port-a-potty.

After an easy run of about five minutes, swinging your arms to get them loose, slip into the water for a short swim. That will loosen your swimming muscles and help keep you from feeling shocked when you enter the cold water at the start of the swim. The water won't seem so cold if you have already been in it. A brief swim will also give you a chance to sight the buoys and orient yourself to the course.

If any of the three warm-up activities is prohibited by the race organizers for some reason, do a little bit extra of what you can to make up for missing one of the others. The main objective is to avoid starting cold.

Surviving Your First Triathlon Swim

As mentioned previously, there are two ways to start a triathlon swim: wave and time trial. In a wave start, all the swimmers start at the same time, although waves can be divided into age groups or other common denominators. Some triathlons have all beginners start together in a wave. The other way to get things going is by time trial. Swimmers line up, also possibly separated into groups, by number, entering the water one at a time, usually with a few seconds in between.

The scene at a wave start can be chaotic as swimmers thrash and flail on surges of adrenaline. If you're in the middle of it, you might be kicked and punched as all the arms and legs go churning through the water. Trunks and swimsuits will be pulled down, swim goggles will be knocked off. It can be pretty rough.

A wave start to the swim in a triathlon can have as many as sixty to eighty swimmers entering the water at the same time. If the crowd looks intimidating to you, there's nothing in the rules that prohibits you from hanging back for a few seconds until everyone is already in the water and on their way.

The way to avoid a lot of the hassle in the water is to position yourself on the edge of the mass of people. It might cut down on your time slightly, but it will be worth it to avoid the trauma of being in the middle of the hectic takeoff.

Positioning yourself on the outside edges of the wave start will affect how you see the buoys on the course, making it even more important for you to get a good look at them ahead of time if you can. Even as late as the morning of the race, go to the water and count the buoys so that you can remember the number and their placement.

A triathlon's website usually has all the details of the competition, including how the swim will start. As a new triathlete, you will enjoy a time trial start more than a wave start. When picking your triathlon, check the details of how it's run.

Plunge Taken

Once in the water, try to stay close to the buoys if you can. If you get into a bit of trouble or simply tire, it's okay to hang onto a buoy or a boat so long as you get no aid from anyone on the water.

As you swim, remember to look up every few seconds to make sure you are staying on course. It's easy to overshoot your objective if you don't keep an eye on where you're going.

It should be evident that the more effort you put into making yourself familiar with the swim course before you get into the water, the better your experience will be. Do your homework. You will be glad you did.

Dealing with Muscle Cramps

There are varying theories about the causes of muscle cramps, but the problem seems to be much more common in hot-weather races, suggesting that the loss of electrolytes is a significant factor. When you are exercising strenuously, your body heats up. To cool itself, your body sends water to the surface of your skin. The process of evaporation has a cooling effect. The perspiration evaporates at different rates depending on the humidity. When it's humid, the perspiration evaporates more slowly, hampering the cooling process. In response, your body sends more water to the surface.

Unless you have a chance to acclimate yourself to warm, possibly even hot, and humid conditions, be careful about entering a triathlon in a part of the country that is likely to present significant weather challenges. At the very least in such a case, arrive a couple of days early to get used to the conditions.

The fluid your body sends to your skin to try to cool you off contains more than water. It also has sodium, potassium, calcium, and magnesium, known as electrolytes. These substances are critical to the proper functioning of the muscles. Many experts believe that cramps come on when electrolytes get too low.

Cramping usually occurs in the legs, especially in the calf muscles and quadriceps. A truly bad case of cramps will make you feel as though every muscle in your legs has frozen.

Prevention

Heading off cramps, of course, is preferable to dealing with them during a race. A seized-up muscle can have a devastating effect on your race, costing you considerably in time, not to mention pride. There are few things worse than feeling as though you are cruising in the final stage of your triathlon only to have to limp across the finish line because running is impossible thanks to a leg cramp that won't go away.

Hydration, of course, is a key, but it is critically important that electrolyte replacement take place along with fluid intake. It's good to drink water, but if that's all you take in, you could end up flushing a significant portion of your body's electrolytes from your system as you urinate.

Not Only H2O

During a sprint or Olympic-distance triathlon, if you started with your electrolytes at proper levels, it is unlikely you would be in any danger. In a longer event—a Half Ironman, for example—it is very important for you to drink something other than water.

Aid stations at races always offer a sports drink in addition to water. The sports drink contains a bit of sugar for a quick energy boost. More important, it also contains electrolytes. You can still have a cup of water if you want it, but be sure to include sports drinks at least at every other stop.

Taking in only water for an extended period in hot-weather exertion can lead to a serious condition known as hyponatremia, which occurs when the sodium concentration in the blood gets too low. Hyponatremia can result in death. It is not normally a danger in short races such as sprint triathlons.

As you approach your race, especially if it is going to occur in warm or hot temperatures, increase your intake of salt. Consider electrolyte supplementation starting a week or so before race day, and keep it up at least through the night before. It won't hurt you and could prevent serious problems on race day.

Real Time

If you do enough racing, especially in warm weather or if you perspire heavily, you will probably have to deal with muscle cramps at some point. It is unlikely you will have a muscle cramp during your swim, especially if you warm up first as recommended. If you do, however, it can help to switch from freestyle to the backstroke or some other different way of swimming.

If the cramp is still with you despite a change in strokes, head for a boat or buoy to rest for a bit. Remember, as long as you do not receive aid from anyone, you can hang on to a boat until you feel capable of going on.

Vicious Cycle

During the cycling part of your triathlon, if cramps come on they are most likely to be in your legs, but you could experience cramping in your back. Most often, you will have this experience in hot weather.

In case of cramps on the cycle, stand up on the pedals and try to stretch your limbs for a brief period. Obviously, this will slow you down, but it's better than having to quit because you can't pedal at all. If the cramps don't subside from a bit of stretching on the bicycle, you may have to dismount and stretch.

QUESTION?

Is there anything I can do to prevent cramps besides taking in extra salt and other electrolytes?
There are many ergogenic aids that supposedly prevent muscle cramps. If cramping is a chronic problem and simple electrolyte supplementation doesn't work for you, it would be worthwhile to try something new. Any biking, running, or triathlon magazine will help you find these products.

In a short race such as a sprint triathlon, you probably won't have to deal with muscle cramps. If you do, it will almost certainly be during your run. If you feel a cramp developing, which sometimes start as just a twinge, slow down at that point or stop and stretch the endangered muscle. It might just take some periods of walking, even alternating running and walking.

There are folk remedies for getting rid of cramps, such as pinching your upper lip. Don't bother with them. It's better to remember the folk aphorism about "an ounce of prevention."

Strategies and Protocols for Bikers

There is a lot more to the bicycle portion of your triathlon than simply hopping on your machine and taking off. Unless you are participating in a mom-and-pop triathlon in some backwater burg—and don't even think about doing that—you will be swimming, biking, and riding according to the rules of the national triathlon association, USA Triathlon. Ignorance of the rules will not help you if you violate one of them, and you are most likely to get into trouble before and during your bike ride. The two biggies involve your helmet and the practice of drafting.

Strap It

Triathlon organizers are very strict about your bicycle helmet. Once you are out of the water and into your transition area, your first priority should be to put on your helmet and buckle the chinstrap. Do this before you even touch your bicycle. This is not an overstatement to make a point. There will be monitors everywhere at your triathlon, and if you are seen violating any aspect of the helmet rule, you will be penalized (minutes added to your final time) or disqualified.

It is not customary for monitors to tell you when you have violated a race rule. The monitor will simply note your number and the violation. The penalty, which could be disqualification, will be posted with the final results. It's up to you to know the rules and to follow them.

The helmet rule is in force, of course, all during your bike ride and after the dismount when your ride is finished. You must keep your helmet on with the chinstrap buckled until you rack your bike.

Be a Draft Dodger

Drafting is another major sin in the world of triathlons. As bikers go along, each creates a slipstream, an area in which the air resistance is lessened. Any trailing rider in that slipstream has much less work to do. It is estimated that the energy savings can be as much as 40 percent for a drafting rider.

Each rider has a drafting zone. It is two meters wide and seven meters long, starting at the front wheel of the bicycle and going backward. Riders are not permitted to have their drafting zones overlap. If the rider in front of you slows down, you must slow down also or pass.

An easy way to avoid being penalized or disqualified for drafting is to always stay at least two bike lengths behind the rider in front of you. If you even think you might be getting too close, drop back a bit.

Once you enter a rider's drafting zone, you have fifteen seconds to pass that biker. Once your front wheel moves out ahead, the other biker must drop back to avoid a drafting violation.

Get It Right

Another rule is that bikers must stay to the right at all times unless passing. If you are in the left lane attempting to pass and a faster rider approaches, you must get out of the way or you could get a penalty for blocking.

One of the most common mistakes beginning triathletes make is not staying to the right. A free copy of USAT rules can be downloaded from the organization's website (*www.usatriathlon.org*).

Good Ride

Now that you know the key rules and how to avoid breaking them, you should consider your racing strategy. In the excitement of the competition, it's natural for people to start every part of the race at full speed. You will see adrenaline-pumped bikers blasting off as you begin your ride. If you follow a better strategy, you will see them again, exhausted and struggling, as you pass them on the course.

Aim to start at a moderate pace and build speed as you go. In a sprint triathlon, your bike ride will be 13 to 15 miles. That should take you forty-five to ninety minutes depending on the difficulty of the course and your fitness and riding skill.

More to Do

Remember, you have a run of 3.1 miles to do after you get off your bicycle. It's good to build up some speed as you go, but back off over the last half mile so that you aren't starting your run completely out of breath.

With ten to fifteen minutes left in your ride, take the energy gel you brought along with you. Wash it down with water. That will give the gel time to get into your system for the final phase of your race.

Off the Bike and On the Road

If you have organized your transition area efficiently, you will have your running gear ready to go after you have dismounted and walked your bicycle to the rack (you can go faster than a walk, but be careful). Remove your helmet, put on your running shoes, grab the belt containing your race number, and take off. You can put the belt on as you go.

After cycling for an hour or so, your legs will feel heavy when you first start the run, but all will return to normal in about half a mile. Remember all that practice with bricks? This part of the race is why you did all those workouts.

Start your run at a slow to moderate pace and get your breathing under control. You can then start to push, although there's nothing wrong with cruising through the run if your goal for your first triathlon was just to finish. You will be able to judge how much effort you can afford by how you feel.

Cautions

If the weather is warm on race day, take extra care to stay hydrated, and beware the symptoms of heat exhaustion. If you feel dizzy or have the chills, find an aid station and get some fluid. Pour some water over your head and body and take in a sports drink. You can finish, but you must take it easy. Listen to your body.

Of course, if things are going well and you feel good, you can quickly build up the run to a strong effort, planning to go all out over the last mile of the run. Finishing strong will give you confidence for your next race.

Keeping Your Head in the Race

In most competitive endeavors, concentration and focus are key elements of success. Keeping one's eye on the ball is more than just a saying. It's a must. In the triathlon, it is vital to stay in the moment.

If you are worried about how you're going to manage on the bike course while you are swimming, you are not focused on what you should be doing in the water. You could easily find yourself way off course when your mind returns to where it should be.

Fretting about things you can't control—the weather, other competitors—will distract you from the task at hand, and it will not help you in your race.

If you start out on your bicycle and people are passing you in a steady stream, it will not help to worry about that. Remember, you will probably catch and pass many of them later in the ride. Even if you don't, so what? Your only real competitor is you, especially if you are a first-timer.

On the Alert

On the ride, focus is even more important because a lapse in concentration can result in a crash and potentially serious injury. Bike courses are not perfect. You must be alert to possible hazards, turns, other riders, and your position on the course (remember those penalties). While you're riding, don't be thinking about the run or how you can cut ten seconds off your transition time. Concentrate on the road and your cadence.

Approach each competition with the idea that you will learn something (you probably will), and don't be discouraged if you're having a bad day. That happens to everyone, even the elite athletes. No matter how badly things might be going, don't let negative thoughts into your head. Always keep it positive.

Remember, you are fit and strong. One bad performance doesn't change that. You will return to fight another day.

CHAPTER 17

After the Race

When you cross that finish line in your triathlon, you will feel the exhilaration of accomplishing a difficult task. That feeling will be intensified if the triathlon was your first. All those early morning workouts, bike rides, and runs in the dark, and all those bricks, were worth it after all! Hold on, though. You aren't quite finished. There are still a few things left to do right now and in the weeks to come.

Immediately After

Someone will hand you a bottle of water as you make your way through the chute. Drink it in small sips. Even if you didn't have to cope with heat and humidity during the race, you lost fluid, so get started putting it back. If there is a sports drink available, have one of those, too.

Keep moving for a few minutes before finding a place to stretch your tight muscles. You will regret it if you head for a chair or bench and sit right away. Those tight muscles will get tighter, and you may be shocked at how hard it is to get up. As you stretch, make sure you target the hamstrings, quadriceps, glutes, and anything else that feels tight.

A Stretch in Time

There will be distractions. You may want to share your triumph with friends and family, perhaps call home and tell someone how you did. That's okay, but try to do your stretching during the first thirty minutes after your race.

You can do a light jog if that helps you get loose. You were probably pushing pretty hard at the end of your run, so whatever helps you relax will be beneficial. Remember, stretching is more effective when the muscles are still warm.

Cool Spot

It might not occur to you to do this, but getting back in the water for a few minutes can help you cool down, stave off a bit of muscle soreness, and promote faster recovery of the muscles.

It always feels good to immerse your legs in cool water after a hard run—spraying your legs with a hose works, too—and no matter how warm the ambient temperature, the lake water will feel cool and soothing. It is not necessary to do a lot while you're in the water. Go in to the point that the water hits your waist, then relax as you move around slowly, letting the water do its tricks on your legs. You will have company. There will be plenty of experienced triathletes in there with you.

Important Info

By the time you have had a drink, a stretch, and a dip in the lake, you can go and check the leaderboard to see how you did. If your race was chip timed, the results will be posted pretty quickly and will include your times in the swim, ride, and run. The results will also include how long you took in the two transitions.

What You Should Eat and Drink

You will get water right away when you finish the run, and there will be more available in various locations, but don't forget that an important part of your recovery will be restoring the glycogen that you used during the triathlon. That means getting some carbohydrates into your system.

The body is most receptive to glycogen replacement for thirty minutes after exertion stops. After half an hour, absorption of carbs is not as efficient. The same goes for protein, although your window of opportunity there is slightly longer. Start by switching from water to a sports drink. Most have sugar, which is a start, and they also have electrolytes.

Oranges and bananas, often provided for the competitors, are ideal postrace snacks. Oranges have sugar for carbohydrate replacement. Bananas also contain carbs, with the added benefit of potassium, one of the electrolytes.

Look around for some pretzels. The salty snack will help replace some of the sodium you lost during your race. Pretzels are much better than potato chips because of the difference in fat content (chips have lots more).

You will have a lot of things to think about and do in a short period of time, including stretching, so look around right away for some kind of food. If you were smart enough to pack a protein bar, head for the transition area—if you are allowed to enter it—and fish it out of your gear bag.

If you planned well, you or someone in your party will have a cooler with a postrace protein shake. You can make your own, of course, but it is easier to buy shakelike recovery drinks ready to drink. You can find them at health food stores and nutrition centers. However you take it in, protein is needed for recovery soon after you finish.

Party Smartly

Of course, in your state of exhilaration and remembering how good you were, nutrition-wise, during your training, you will be in the mood to bust out and have something you might not ordinarily eat or drink. Yes, that could mean a cheeseburger if you are so inclined.

Triathlon organizers often offer grilled meat—hamburgers and hot dogs—chips, barbecue, and other foods you might reject at other times. It's okay to indulge. You earned it. Just don't depend on such greasy or fatty fare for carbohydrate and protein replacement.

Have a couple of pieces of fruit and your shake or protein bar. Then you can be bad if it suits you.

Many triathlons also have a few kegs of beer for the competitors. What's a party, after all, without the suds? As with the fatty or fried food, moderation is best. Don't forget that your fluid levels may be down somewhat after your race, and alcohol has a dehydrating effect. If you overindulge in a dehydrated state, you could easily get sick, and you don't want to end your triumphant day with a vicious hangover. Another important point: if you are by yourself or are the driver in your party, be very careful about your alcohol consumption.

Later That Day

The first thing to address is the transition area, where your bicycle and other gear have been sitting since morning. The rules differ, so be sure you know how your triathlon organizers manage the transition area.

Some triathlons do not permit anyone who is not still competing to enter the transition area until a certain time that day. Others require everyone to be out of the area by a certain time. All in all, it's best not to plan any activity on race day that will require you to get away immediately after the competition. There are also strict rules about leaving trash behind, so plan to bring a plastic sack for empty gel packs or energy/protein bar wrappers.

While you're relaxing and reflecting on your accomplishment, you will have time to return to the leaderboard. Most races update the standings continuously as finishers come in. Complete results are usually available on the Internet almost immediately.

High Fives

Once you're done and have cooled off, stretched, started rehydrating, and put some food in your stomach, go back to the finish area and see if you know anyone, perhaps some of your training partners. Find someone to congratulate. Share hugs and war stories from your race.

If it's your first triathlon, there will never be another. Savor the experience. Take photos if you have a camera, and look around so you can remember the scene. There will be lots of thoughts running around in your head. Dismiss anything resembling recriminations—what you could have or should have done differently. There will be time for that later. For now, just relax and enjoy the feeling of achieving your goal.

Winding Down

If you are not under pressure to get away quickly, consider lending a hand to the organizers who put the race together. A significant number of them, probably the majority, will be volunteers, and they will definitely appreciate any assistance in tearing down the finish line and packing up the gear. Even if they don't need your help, you'll get credit for offering.

Once you're done and have stowed your bicycle and other paraphernalia, head for home or the hotel to clean up and plan for a brief nap. Sleep is a very good recovery tool. You don't have to stay in bed for a long time, but the rest will leave you refreshed and ready for more fun that evening.

Taking Stock: What Went Well, What Went Wrong

Once you have rested and cleared your head, review the triathlon step by step while your memory is still fresh. You may be surprised at how vivid some of the memories will be. Make some notes as you go over each phase of the race. Be objective, but don't beat yourself up over perceived mistakes. You will probably learn something in every race you do. Make that your objective, along with doing better next time. Compare only with yourself, not others.

Important Issues

Here are some key questions for your review process:

- Did I get to the venue soon enough? Did I have to walk a long way after parking? Did I have enough time to warm up after placing my bicycle and gear in the transition area?
- Did my checklist contain everything I needed? Should I add to it?
- Did I position myself correctly to avoid problems in the swim start? Did I go off course?
- Did my first transition go smoothly? Was all my gear arranged in the right order and easy to get to? Did I have the right socks for the ride and the run?
- Did I have my bicycle in the correct gear starting out? Were there mechanical issues with the bike I could have or should have addressed before the race?
- Did my second transition go well? Do I need more practice going from bike to run?
- Did I go too hard near the end of the ride? Should I start backing off earlier to get ready for the run? How long did it take my legs to adjust in the run?
- How did my nutrition plan work out? Did I eat enough, or too much, before the race? Do I need a second water bottle for the bicycle phase? Were the gels easy to get to as I rode?

- Did I see another athlete using something—food, drink, equipment—that could be useful for me?
- Were my running shoes right for the triathlon?

Going Forward

You may not know all the answers to all of these questions, particularly the ones that call for some judgment or experience. If you had a problem in some area, or if you just have a feeling something should have gone differently or better in some way, find a coach or a veteran triathlete and ask. Most are delighted to share their knowledge with someone trying to improve.

As you review the race, try to adopt a big-picture perspective. Look at the swim, for example, as a warm-up, the bicycle ride as building more speed, culminating with the run, where you keep building up speed and lay it all on the line in the final mile or so. Ideally, when the race is over you want to reflect that you could have pushed a bit harder rather than feeling as though you were in a death march to the end.

FACT

Each component of the triathlon is important, but the reality is that triathlons are won in the cycling and running phases. The best swimmers rarely come out on top unless they perform equally well in the other two phases.

Chances are you will never feel that everything went just perfectly in your triathlon. There will always be something you believe could have gone better, some aspect of the race that needs improvement. As long as you don't obsess over these issues, it can be healthy and productive to keep trying to do better.

Final Review

Sometimes, things beyond your control, usually the weather, will throw a monkey wrench into your plans, and your race will turn out to be a disaster, or something that feels like one. For example, if race day greets you with temperatures approaching or exceeding 90°F, with some extra humidity thrown in for good measure, you and just about everyone else will struggle. Many of the elites, of course, will still dazzle you even as they record much slower times than usual for them.

Instead of comparing yourself to others or feeling that you should have done better despite the conditions, just chalk it up to bad luck and move on. Keep a positive outlook. If the weather was horrible but you finished anyway, enjoy the satisfaction of overcoming the elements, however slowly you had to do it. If an injury slowed you down, feel good about not quitting.

The Next Week

The day after your race should be devoted to rest or light activity. You will probably find that extra stretching is beneficial. A hot bath in Epsom salts will get some of the soreness out of your legs.

Remember, even in your training, you never did all three sports in the same day, certainly not compacted into a couple of hours. Chances are your heart rate was at its highest for the longest period ever in your life. You stressed your body like never before, so you need time to recover.

You will recall from your training that every week had time set aside for recovery, and there were recovery weeks of lighter-than-normal activity. You need that recovery time just as much, if not more, after your race.

If your triathlon was on a Sunday, keep the exercise light for at least Monday and Tuesday. Acceptable activities are stretching, yoga, easy swimming, and light biking. Avoid running, even slowly, until Wednesday. Keep the heart rate low.

Brakes, Please

If your race went well, you might be feeling superhuman, ready to leap tall buildings or run a 10K at full speed. If so, you are an injury waiting to happen. Many a new athlete has suffered a devastating injury by overdoing it in the euphoria of success after the first venture into sports. Think long term. Give your body a break.

If you just have to get out on the road, go for a ride, but keep your bicycle in an easy gear. No elevated heart rates or hard riding. An easy ride can actually take some of the soreness out of your legs, and you can get the same benefit from an easy swim.

It's different if your goal in your first triathlon was just to finish and you did not push particularly hard. In that case, your recovery time will be shorter. You should still exercise caution, however. The triathlon was a new experience for your body. If you want it to be healthy and ready for the next attempt, use common sense.

You will have some soreness for a couple of days after the triathlon, no matter how easy, relatively speaking, your effort was. That's normal. If fatigue lasts for more than a day or two, that may be a sign that you need more rest. Some people recover more quickly than others. As you gain more experience, you will learn to read your body regarding its limits and recuperative abilities. In the meantime, it will be wise to be conservative.

If any workout after your race seems more difficult than usual, bag it for the day. The same symptoms that signal overtraining can also indicate a less-than-full recovery from your triathlon.

A day or two after your triathlon, consider treating yourself to a full-body massage. Besides feeling good, a massage promotes recovery and helps rid your body of the lactic acid that accumulated during your race. Make a postrace massage part of your triathlon plan.

By the third day after your race, it's okay to start running again if you are so inclined, but keep it easy. If you just have to push a little, go at a moderate pace. No hard stuff, period.

Of the three sports, running is the most likely to result in injury if you go too hard too soon after the triathlon. Be aware of tweaks and pains once you start running again. If something hurts, slow down or stop. You won't be able to do that next race if you end up sidelined for weeks with a hamstring pull, sore Achilles tendon, or worse.

Back to Normal

On race day, you had to eat a bit extra to replenish glycogen stores. You can resume normal eating the day after the race, always mindful of your different nutritional needs when training. As always, think carbs, protein, and plenty of fluids, and go easy on saturated fat.

Try to get back into your prerace sleeping regimen (eight hours or whatever works for you). Your body does a wonderful job of repairing itself and getting ready for the next challenge, and a lot of that self-healing occurs during rest.

You are now a triathlete with a new view of the sport, excited at the prospect of achieving more as you recover and plan your next race. The key is not to let the exhilaration of finishing a triathlon cloud your judgment when it comes to resuming your activities.

When to Resume Serious Training

Your first triathlon went well, and you can't wait to get back out there to take the challenge again, with all kinds of plans about how to do better the second time out. Perhaps you have even signed up for another race. How soon, you might ask, can a new triathlete resume more than light workouts?

If your first or just-completed triathlon was a sprint distance, it's okay to put another sprint-distance race on the schedule as soon as two weeks later. Say you did just that: scheduled your second sprint triathlon for two weeks after the first one. Do little or nothing the first couple of days after your just-finished race, followed by light to moderate workouts for the rest of the week.

Follow Directions

In the week leading up to the second triathlon, go back to your training schedule and do the workouts recommended for the week leading up to your first race. Basically, train on Sunday, Monday, Tuesday, and Wednesday, then back off on Thursday, Friday, and Saturday for a Sunday race.

Don't worry that you will lose fitness in this period. If you trained properly for your first race, you will be more than ready for the second with some short tune-ups and brief workouts. Just don't do any long, hard workouts. It's okay to have some intense runs or rides, but only for short distances.

If you are moving up from a sprint triathlon to a longer distance, perhaps Olympic distance, add time, distance, and numbers of repetitions to the workouts in the beginner training charts in Chapter 11. The increases should be equivalent to about 25 percent.

Check the course for your next triathlon to determine if there are any challenges you didn't face the first time around. For example, the next run or bike course might have some significant hills. If the next triathlon is two weeks away, you probably won't have time to get much hill work in before you race again. With more time, however, plan to add at least one good hill workout per week in biking and running, not including the week before the triathlon.

Also, do your best to ascertain whether there will be issues with heat and humidity in your next triathlon. If so, you will know to take extra precautions in your prerace preparations relative to hydration and electrolyte stores.

More Time

If your next race is a month or more away, go back to the training schedule and pick it up at a point that matches how long you have before you race again, minus the week you are spending in recovery from the triathlon you just completed.

With more time, you can do more workouts that are longer and harder. For an Olympic-distance triathlon, you can increase your long run time to as much as seventy-five minutes. Your long bicycle rides will be up to an hour and forty-five minutes, and you should plan to swim for close to an hour once a week. It is essential to get your body used to the longer durations so that you can cope with the change in your next race.

Adjustments

The extra time will also give you a chance to work on some of the issues you might have had in your first race. For example, if you had trouble staying on course during the swim, you can practice swimming with your head up so that you don't waste time and energy in the next triathlon.

Was the swim more difficult than you expected it to be? You might need to adjust your workouts at the pool. Tell your swim coach how it went and how you would like to improve. The coach will provide workouts aimed at helping you improve in your next triathlon swim.

Running on Empty

Did you feel really spent at the end of the run? That could indicate you should do a bit more speed work in the next couple of weeks, assuming you have about a month to prepare for your next race.

Also, revisit your nutrition plan for the race you just ran. You might conclude that you need to take more than one energy gel before you start running. Perhaps you should consider a different gel or other energy source.

These issues are why you made those notes at the end of the race. Use the information to your advantage now.

CHAPTER 18

Planning for Your Next Race

Now you've gone and done it: you are a triathlete, one of a select group. Chances are you are happy about it and already thinking about when and where the next triathlon is happening. Once you find yourself completely hooked (it can happen), other considerations will loom into view, matters such as equipment, bigger challenges, and better training. Take it one step at a time. Multisport racing is a big, wide world.

Do You Have the Triathlon Bug?

When you cross the finish line in your first triathlon, you will experience an array of feelings, physical and emotional. You may be out of breath and hurting from the exertion of the final, crazy sprint to the finish. You may be feeling the thrill of doing something that a few months ago you probably wouldn't have thought possible. It's not uncommon for tears to flow at such a time.

If you got through the triathlon without major problems and finished feeling pretty good, you were probably hooked then and there. If you thought it was fun and you're high as a kite from the excitement of finishing, you don't need any motivational speeches. Sure, you're sore, but the pain won't last. It will be forgotten tomorrow. You can't wait to get out there again, and you know you'll do better. What a charge!

If you did not do as well in your first triathlon as you expected, focus on the fact that you are active and healthy, capable of undertaking the physical challenges of such an event. How many people do you know who would even try it?

Second Thoughts

On the other hand, you may simply be exhausted, sweaty, and sore when you get to the end. You may feel that your triathlon adventure was a mistake and that you aren't cut out for this sort of thing. Such feelings are usually the result of a disappointing performance. You thought you would do a lot better, but most of the race was a struggle.

Don't be too quick to judge yourself or your performance. If you made some mistakes, most of them can be corrected, and perhaps there were external factors that affected your times. If, for example, the weather turned out unexpectedly hot on race day, it would take you a lot longer than you anticipated to finish, especially if you trained in a more favorable climate. Don't get down on yourself or the triathlon experience because you had a bad race in the heat, rain, or whatever slowed you down.

Tough Day

Try not to be upset with yourself because of a bad race even if conditions were perfect. Everyone has a bad day or two. You just got yours out of the way early in your triathlon career. Remember those training days that didn't go so well? The same thing can happen on race day.

If things didn't go very well and you're feeling miserable, have a beer, a hamburger, and some chips, maybe some cookies afterward, and put it all out of your mind. Don't even consider future triathlon plans until tomorrow, after you have had a chance to reflect on some of the things you might have done better.

Don't listen to people around you complaining or swearing they'll never do another triathlon. Most of them will be at their computers the following day signing up for the next race. They're just talking. It's human nature to gripe. Don't take it seriously.

Do you remember learning to ride a bicycle? Did you jump right on and pedal down the street the first time? No, you kept trying despite falling down a few times. Don't quit the triathlon just because you didn't "get it" the first time.

For some, even a bad first experience won't be enough to put them off triathlons. There is a lot of positive energy flying around the venue, and if you review your race dispassionately, you will probably recognize many things you could improve on next time.

Looking at it another way, if you didn't do very well the first time, your next triathlon will surely be an improvement, and that's what everyone strives for, right?

Other Multisport Events

The triathlon is challenging because of the three different sports you must tackle in the competition. The triathlon is not, however, the only challenging multisport event available to those willing to try something different.

A well-known alternative to the triathlon is the duathlon, which features a run, bicycle ride, and another run. This is sometimes confused with the biathlon, an event in the Olympic Games featuring skiing and shooting. A kind of starter distance for a duathlon is known as a Formula One: 2-mile run, 10-mile bike ride, 2-mile run. There are other distances, all the way up to the Powerman Duathlon: 10K run, 60K bicycle ride, 10K run.

Your local bike store will have a calendar of multisport events, including duathlons, and there are ample resources on the Internet to find a duathlon if you're interested. For people who don't like swimming or aren't very good at it, the duathlon is a fine alternative to the triathlon. If you can run and ride, you can take part.

Unless you are a veteran of the duathlon and in peak shape, your best strategy in the duathlon is to go relatively easy in the first run to avoid blowing up in the second. You want to finish in a sprint, not a crawl.

Tough Enough

Although duathlons once enjoyed widespread popularity, they've taken a back seat to triathlons lately despite the fact that the two-sport race provides a good opportunity for triathletes to sharpen their biking and running form before and during the triathlon season. USA Triathlon is working to promote more duathlons, so keep your eye out for opportunities in your area.

Competing in two sports instead of three might sound easier, but the duathlon is actually a bit tougher than the triathlon. In a triathlon, the swim phase does not usually elevate your heart rate to a significant degree. In a duathlon, you start out with a run, which gets your heart pumping pretty hard. The cycling phase provides no letup, and your second run is usually harder than the first. The two runs can represent some serious stress to your body.

For organizers, duathlons are a lot easier than triathlons because no large body of water is needed, and a typical duathlon takes a lot less time from start to finish. See Chapter 19 for information on the popular XTERRA off-road duathlon.

Water Worlds

It's not common, but some triathlon organizers have been known to add an event called aquabike, created to give a competitive option to people who have injuries that keep them from running but not from biking or swimming.

It's a relatively new sport that usually allows participants to swim with the triathlon swimmers and bike with the bikers. When an aquabiker finishes the ride, however, it's over. No running is needed, and there is no second swim. With chip timing, it's easy to keep track of the aquabikers and to produce results.

Running Water

Another new multisport opportunity can be found in the aquathlon, sometimes called aquathon, for people who don't have or want to purchase a racing bicycle. The sport of aquathlon is attractive to many athletes because the typical distances are shorter, meaning less training time is needed to compete, and it's a good way to train for two of the three triathlon sports.

Even better, the equipment costs are relatively low. All you need are a swimsuit, goggles, running shoes, and shorts. You don't have to lay out the bucks for a bicycle or lug it around to your competition.

As with a duathlon, the logistics of setting up an aquathlon are easier than a three-sport event, and it can be contained in a relatively small area. An aquathlon can be organized as a run-swim-run or simply as a swim-run. You may have never heard of the aquathlon, but hundreds of swimmer-runners take part in the growing International Triathlon Union Aquathlon World Championships each year.

Cold Competition

Is there such a thing as a triathlon without water? You bet. It's the winter triathlon, featuring running, mountain biking, and skiing—all done in snow. The run is usually 5K, but it can be longer, and it takes place on packed snow or ski trails. Next you hop on the mountain bike for a 10 to 15K ride on a ski trail. When that's done you get to hit the ski trails for an 8 to 12K cross-country ski.

This is an event limited to places where there is plenty of snow, and strategies and gear are lots different from most races. But if you have a pair of skis and a mountain bike, this is a great way to get started in multisport events if you're inclined to try something very different. If promoters of this sport have their way, the winter triathlon will be part of the 2010 Winter Olympic Games in Vancouver, British Columbia.

Upgrading Your Equipment

Once you decide you're into triathlons for the long haul, your next step is to review your gear, starting at the top. No need to break the bank here, but you can make some modest changes that will improve the triathlon experience and provide the potential for better results. It's still up to you and how well you train, but all things being equal, better gear can take minutes off your triathlon time.

Wheel Deals

Start by making an assessment of the bicycle you used in your race. First, does the bike belong to you? It's not uncommon for a first-time triathlete to borrow a bicycle to avoid the expense of buying one for an event that might not be repeated. If the bike you rode is yours, ask yourself some questions. Does it fit you well? Is it comfortable when you ride? Is it in good mechanical shape? If the answer to these questions is yes, turn your attention to the wheels.

Big Gains

Your bike frame might not be as sleek as the frames of some of the riders you have seen, but unless it's a pure clunker, you can make a major upgrade to your bike with better wheels. Regular training wheels are heavy and have lots of wind-resistant spokes. They are sturdy but not very aerodynamic.

Head for the bike store and let the experts help you select a set of racing wheels for your machine. Plan to spend $700 to $1,100 for the new wheels. That might sound like a lot, but it's considerably less expensive than a whole new bicycle (that's your story for the spouse, anyway, and you should stick to it). Because the wheels can make such a dramatic difference, you usually get more bang for the buck by simply investing in race wheels rather than a new machine.

Don't throw away the old bicycle wheels after buying a set of racing wheels. Keep training with the heavier wheels, saving wear and tear on the expensive new set. On race day, your new wheels will feel extra light after all the training on the heavy ones.

Racing wheels are lighter and more aerodynamic with better bearings for easier spin. Some racing wheels are solid, called discs, and offer virtually no wind resistance straight on. These solid wheels are used only on the rear. Discs are sometimes banned in races where high crosswinds could blow bikers over and greatly increase the risk of accidents.

Your bike shop will have lots of options when it comes to race wheels. You'll see titanium, carbon fiber, and wheels with thick rims (called "deep dish"). Let the experts match the wheels with your bicycle frame and your objectives in upgrading.

New Ride

If you decide that you need a new bicycle after all, keep the issue of wheels in mind. In general, you will be better off early in your triathlon career to opt for a modest frame, dressing it up with better wheels and gears.

Before you start shopping, in person or online, set a price range and stick with it. The local triathlon club might know someone looking to sell a bicycle that would be a significant upgrade to yours. You could make a major move up without spending a fortune.

Remember, the fit of your bicycle and the wheels are the most important considerations. Get your money's worth out of the bicycle you own before you move up.

High Tech

Ultimately, you and your effort in training will have the greatest influence on how well you do on race day, but there are a few training aids that can help you get better. There are many electronic devices that help you keep track of your workouts. Some are capable of downloading data directly to your computer. Devices connected to global positioning system (GPS) satellites are discussed in Chapter 10. Look for the ones that can be used for running and biking.

Heart rate monitors (also discussed in Chapter 10) are very useful in helping you avoid overtraining. Most are very easy to use.

Light on Your Feet

Lastly, consider an upgrade in your running shoes. If you have no biomechanical issues, consider a pair of racing flats. They are very light, weighing as little as 7.5 ounces per shoe, compared to regular training shoes that typically hit 11 or 12 ounces or more. You might not think a difference measured in ounces could be very significant, but at the end of a hard race, your 12-ounce shoes can feel like a pair of bricks compared to a set of racing flats.

Bear in mind that racing flats typically do not have a lot of support or stability and generally are best for short races (5K and 10K) and lightweight runners. If you're at 180 pounds or more, stick to your regular shoes.

Higher Aspirations

It's natural to want to do better. If you competed in your first triathlon with the goal of simply finishing, it is very likely you will improve next time with a bit more work. As you assess your situation and consider your goals going forward, the first consideration is the next race.

Are you planning another sprint triathlon with the goal of improving your times, or have you decided to move up to a longer race, perhaps Olympic distance? If it's the latter, there are a couple of considerations.

First, do you have enough time to train for the event? It would be unwise to try to go from a sprint distance to an Olympic-distance triathlon without at least a month to prepare, and that's just to finish. Forget about any time goals.

Second, do you realize what you are getting into? If you are a typical new triathlete, your sprint distance race probably took one to one and a half hours to complete, not counting transition times. It will take you at least double that to complete an Olympic-distance triathlon.

If you were injured during your most recent triathlon, don't even think about the next race until you are healed. You won't be able to train effectively while injured, and racing while injured is a recipe for disaster.

Numbers

Here is what you will be facing in the Olympic-distance triathlon: a swim of 1.5K, a 40K bicycle ride, and a 10K run. You will have to swim nearly a mile (.93), ride nearly 25 miles (24.85), and run 6.2 miles. Compare those numbers to your sprint distances, most likely one-quarter to one-half mile for the swim, a 10- to 15-mile bike ride and a 3.1-mile run.

It will pay you to be objective and realistic in assessing your prospects. It's great to have higher ambitions, but if you are not prepared for the next race it will not be fun, and the misery could be compounded by an injury.

If you were a nonswimmer going into your first triathlon, look back on how the swim went in your recent race. If it was tough, consider how much trouble you could get into by entering a swim that could be more than three times as long.

Forging Ahead

All this is meant to make you aware of the challenge in moving up in distance. Athletes with more experience and fitness probably will not be discouraged, nor should they be. Also, those with two or three months to prepare can feel confident they can try the next level without undue risk of blowing up or suffering injury.

If you came out of your recent triathlon feeling good and with all parts working well, and if you have the time to train for your new distance, refer to the intermediate training chart in Chapter 11. You are probably ready for the increase in the training load.

If you are graduating from a sprint distance to Olympic distance, add some time to the long rides and runs on the intermediate chart. Your long rides should be two to two and a half hours, and your long runs about one and a half hours.

Not so Fast

If you are so excited about your new sport that you have ambitions beyond the Olympic-distance triathlon, here's some advice: wait 'til next year. See if you can get through a full triathlon season without injury or burnout before launching yourself into a race such as a Half Ironman, which will be very taxing and will require a lot more training than you have under your belt at this time or are likely to get in even a couple of months.

Here's a suggestion: enter and complete a half marathon (13.1 miles) and see how that feels. Now ask yourself if you would be ready to undertake a run of that distance after swimming more than a mile and riding for another 56 miles.

If you answer yes, think it over for a day and ask yourself again, with a reminder of how much more training will be required. If you still say yes, good luck—and be sure to pack lots of ibuprofen and muscle ointment for your trip.

Sense and Sensibility

If your goal in the near future is simply to improve your times in another short triathlon, you have an excellent chance to succeed. First, go to the website of the race you just completed and look at the results. Check your position in your age group in each of the sports. If you were about in the middle on two of them and, say, closer to the bottom in the third, it's clear where you should focus your attention in your next round of training.

If the results don't reveal anything significant, resume your training with a moderate increase in the intensity of your workouts. All steps in your first triathlon season should be small ones.

Going Beyond Just Finishing

If you are staying with the shorter distance for your next triathlon and you feel your body can handle the extra workload and intensity, start doing the workouts found on the intermediate training chart in Chapter 11. You probably won't have time to start at the beginning, so be cautious about overdoing it, especially at first. You should, however, be able to ease into the final four to six weeks of the intermediate regimen. The more demanding schedule will leave you poised to do better in each sport the second time around. You will also, of course, check out the next triathlon to see if there are major differences from your first, perhaps more hills on the ride or the run.

As you move deeper into the triathlon season, weather—specifically heat and humidity—will become more of a factor in your race preparation. Always make your best effort to determine conditions so that you can train and make race plans accordingly.

For those who jump to an Olympic-distance triathlon, the goal should in most cases remain just to finish. For one thing, comparing your sprint triathlon to the longer distance will be an apples-to-oranges proposition. They are different courses, different distances, and possibly radically different conditions.

You will be able to determine your pace in each sport in both events, but unless you have a long time to train for your next triathlon, it's unlikely you will get a lot of satisfaction from comparing your 5K pace in the sprint to your 10K pace in the Olympic-distance race. The same goes for the other sports.

Joining a Triathlon Club

It's natural for people with a common interest to get together, and triathletes are no different in that regard. As noted in Chapter 2, there are more than 500 triathlon clubs in the United States, so there's a good chance you can find one near you.

As you learned in Chapter 3, training with a group seems much less like drudgery than running or riding alone. Joining a triathlon club will also give you access to a lot of information that can be very useful to you in your training and racing. Veteran club members can answer your questions and provide tips, often through lectures or other group activities. You can learn about better racing, the latest gear, and the best races to sign up for.

Tri clubs are often the organizers of or are heavily involved in local multisport races. Many offer training programs tailored specifically for a race that they sponsor. This provides the perfect opportunity to gauge your progress as you'll most likely be training with people in your age group or experience level. You will probably even find yourself planning road trips to various multisport events with members of your training group.

As you learn to enjoy the sport and benefit from it in many ways, you will have a natural inclination to give back. Tri club membership will provide ample opportunities for volunteering, organizing, and learning.

In addition to organizing races, your local club also probably has purely social functions such as cookouts and group rides or runs followed by breakfast or another meal. The people you meet in the tri club will become your friends and will be there to support you in many ways, some completely separate from sports.

The USA Triathlon website (*www.usatriathlon.org*) has a list of triathlon clubs, by state, with web links. Go to the USA Triathlon's home page and under the Resources menu click on "For Clubs," then click on "Find a Club."

Club Perks

Most clubs have riding gear or T-shirts available for members to give them a sense of belonging and identification. If there are a variety of sports clubs in your area, the tri club may organize or participate in interclub competitions, such as competitive rides, runs, or swims. It is not uncommon for businesses such as running shoe stores and bike shops to offer discounts on purchases to members of local running, biking, and triathlon clubs.

Most triathlon clubs maintain websites, and many have regularly published newsletters. The dues for most triathlon clubs are either nonexistent or very affordable. They're not in it for the money; they're in it for the fun. Join in and have some.

CHAPTER 19

Mud, Sweat, and Gears: The XTERRA

As you learn more about the sport of triathlon, you will detect the kind of spirit, some might call it bravado, that leads participants, of their own free will, to plunge into water, ride a bicycle like a maniac, and cap it off with a hard run. From there, it's not difficult to perceive the kind of mindset that could create the wild and crazy world of XTERRA, the off-road triathlon that has been growing in popularity since its inception little more than a decade ago.

The Adventure of Off-Road Racing

The first XTERRA race took place in Hawaii in 1996 and was called the Aquaterra. It was later renamed XTERRA. The car company Nissan chose the name for an SUV, calling it the Xterra, and was the sponsor of XTERRA races for many years until 2006.

The basics of the XTERRA for high-level competitors are a 1.5K swim, 30K mountain bike ride on a trail, capped off by an 11K trail run. A small, local race might feature at 500-meter swim, 15K mountain bike ride, followed by a 5K trail run. At the local level, the distance may be dictated by the length or layout of the available trail.

The XTERRA is meant to be rugged, and it is. It's a seriously tough race requiring a lot more athleticism than a regular triathlon. You must have good balance to stay upright on the bike and to negotiate the terrain as a runner. You could easily end the mountain bike ride with a thick coat of mud from head to toe. The pace will seem frantic at times, with twists, turns, bumps, and obstacles that will make you wonder, once you have finished, how you stayed on the bike.

FACT

You can wear a wetsuit in an XTERRA, but the upper water temperature limit for wetsuit use is 72°F. In a regular triathlon it's 78°F. Face it—you have to be tough to even think about the XTERRA. It's a point of pride for competitors.

Easy Beginning

The swim starts pretty much like any other triathlon, although at some regional or national events the swimmers exit the water briefly and run to another point where they re-enter the lake or ocean. The swim and the transition area are the only elements of the XTERRA that you will view as "normal" relative to multisport racing.

Once on land, XTERRA competitors face constantly changing terrain, with ditches, logs, rocks, sand, branches, tree roots, mud puddles—all the sorts of things likely to be found on a trail in the woods. And there are, hills; some courses will have lots and lots of steep, rock-covered, blankety-blank hills. It takes a lot of upper body strength to maintain balance and keep from crashing your mountain bike or sailing over the handlebars after running into something on the forest floor or failing to make it over a big log in your path.

XTERRA organizers usually use separate trails for biking and running, although there sometimes may be a common start. Most trails are too narrow, however, for bikers and runners to compete together, and both courses will be loops. Two-way traffic just won't work.

The XTERRA may sound pretty harrowing, but it's not all bad. The soft trail surface is easier on the legs than asphalt or concrete, and you usually get to do your ride and run in the shade. Aficionados consider their sport more fun than regular triathlons.

Trail running and riding are necessarily slower because of the turns, the obstacles, and the need to watch where you are going at all times. Also, your mountain bike is not really built for speed. It's designed to get you through the race in one piece, albeit in serious need of a bath.

Don't enter an XTERRA with the idea you are going to duplicate your time or pace from some similar distance on the road. Don't even try to guess how much difference there will be. Just relax and enjoy the new experience.

Rough and Tumble

You may look and feel like you have been in a war—or a mud bath, anyway—when you finish, but you will have a high sense of accomplishment that you made it through the ordeal despite the difficulties presented by Mother Nature. There will be times during the race that you have to get off your bike just to keep moving forward. There are photos in circulation of XTERRA competitors carrying their mountain bikes up a rocky slope. You might think you know the course, but there are always surprises. That's part of the attraction of the event.

The sport has grown so fast that there are XTERRA races practically year round, concentrated, of course, in warmer climates during certain times of the year. Pro competitors can earn serious XTERRA prize money in races all over the world, and the XTERRA World Championship annually attracts more than 500 racers. Obviously, lots of people who like to play in the dirt have found the perfect outlet.

If ever there was an activity that called for concentration, it's the mountain bike phase of the XTERRA. Even a moment of distraction could send you careening into a tree or some other impediment on the trail. You also have to be ready, even as you zoom through the forest, to deal quickly with a large obstacle in your path. It really helps to know the course.

Equipment

This will come as good news to those of you who like to buy stuff. If you want to compete in an XTERRA, you're going to have to get a new bike, specifically a mountain bike. Yes, it's got two wheels and a seat, but there are big differences between the mountain bike and your road cycle. For starters, the tires are thick and covered with knobs for extra traction. Your mountain bike also comes with suspension because of all the bumps you will experience out on the trail. Without the suspension, you would be bouncing all over the forest. Mountain bikes without rear suspension are called "hard tails."

The mountain bike is not sleek or graceful. It is heavy and sturdy, made to take a pounding on an uneven surface. Out on the trail, aerodynamics is not an issue. You want a machine that will get you from point A to point B without shaking your teeth loose or falling apart.

Besides having funny-looking tires, the mountain bike has more gears than a road bike. A regular machine has two front rings for the chains. Your new mountain bike has three rings. The smallest of the rings is the "easy" gear, often called the "granny" gear because it's so easy to turn that your granny could do it. You often need this gear to get through the mud and sand, and for steep climbs.

Your mountain bike gets very dirty, with lots of grit getting into the gears and on the chain. This kind of bicycle requires more service than a road bike. Your gears will wear out a lot sooner from trail riding.

As described in Chapter 9, fit is very important with a road bike. Fit still matters with a mountain bike, but not as much because the ride is bumpy and you may be standing up on the bike or hopping off periodically.

QUESTION?

How much should I expect to spend on my new mountain bike?
An entry-level mountain bike can be had for $500 to $700. As you might expect, fancier versions are available for a lot more money.

Need to Push

To go along with your mountain bike, you will need a pair of special shoes designed for trail racing. Mountain bike shoes are similar to road bike shoes in that they attach to the pedals, but they have a thick, aggressive tread with lugs in case you have to get off your machine and push it. Regular bike shoes are slick on the bottom and would not work well on a muddy trail.

Because of the rough terrain, you are more likely to have a flat as you make your way along the uneven trail. Most experienced XTERRA competitors carry two extra tubes as insurance.

On Hand

Don't start your XTERRA mountain bike without gloves. You must maintain a solid grip on the handlebars as you ride. Out in the heat and humidity, a likely scenario, perspiration will make your hands very slippery. One good bump on a rock or tree root could cause you to lose control. If that happens, you know there's a tree with your name on it.

On Foot

There are running shoes designed for trails. Most come with lugs for better traction. Trail shoes would probably be useful for your XTERRA adventure, but you could get by with regular running shoes. Actually, a pair of gaiters, coverings for your shoes to keep the rocks out, might be more useful than trail running shoes if the terrain calls for it and the run is long.

While you are riding and running in the XTERRA, bright sunlight may not be a concern on the trail, but you still need glasses for your race. You will be flying along with all kinds of branches and leaves hitting your face, and the bikers in front of you will be kicking up rocks and gravel, so protection for your eyes is a must.

Cover Up

In a regular triathlon, it's not unusual to see competitors, men and women, biking in their swim trunks and swimsuits. It's quicker than putting on something else. In an XTERRA, you need more cover than that because of all the branches and other vegetation that will be encountered on the trail when riding and running.

Invest in a triathlon suit with shorts, enough to cover the thighs. If you wear that for your swim, you won't have to worry about adding any clothing in your transition.

Drink Up

On your bicycle ride in a regular triathlon, your machine has a cage for your water bottle. It's easy to reach down as you go, pull out the bottle, and take a swig. No problem putting it back. Just one hand needed.

In the XTERRA, you should not be riding with only one hand on the bars for as long as it would take to drink. Hit a rock with just one hand on the front and you could find yourself face down in the dirt or driving into the brush.

You still need water, of course, so what can you do to drink while you ride without risking a wreck? Help is there in the form of a hydration pack that looks like a backpack, and you can get one designed for bikers. The backpack has a plastic reservoir, more or less a large bladder, for the water and a tube that goes over your shoulder to draw the fluid from the pack. It takes just one quick motion to pull the tube to your mouth whenever you need a drink.

The tube is made so that water won't leak out. The packs come in several sizes and can hold a lot of water, up to 100 ounces or more. That's probably more than you need for a short XTERRA, but there are many choices. You can put ice in it before the race starts so that you don't have to drink warm water on your ride.

Swim Training

Swim training for an XTERRA is not much different from what you would do to get ready for a regular triathlon. You will still probably be swimming in a lake in a wave or time trial start.

A twelve-week swim training schedule identical to the one in this book will serve you just as well for an XTERRA. The one difference is that you have more of an incentive to get out of the water in an XTERRA. If you take too much time in your swim, you could easily get caught behind a very slow rider on the trail with little or no opportunity to pass.

On Draft

One way to address this problem is to practice drafting in the swimming pool. In regular triathlons and in XTERRA, drafting in the water is legal. Just remember to pick someone faster than you to follow. Swimming directly behind someone else will make things easier for you, and the effort of staying in that person's wake will make it feel as though you have a pacer to make you go faster.

Here's how drafting practice works. First, find a partner. You can practice drafting behind the partner for a couple of lengths. Then you can switch roles. Both of you get the practice. Get in the water and follow as closely as you can without touching the feet of the swimmer ahead of you. In a regulation pool, each lane has a black line down the middle. Practice drafting in a circle, always keeping the black line on your left shoulder and the lane rope on your right as you follow your partner to one end of the pool and back. Do this drill at least once a week.

Bike Training

In the XTERRA, the bicycle course is considered much more technical than a regular triathlon riding course. That's because of all the maneuvers needed to get through the XTERRA ride in a reasonable time with a minimum of downtime (translation: spills).

Your XTERRA bicycle training should have two phases: putting in sufficient riding time to achieve the fitness you will need on race day, and learning how to negotiate the trails under the pressure of race conditions. You can use your regular bicycle and normal triathlon training to get into race shape. Add some intense workouts—hills would be ideal—to get your body used to an elevated heart rate, which is what you will experience when you hit the trail on your mountain bike in the XTERRA. Do trail work at least once a week leading up to the XTERRA.

Skill Set

The key to your XTERRA ride is acquiring the skills to maneuver over rocks and logs and through water. You have a distinct advantage if you are already a mountain biker. You know what it's like out there, and you have learned the tricks, or at least some of them.

An XTERRA racer in training should find someone who can show how it's done in real situations rather than trying to learn in the abstract. If you don't know an experienced trail rider, check with your bike store. A staff member might be available to help or might know someone who could demonstrate the techniques.

If you are lucky, you won't have to travel far to find a trail that can test you on your biggest trail challenges: logs, big rocks, and water. Most of your learning will be by doing, but an essential element of your training will be figuring out how to unweight the front of your mountain bike while continuing to ride.

Streaming Along

To illustrate how important this bit of balancing can be, picture yourself entering a stream or large puddle. If you charge ahead full bore and your front wheel becomes stuck in the mud or the creek bed, what do you think will happen to your forward movement? Yep, you're going to keep going while the bike settles in for a rest. What you want to do is put your weight on the seat of the mountain bike and lift up on the front end.

A good rule of thumb for riders new to the XTERRA is to trust your mountain bike and let it all hang out. In other words: "When in doubt, speed up."

Logging Time

When approaching a log that you can't go around, you want to lift up the front of your mountain bike. If you can get the front wheel over the log, don't worry about the back wheel. It will follow.

The essential element of your training will be finding a venue for practicing these difficult maneuvers, learning the art of balancing and seated hill climbing. If you have to learn on your own, you will need more time on the trails and less on the roads while you figure out the techniques and become accustomed to a different way of riding.

See It, Do It

Make it part of your planning for your XTERRA to get to the venue at least one day early so that you can ride the course. Getting a look at the course in advance is actually more important than a rest day. The more you know, the more you will enjoy your race.

During the race, don't concern yourself with cadence or time. Your mountain bike won't have a computer anyway, and it would be little more than a distraction if it did. Just ride.

Run Training

First things first: don't expect to duplicate your road time in this XTERRA trail run. It is much harder to get into a rhythm on a trail because of the rocks, logs, hills, and other impediments to your swift progress. Some of the hills you will encounter on the trail will be much steeper than you're used to, and many will be strewn with rocks. There may be water to get through. Okay, you have been warned. So what can you do about it?

To start with, add some strength training, especially in the legs, to your XTERRA training. Remember, the bike ride that precedes your run is going to be more difficult than the ride in a regular triathlon. Out on the trail, you won't have the opportunity to cruise if you grow tired, and your fight with the elements will take more out of you.

Besides helping you with your conditioning and strength, stair climbing will get you into the habit of picking up your feet as you run, which is very important on a trail with rocks, roots, and stumps that can trip you.

Climbing

If you have a trail nearby with hills, substitute hill work on the trail for a track workout at least once a week. In addition to building leg strength, running on the trails will help with your balance and agility, both of which will be needed on race day.

You can also add to your leg strength and endurance with stair climbing. Find a building tall enough to allow you to climb for two minutes at a moderate pace (between simple climbing and a sprint). If two minutes on the stairs is too much at first, start with one minute and build up. Once you can do two minutes, repeat six to eight times once a week. If you don't have access to a tall building, perhaps there is a stadium you can use for stair running. Go up and down five or six times once a week.

If you have access to a trail, do the same tempo runs found in the training chart in Chapter 11. The more you get used to the rough, uneven surface, the better your run will go on XTERRA race day. If you can get any information about the run course, try to find a trail for your training that has at least some of the same features. As with the riding phase, try to get to the XTERRA venue early enough to scout out the trail and run it at least once if possible.

Transitions

As with just about everything else at the XTERRA, it's going to take longer in the transition than in a regular triathlon. There's more to do, after all. With everyone's times extended because of the conditions, time spent in the transition is not critical. That doesn't mean you can just lollygag around, but don't get too worked up over the extra time. In a regular triathlon, your bicycle will have your water bottle in a cage. For the XTERRA, you will be putting your water supply on your back.

XTERRA rules are basically the same as in a regular triathlon. The most important equipment-related rule involves the helmet, which must be buckled before you touch your mountain bike on your way to the mount/dismount area. You also have gloves, socks, and safety glasses to worry about. The glasses are not required but are highly recommended.

After you ride, you will be shedding your hydration pack and gloves, perhaps putting on a hat or visor for sunshade and to keep perspiration out of your eyes. Don't forget, by the way, that your run will be on the same kind of rugged trail as the ride, with branches and leaves in your way. Keep the glasses on.

Dirty Work

In Chapter 16, you were advised to put down a towel to help organize your gear in the transition area. For the XTERRA, a towel is a must but for a different reason.

It would not be a big surprise if you returned to the transition area after the ride covered with mud. This is not the ideal circumstance for the start of your run. Even if you aren't covered, there will be dirt and grit on you. Take a moment to get rid of some of that before you get going again.

You won't find aid stations where the bikers ride, but there should be stops on the run course with water and a sports drink. You should be able to get by without carrying any fluid.

Race Day

Common sense and experience will guide you on the big day, starting with your arrival time. You will, of course, get there early and set up in the transition area with enough time to allow for a warm-up ride, perhaps a light jog and a quick swim to get loose.

Your prerace nutrition should include more calories because the XTERRA demands so much more of you than a regular triathlon. Plan to take some kind of nutritional supplement on the ride, a couple of gels maybe, or if it looks like grappling with a gel pack on the course might be dangerous, take some kind of liquid energy source. If neither plan seems viable, plan to carry a couple of gels on the run. Check with the organizers to see if one or more of the aid stations will be handing out some kind of energy source.

Gloves usually come off after the ride in the XTERRA, but they might be needed if you have to climb over some rocky terrain during the run. That's another reason for checking the course in advance.

Your prerace preparation should include a ride on your mountain bike of about fifteen minutes. Ride the course if you are allowed to. If not, ride wherever you can to warm up and make sure the gears are shifting properly.

Take a little extra time in the water, with two or three 25-yard sprints to get your heart rate up. The water might be pretty cold—remember, no wetsuits unless it's 72°F or lower—so acclimating to the temperature will be beneficial. You can jog lightly if you want, but it won't hurt if you skip it.

Race Strategy

If you are a first-time XTERRA competitor, forget about the big picture and any goal other than getting to the finish line. Stay within yourself and concentrate on making it from point to point in a literal sense, that is, from this log to that creek, from that creek up the next hill, and so forth.

Chances are this sport is like nothing you have ever done. Your times won't have much meaning because the courses are so different, and you don't know how you will manage in the twists and turns and in your battle with the obstacles and the elements.

You trained for the XTERRA, learning tricks and techniques. You are fit and competitive, and you will try your best, pushing when you can, but without a frame of reference, times are meaningless. Save all that for next time. Just do your best and enjoy the adventure. Near the end, if you're tempted to try to pick up a few seconds with an all-out burst, consider whether it's worth it if you crash into a tree and end up out of commission for days or weeks.

All Done

Your postrace routine for the XTERRA should be much the same as for a regular triathlon. Take in carbohydrates as quickly as possible to replenish glycogen stores (remember the thirty-minute window), and don't forget protein for muscle recovery.

In the highly likely event that you are covered with mud or dirt, head for the lake to remove the grime, then go get some food (don't overdo the greasy, fatty fare).

You will probably be more tired than usual, but you may also discover the next day that you don't feel as beat up as you often do after the pounding of a hard run on the asphalt. Keep taking in fluids, carbohydrates, and protein during the day, just as you would after a road event.

Go by how you feel after your XTERRA in deciding when to resume training. Even if you feel better than usual, don't do anything intense for at least a couple of days. Make sure your heart rate stays low in all activities.

CHAPTER 20

Moving to the Next Level

In any group, even one whose members have a common interest, there will be a variety of motivations for participating. A typical triathlon will have people whose primary motivation is prize money and others who seek the satisfaction of completing a difficult task. Still others are happy just to participate. Perhaps your motivation is to find out how good you can be. In the end, only you can decide on the dream you want to chase.

Periodization

The word *periodization* does not refer to sentence punctuation. It is a term that describes an overall, year-long plan for rest and recovery, base building, and training for athletic competition. The goal is keep the athlete fit and ready to compete at the appropriate times and free from injury.

As much as you might enjoy the training and racing, you can't do it all the time without burning out, suffering serious injury, or both. There's an excellent plan for matching your ambition with your capacity for achieving it. The idea is to break up your year into periods, thus the terminology. There are four periods:

- **December, January, and February.** After a period of downtime, you begin building your base again. Your workouts have structure. You are following a training plan, adding strength with weights, and putting in more time in all three sports. You can use the beginner's training schedule from Chapter 11, replacing any hard workout with a longer but easier session in the same sport. You aren't trying to get race ready yet. Your goal in this period is to regain enough fitness to be able to move on to the next period.

- **March, April, and May.** Now you add hard workouts such as tempo sets, intervals, and hill repeats. You show up at the track more often for speed work. Your goal is to build on the foundation, the base, you laid in the previous period to get into race condition. You cut back on the weight training but focus your hard workouts on certain drills depending on coming races, for example, more hill workouts when your next race will present that kind of challenge.

- **June, July, August, and September.** This is the race season in most areas. You do less training during this period because the competition is keeping you in top condition. More important, you need time to recover from the races you have been doing. In race season, your weight training is cut back significantly. If you are new to the triathlon, limit yourself to two races per month and schedule at least one week a month for rest and recovery. All workouts during your rest week should be light. If you don't schedule some time for rest during the triathlon season, you risk burnout. No one can go hard week after week without a break. Even the pros back off regularly.

- **October and November.** You don't have to take the full two months, but schedule four to six weeks of light, unstructured activity. You still run, swim, and ride, but always at low intensity. There are no hard workouts or any kind of structured activity. This is the period during which your body recovers from the training and racing you have put it through in the previous ten months. Don't listen to the demons inside telling you to throw off the shackles and get out there for a hard run. Your discipline will pay off with a better racing season next year.

During your rest period, use your training log and heart rate monitor to make sure you are sticking to your plan for taking it easy. The light workout schedule will leave you with some excess energy, which will tempt you to overdo it.

These periods are, of course, subject to change based on a variety of factors, including climate and the availability of certain races. If your racing season starts earlier, you should start building your base on a different schedule.

The details are less important than sticking to the plan. As long as you build in rest periods and schedule some time off at the end of the season, you can keep this going almost indefinitely.

Good Timing

In periodization, you train with the objective of hitting your peak at the same time that you toe the starting line in your next triathlon, and the one after that. Planned correctly and followed with discipline, periodization will help keep you in the game instead of sitting on the sidelines with an injury or simply burned out because you overdid it.

The Half Ironman

The Boston Marathon is the Mecca in the world of running. With an experienced runner, you need only say the word "Boston," and you're understood. In triathlons, it's the Ironman Triathlon in Kailua-Kona, Hawaii. The magic word is "Kona." Both races are more or less exclusive; most participants have to qualify.

Just as marathons have made themselves more accessible to runners without "Boston ability," triathlon organizers have attached the Ironman cachet to a race that is doable for a wider variety of athletes. If you have the fitness plus the time and the will to train for it, you can probably complete a Half Ironman (1.2-mile swim, 56-mile ride, 13.1-mile run).

The question you have to ask yourself is, "When?"

Reality Check

The answer depends on where you are right now. If you have just completed a sprint triathlon and that's the extent of your experience, the Half Ironman should be a project you plan to work on for at least a year.

In the next twelve months, get some more triathlons under your belt, increasing the distance to at least Olympic range. Train for and run a couple of half marathons, and adopt a serious program to get your body ready for the event. The Half Ironman is possible for anyone determined enough to put in the work, but it's not a lark.

QUESTION?

I want to experience the Half Ironman but I don't have the time to train adequately in all three sports. Do I have any options?
Consider signing up for a Half Ironman on a relay team. Most people can find the time to train for one of the sports, and the team aspect increases the fun.

Say you have just completed a sprint triathlon that took you an hour and forty-five minutes. Compare that to what you will probably face in your first Half Ironman even if you train well and feel prepared:

- Your 1.2-mile swim will take forty-five minutes, possibly longer.
- The 56-mile bicycle ride will keep you in the saddle at least three to three and a half hours.
- You will be tired after all that riding when you start the half marathon, so covering the final 13.1 miles of your race will probably take at least two and a half hours.

You could be looking at five hours or more on the Half Ironman course. If the weather presents additional obstacles, the Half Ironman could very well be the longest day you ever spent completing a sporting event.

Prep Work

So what will it take to get ready for a Half Ironman? Finding the time to train adequately will surely be at least as challenging, if not more so, than the race itself.

For a Half Ironman, you will have to do some four-hour bike rides, and your runs and swims will be proportionately longer. You should plan to set aside ten to twelve hours a week to train for your half triathlon. Granted, the demands are not as oppressive as if you were training for a full Ironman—think bike rides of 100 miles, seven hours long—but it's a lot for a person with a job and family.

Rosy View

These cautions are not intended to discourage you from reaching higher in your athletic goals, and if you have experience at greater distances, you are in a much better position to move up more rapidly. Go-slow caveats aside, there are positives to consider about the Half Ironman. For starters, it is much less intense than the full Ironman and its daunting challenges. There will be a confidence factor at the start of the Half Ironman you might not feel in a full Ironman, no matter how diligently you prepared. Because you know you can do it, you will be more relaxed and you won't worry about going slow in spots, and your first one is definitely a just-get-to-the-finish race.

No Need for Speed

The Half Ironman is a good race for people who aren't very fast, and it's sufficiently challenging that completing the journey will be very satisfying. Most Half Ironman races are open to everyone, and there are enough of them on the calendar that you should not have great difficulty finding one that suits you and provides the time to get ready.

A training schedule for a Half Ironman is beyond the scope of this book, but there are many excellent, and free, training resources on the Internet. Many race organizers offer training programs on the same website where you register for the event.

What It Takes to Be Competitive

You may not be satisfied with just participating. You may want to break free of the middle of the pack and put yourself in contention for some age-group hardware. The first thing you must do is figure out what it will take to get where you want to go. Remember, the triathlon is a three-sport event. When the final standings are posted, one really good race and two poor ones will leave you out of the money.

You don't get a medal or a trophy for placing first in your age group in the run. You get it for accumulating one of the top times in your age group for all three sports, with transition times added in. That said, it might be just one sport and a relatively few minutes that kept you from an age-group award.

The Count

Say your triathlon swim was twenty minutes. You check out the finishers in your age group and see that you fell short of making the top three, the normal depth for awards, by six minutes. You are not going to go from a twenty-minute swim to a fourteen-minute swim; that's a 30 percent improvement. It just isn't going to happen. Taking one, perhaps two, minutes off is possible, so you've got to look at your other two events to see if you can find four minutes.

Perhaps your 5K run was twenty-seven minutes, a pace of 8:41 per mile. If you can speed up by eleven seconds per mile, you time goes to 26:24.

Improve by twenty seconds per mile and you're at 25:53, more than a minute better.

Now look at your triathlon ride of, say, 12 miles. If you averaged 16 miles per hour on the ride, it took forty-five minutes to complete the distance. By averaging 18 miles per hour, you can cover the distance in forty minutes.

Honest Appraisal

The key is to be objective about the performance you are trying to improve on while being realistic about how far up the ladder you can go in the short term. For example, perhaps your twenty-seven-minute 5K occurred on a good day, and there's not much room for improvement, at least in this season. That puts a lot more pressure on the other two sports for the minutes you need to achieve your goal. If the gap is pretty big, lower your sights and shoot for simply improving your age-group position in the next race. Nothing is impossible for a fit person with determination and the time to put in the right kind of training, but goals must be realistic.

In assessing your performance for the purposes of improvement, don't fail to consider the elements or other factors such as injuries. Compare your target times to your results in the best conditions for a true measure of how far you have to go.

Improvement Plans

To become more competitive as a swimmer, work on technique before you start in with the harder workouts. Harder or longer sessions in the pool with poor technique will only reinforce your mistakes and turn them into habits. If you're swimming at a club, have the coach check you out before you start in on the hard workouts. When you are satisfied that your form is good, add some interval workouts, ten to fifteen minutes at a time, at least once a week.

Your run training should also include more speed work, say a 3-mile tempo run once a week. If you are shooting for an eight-minute pace in the 5K, do the tempo runs at 8:20 to 8:30 pace. As you get used to the tempo pace, speed up a bit or do longer workouts. As always, be cautions about ramping up the speed too quickly. Injuries will only set you back in your quest to move up in the standings.

On a Roll

You will have your best opportunity for a big gain in the bicycle phase, and it is possible to buy speed, as you will see later in this chapter relative to super bikes. If you prefer to add speed on the bicycle through training, refer to the intermediate training chart in Chapter 11 and add time and distance to the hard workouts. Find some hills and take them on.

Your goal is to achieve a comfort level at the kind of intensity you will experience in the race. The harder you work in training, the easier it will go for you on race day.

Expectations

Here's a caution: you can work your butt off, make major improvements in all three of your sports, feel great going into the race, and still not achieve your goal. There are some awesome athletes who are attracted to triathlons, and if two or three of them in your age range show up at your event, you might end up out of the money despite your best efforts. It's a tough sport, and not just in physical terms.

Learn to take setbacks in stride. If you are outgunned by the talent, think of it as no different from bad luck with the weather and keep trying. You'll get 'em next time. It's corny but true: quitters never win and winners never quit.

Working with a Coach

If you haven't already decided to get a coach after reading Chapter 8, it bears repeating here: it's a rare athlete who knows instinctively the right way to do everything. To take it to the next level, having someone assess your performance will pay huge dividends. Technique is critical in many areas, none more so than in swimming. As noted in Chapter 8, poor technique can result in more fruitless effort in the water than you would care to contemplate, and it's hard to see where you're going wrong when you're just trying to make it from one end of the pool to the other faster than you did last week.

A good coach will detect your flaws and give you drills to help promote good habits, smoother moves, and easier laps. All that will pay off on race day with a much better swim. Most health clubs with pools also have coaches, giving you greater access to assistance where you need help the most.

QUESTION?

I've heard there is coaching available on the Internet for different sports. Could I get that kind of help to improve my swimming?
Stick to live coaches to help you with swim technique. The coach needs to observe you in the water to get a grip on what you're doing wrong and to see where you need the most work. Swimmers need hands-on, not virtual, coaching.

If your swim practice occurs where a coach is not available, you can get help from some of the more experienced swimmers. They might not be certified coaches, but they can help you with technique or at least answer some of your questions. They probably also know some good workouts to share with you.

Cyberworkouts

For most runners and bikers, it's not problems with technique that slow them down or leave them short of their potential. It's the design and quality of the workouts that matter, assuming that the work ethic is there.

If you look around, you can find goal-specific programs that are designed to help you achieve a certain time at a specified distance. There are plenty of these in books and training manuals, but they are becoming more and more available nowadays on the Internet.

There are even software programs that allow you to enter data about yourself along with your specific goals. The end product is a training program for what you want to accomplish. Many of these programs are free. Some online coaching programs are packaged with the opportunity to interact with a real person from time to time. The coach on the other end can answer questions and provide advice and encouragement. The cost of this kind of coaching varies, but it's usually in the range of $30 to $40 per week.

Accountability

Besides the obvious advantage of personal attention, having a coach can also serve as a motivator through encouragement as you go and from your natural urge to want to work harder to meet expectations. A good coach will assess your overall fitness and the likelihood that you can meet the goal you have in mind, then custom design a program to help you get there. Even if you are just part of a group under the care of a coach, a small amount of individual attention can change you from a wannabe to an accomplished athlete.

Super Bikes: Worth the Price?

Okay, you're really into this triathlon thing. You're committed to the tough workouts, the time away from family, and the aches and pains of the training. You're looking for every legal edge you can find in the training shoes, heart rate monitor, nutritional supplements, and the bicycle.

In your last triathlon, some biker flew past you on a machine that looked like no set of wheels you have ever seen. You couldn't believe it: the rear wheel was solid! The next day you were down at the bike shop checking out all the fancy bicycles that make your machine look like a Pinto among Cadillacs. If only you could afford one.

Big Bucks

Yep, that's the rub. The super bikes available today can cost $10,000 or more. They come with ultralight carbon fiber frames, $1,400 wheels, state-of-the-art gear shifters, ceramic bearings, the best pedals…everything an elite athlete might need to get to the finish line first to claim the prize money.

And that, all you men and women in the middle of the pack, is the bottom line. Unless you're good enough to believe you can pocket a big check at the end of the race, you should stick to upgrades that will help you in your races without deflating your wallet.

What to Upgrade

You don't have to be an elite competitor to look into an upgrade. You can make major improvements for a fraction of the cost of a super bike.

As described in Chapter 18, one of the biggest improvements you can make is in the wheels. Adding racing wheels will set you back about $1,000. You can also upgrade to a carbon fiber frame, which weighs about two to three pounds, for around $3,000 that will perform extremely well. For sure, it will blow away your entry-level bicycle.

FACT

Believe it or not, you can gain speed in your bicycle ride by changing helmets. New-model helmets that go for $150 to $200 have been known to save up to four minutes in the 112-mile bicycle ride in the Ironman Triathlon.

Even if you have the funds, you would do better to take the money saved by investing in a midrange bicycle, about $1,000 to $3,000 and use it to hire a coach or upgrade your heart rate monitor. If you do invest in the ultimate riding machine, don't expect it to produce results unless you put in the training. Triathlon success is still mainly about hard work and determination.

Are You Ready for the Ironman?

Every Little League baseball player dreams of playing in the World Series. Golfers picture themselves sinking the winning putt in The Masters. Sooner or later, the new triathlete will hear about the Hawaii Ironman or see it on television, and another fantasy will be born.

Yes, fantasy is just that, but picturing yourself at the top can inspire you to worker harder. While you might never qualify for Kona, there are Ironman triathlons available to those with grand ambitions, a taste for adventure, and a will of iron.

You have to know what you're getting yourself into. The Ironman is not a race you should consider without at least two triathlon seasons in which you participated pretty heavily.

The Grind

The Ironman has been discussed previously, but here are the essentials: you swim 2.4 miles, then ride your bicycle for 112 miles, and top it all off with a full marathon (26.2 miles).

You have seventeen hours to get to the finish line, and it might take you all of that. If you have a great day, you might finish in twelve hours, but it's a lot more likely to be fourteen or fifteen. To prepare for an Ironman, plan on training eighteen hours a week, easily three times what you committed to for your sprint triathlon.

FACT

Competitors in the Kona Ironman Triathlon are members of a rather exclusive club. To qualify, you must win your age group at one of the other Ironman qualifying races or place in the top three if there are lots of entries.

Century Marks

You will have to do some centuries—100-mile rides—on your bicycle, and you can look forward to some six- and seven-hour rides in your training. Plan on swim training until you feel like you're going to grow gills.

To prepare for the Ironman marathon, you're looking at building slowly and steadily in your training to two or three runs of 20 miles, plus hill work, speed sessions, and more. Many coaches recommend that you complete at least one full marathon before you try the Ironman. The marathon itself is a grueling test of stamina and will, and you should envision the odyssey after the swim and hours of riding.

It is also recommended that you get a couple of Half Ironman races under your belt. Above all, find a training program that will adequately prepare you for one of the hardest thing you will ever do.

The Ironman is a serious race requiring serious preparation, but you will find the deepest part of yourself in meeting the challenge. Crossing that finish line may overwhelm you.

To get a glimpse of what is in store, find someone who has completed an Ironman and ask questions about preparation and likely race-day challenges. Ask if it was worth the price, the effort, and the pain. Prepare to be blown away by the response.

You don't have to do an Ironman to feel good about yourself. Dare to dream, dare to try, and never give up.

Good luck.

	Sunday	Monday	Tuesday
Yard/ Meters Comments	*Swim*	*Swim*	*Swim*
Mileage/ Time Comments	*Bike*	*Bike*	*Bike*
Distance/ Time Comments	*Run*	*Run*	*Run*
Comments	*Weights*	*Weights*	*Weights*

Log

Wednesday	Thursday	Friday	Saturday
Swim	*Swim*	*Swim*	*Swim*
Bike	*Bike*	*Bike*	*Bike*
Run	*Run*	*Run*	*Run*
Weights	*Weights*	*Weights*	*Weights*

Resources

There are many sources of information about triathlons, training, nutrition, and equipment.

Here are some of the most widely used.

The American Dietetic Association
What you eat will make a major difference in how you perform.
www.eatright.org

USA Triathlon
The starting and ending place for information, rules.
www.usatriathlon.org

USA Cycling
Everything and anything you want to know about cycling is available at USAC, located in Colorado Springs, CO.
www.usacycling.org

Triathlete Magazine
Circulation more than 100,000. The bible of one of the fastest growing sports in the world.
www.triathletemag.com

Active.com
A great resource for a wide variety of sports. Regular newsletters provide an array of helpful information. Members receive discounts on race entries.
www.active.com

Ironman
All about one of the toughest sports on the planet.
www.ironmanlive.com

Slowtwitch
A California-based organization, Slowtwitch has lots of multisport information.
www.slowtwitch.com

Triathlete.com
Interact with other triathletes.
www.triathlete.com

Tri Newbies Online
A ten-year-old organization specializing in helping beginners get into the sport.
www.trinewbies.com

BeginnerTriathlete.com
Another site devoted to new triathletes.
www.beginnertriathlete.com

Inside Triathlon
Based in Colorado, this magazine is all about the multisport life
www.insidetri.com

Training Peaks
Loaded with software for self-coaching, and also a good resource for finding a real, live coach. Many training and meal plans and virtual coaching.
www.trainingpeaks.com

Duathlon.com
Everything you always wanted to know about duathlons.
www.duathlon.com

XTERRA
The triathlon for the rough and tumble crowd has a snazzy website that will fill you in on one of the wildest sports around.
www.xterraplanet.com

Running/Biking/Swimming Clubs

If you are looking for a club in your area, the quickest and easiest way to find what you want is to use the Internet.

Triathlon Clubs
USA Triathlon
✍*www.usatriathlon.org*

Cycling Clubs
USA Cycling
✍*www.usacycling.org*

Running Clubs
Road Runners Club of America
✍*www.rrca.org*

Swimming Clubs
USA Swimming
✍*www.usa-swimming.org*

Index

THE EVERYTHING SERIES!

BUSINESS & PERSONAL FINANCE

Everything® Accounting Book
Everything® Budgeting Book, 2nd Ed.
Everything® Business Planning Book
Everything® Coaching and Mentoring Book, 2nd Ed.
Everything® Fundraising Book
Everything® Get Out of Debt Book
Everything® Grant Writing Book, 2nd Ed.
Everything® Guide to Buying Foreclosures
Everything® Guide to Fundraising, $15.95
Everything® Guide to Mortgages
Everything® Guide to Personal Finance for Single Mothers
Everything® Home-Based Business Book, 2nd Ed.
Everything® Homebuying Book, 3rd Ed., $15.95
Everything® Homeselling Book, 2nd Ed.
Everything® Human Resource Management Book
Everything® Improve Your Credit Book
Everything® Investing Book, 2nd Ed.
Everything® Landlording Book
Everything® Leadership Book, 2nd Ed.
Everything® Managing People Book, 2nd Ed.
Everything® Negotiating Book
Everything® Online Auctions Book
Everything® Online Business Book
Everything® Personal Finance Book
Everything® Personal Finance in Your 20s & 30s Book, 2nd Ed.
Everything® Personal Finance in Your 40s & 50s Book, $15.95
Everything® Project Management Book, 2nd Ed.
Everything® Real Estate Investing Book
Everything® Retirement Planning Book
Everything® Robert's Rules Book, $7.95
Everything® Selling Book
Everything® Start Your Own Business Book, 2nd Ed.
Everything® Wills & Estate Planning Book

COOKING

Everything® Barbecue Cookbook
Everything® Bartender's Book, 2nd Ed., $9.95
Everything® Calorie Counting Cookbook
Everything® Cheese Book
Everything® Chinese Cookbook
Everything® Classic Recipes Book
Everything® Cocktail Parties & Drinks Book
Everything® College Cookbook
Everything® Cooking for Baby and Toddler Book
Everything® Diabetes Cookbook
Everything® Easy Gourmet Cookbook
Everything® Fondue Cookbook
Everything® Food Allergy Cookbook, $15.95
Everything® Fondue Party Book
Everything® Gluten-Free Cookbook
Everything® Glycemic Index Cookbook
Everything® Grilling Cookbook
Everything® Healthy Cooking for Parties Book, $15.95
Everything® Holiday Cookbook
Everything® Indian Cookbook
Everything® Lactose-Free Cookbook
Everything® Low-Cholesterol Cookbook

Everything® Low-Fat High-Flavor Cookbook, 2nd Ed., $15.95
Everything® Low-Salt Cookbook
Everything® Meals for a Month Cookbook
Everything® Meals on a Budget Cookbook
Everything® Mediterranean Cookbook
Everything® Mexican Cookbook
Everything® No Trans Fat Cookbook
Everything® One-Pot Cookbook, 2nd Ed., $15.95
Everything® Organic Cooking for Baby & Toddler Book, $15.95
Everything® Pizza Cookbook
Everything® Quick Meals Cookbook, 2nd Ed., $15.95
Everything® Slow Cooker Cookbook
Everything® Slow Cooking for a Crowd Cookbook
Everything® Soup Cookbook
Everything® Stir-Fry Cookbook
Everything® Sugar-Free Cookbook
Everything® Tapas and Small Plates Cookbook
Everything® Tex-Mex Cookbook
Everything® Thai Cookbook
Everything® Vegetarian Cookbook
Everything® Whole-Grain, High-Fiber Cookbook
Everything® Wild Game Cookbook
Everything® Wine Book, 2nd Ed.

GAMES

Everything® 15-Minute Sudoku Book, $9.95
Everything® 30-Minute Sudoku Book, $9.95
Everything® Bible Crosswords Book, $9.95
Everything® Blackjack Strategy Book
Everything® Brain Strain Book, $9.95
Everything® Bridge Book
Everything® Card Games Book
Everything® Card Tricks Book, $9.95
Everything® Casino Gambling Book, 2nd Ed.
Everything® Chess Basics Book
Everything® Christmas Crosswords Book, $9.95
Everything® Craps Strategy Book
Everything® Crossword and Puzzle Book
Everything® Crosswords and Puzzles for Quote Lovers Book, $9.95
Everything® Crossword Challenge Book
Everything® Crosswords for the Beach Book, $9.95
Everything® Cryptic Crosswords Book, $9.95
Everything® Cryptograms Book, $9.95
Everything® Easy Crosswords Book
Everything® Easy Kakuro Book, $9.95
Everything® Easy Large-Print Crosswords Book
Everything® Games Book, 2nd Ed.
Everything® Giant Book of Crosswords
Everything® Giant Sudoku Book, $9.95
Everything® Giant Word Search Book
Everything® Kakuro Challenge Book, $9.95
Everything® Large-Print Crossword Challenge Book
Everything® Large-Print Crosswords Book
Everything® Large-Print Travel Crosswords Book
Everything® Lateral Thinking Puzzles Book, $9.95
Everything® Literary Crosswords Book, $9.95
Everything® Mazes Book
Everything® Memory Booster Puzzles Book, $9.95

Everything® Movie Crosswords Book, $9.95
Everything® Music Crosswords Book, $9.95
Everything® Online Poker Book
Everything® Pencil Puzzles Book, $9.95
Everything® Poker Strategy Book
Everything® Pool & Billiards Book
Everything® Puzzles for Commuters Book, $9.95
Everything® Puzzles for Dog Lovers Book, $9.95
Everything® Sports Crosswords Book, $9.95
Everything® Test Your IQ Book, $9.95
Everything® Texas Hold 'Em Book, $9.95
Everything® Travel Crosswords Book, $9.95
Everything® Travel Mazes Book, $9.95
Everything® Travel Word Search Book, $9.95
Everything® TV Crosswords Book, $9.95
Everything® Word Games Challenge Book
Everything® Word Scramble Book
Everything® Word Search Book

HEALTH

Everything® Alzheimer's Book
Everything® Diabetes Book
Everything® First Aid Book, $9.95
Everything® Green Living Book
Everything® Health Guide to Addiction and Recovery
Everything® Health Guide to Adult Bipolar Disorder
Everything® Health Guide to Arthritis
Everything® Health Guide to Controlling Anxiety
Everything® Health Guide to Depression
Everything® Health Guide to Diabetes, 2nd Ed.
Everything® Health Guide to Fibromyalgia
Everything® Health Guide to Menopause, 2nd Ed.
Everything® Health Guide to Migraines
Everything® Health Guide to Multiple Sclerosis
Everything® Health Guide to OCD
Everything® Health Guide to PMS
Everything® Health Guide to Postpartum Care
Everything® Health Guide to Thyroid Disease
Everything® Hypnosis Book
Everything® Low Cholesterol Book
Everything® Menopause Book
Everything® Nutrition Book
Everything® Reflexology Book
Everything® Stress Management Book
Everything® Superfoods Book, $15.95

HISTORY

Everything® American Government Book
Everything® American History Book, 2nd Ed.
Everything® American Revolution Book, $15.95
Everything® Civil War Book
Everything® Freemasons Book
Everything® Irish History & Heritage Book
Everything® World War II Book, 2nd Ed.

HOBBIES

Everything® Candlemaking Book
Everything® Cartooning Book
Everything® Coin Collecting Book
Everything® Digital Photography Book, 2nd Ed.

Everything® Drawing Book
Everything® Family Tree Book, 2nd Ed.
Everything® Guide to Online Genealogy, $15.95
Everything® Knitting Book
Everything® Knots Book
Everything® Photography Book
Everything® Quilting Book
Everything® Sewing Book
Everything® Soapmaking Book, 2nd Ed.
Everything® Woodworking Book

HOME IMPROVEMENT

Everything® Feng Shui Book
Everything® Feng Shui Decluttering Book, $9.95
Everything® Fix-It Book
Everything® Green Living Book
Everything® Home Decorating Book
Everything® Home Storage Solutions Book
Everything® Homebuilding Book
Everything® Organize Your Home Book, 2nd Ed.

KIDS' BOOKS

All titles are $7.95
Everything® Fairy Tales Book, $14.95
Everything® Kids' Animal Puzzle & Activity Book
Everything® Kids' Astronomy Book
Everything® Kids' Baseball Book, 5th Ed.
Everything® Kids' Bible Trivia Book
Everything® Kids' Bugs Book
Everything® Kids' Cars and Trucks Puzzle and Activity Book
Everything® Kids' Christmas Puzzle & Activity Book
Everything® Kids' Connect the Dots
    Puzzle and Activity Book
Everything® Kids' Cookbook, 2nd Ed.
Everything® Kids' Crazy Puzzles Book
Everything® Kids' Dinosaurs Book
Everything® Kids' Dragons Puzzle and Activity Book
Everything® Kids' Environment Book $7.95
Everything® Kids' Fairies Puzzle and Activity Book
Everything® Kids' First Spanish Puzzle and Activity Book
Everything® Kids' Football Book
Everything® Kids' Geography Book
Everything® Kids' Gross Cookbook
Everything® Kids' Gross Hidden Pictures Book
Everything® Kids' Gross Jokes Book
Everything® Kids' Gross Mazes Book
Everything® Kids' Gross Puzzle & Activity Book
Everything® Kids' Halloween Puzzle & Activity Book
Everything® Kids' Hanukkah Puzzle and Activity Book
Everything® Kids' Hidden Pictures Book
Everything® Kids' Horses Book
Everything® Kids' Joke Book
Everything® Kids' Knock Knock Book
Everything® Kids' Learning French Book
Everything® Kids' Learning Spanish Book
Everything® Kids' Magical Science Experiments Book
Everything® Kids' Math Puzzles Book
Everything® Kids' Mazes Book
Everything® Kids' Money Book, 2nd Ed.
Everything® Kids' Mummies, Pharaoh's, and Pyramids
    Puzzle and Activity Book
Everything® Kids' Nature Book
Everything® Kids' Pirates Puzzle and Activity Book
Everything® Kids' Presidents Book
Everything® Kids' Princess Puzzle and Activity Book
Everything® Kids' Puzzle Book

Everything® Kids' Racecars Puzzle and Activity Book
Everything® Kids' Riddles & Brain Teasers Book
Everything® Kids' Science Experiments Book
Everything® Kids' Sharks Book
Everything® Kids' Soccer Book
Everything® Kids' Spelling Book
Everything® Kids' Spies Puzzle and Activity Book
Everything® Kids' States Book
Everything® Kids' Travel Activity Book
Everything® Kids' Word Search Puzzle and Activity Book

LANGUAGE

Everything® Conversational Japanese Book with CD, $19.95
Everything® French Grammar Book
Everything® French Phrase Book, $9.95
Everything® French Verb Book, $9.95
Everything® German Phrase Book, $9.95
Everything® German Practice Book with CD, $19.95
Everything® Inglés Book
Everything® Intermediate Spanish Book with CD, $19.95
Everything® Italian Phrase Book, $9.95
Everything® Italian Practice Book with CD, $19.95
Everything® Learning Brazilian Portuguese Book with CD, $19.95
Everything® Learning French Book with CD, 2nd Ed., $19.95
Everything® Learning German Book
Everything® Learning Italian Book
Everything® Learning Latin Book
Everything® Learning Russian Book with CD, $19.95
Everything® Learning Spanish Book
Everything® Learning Spanish Book with CD, 2nd Ed., $19.95
Everything® Russian Practice Book with CD, $19.95
Everything® Sign Language Book, $15.95
Everything® Spanish Grammar Book
Everything® Spanish Phrase Book, $9.95
Everything® Spanish Practice Book with CD, $19.95
Everything® Spanish Verb Book, $9.95
Everything® Speaking Mandarin Chinese Book with CD, $19.95

MUSIC

Everything® Bass Guitar Book with CD, $19.95
Everything® Drums Book with CD, $19.95
Everything® Guitar Book with CD, 2nd Ed., $19.95
Everything® Guitar Chords Book with CD, $19.95
Everything® Guitar Scales Book with CD, $19.95
Everything® Harmonica Book with CD, $15.95
Everything® Home Recording Book
Everything® Music Theory Book with CD, $19.95
Everything® Reading Music Book with CD, $19.95
Everything® Rock & Blues Guitar Book with CD, $19.95
Everything® Rock & Blues Piano Book with CD, $19.95
Everything® Rock Drums Book with CD, $19.95
Everything® Singing Book with CD, $19.95
Everything® Songwriting Book

NEW AGE

Everything® Astrology Book, 2nd Ed.
Everything® Birthday Personology Book
Everything® Celtic Wisdom Book, $15.95
Everything® Dreams Book, 2nd Ed.
Everything® Law of Attraction Book, $15.95
Everything® Love Signs Book, $9.95
Everything® Love Spells Book, $9.95
Everything® Palmistry Book
Everything® Psychic Book
Everything® Reiki Book

Everything® Sex Signs Book, $9.95
Everything® Spells & Charms Book, 2nd Ed.
Everything® Tarot Book, 2nd Ed.
Everything® Toltec Wisdom Book
Everything® Wicca & Witchcraft Book, 2nd Ed.

PARENTING

Everything® Baby Names Book, 2nd Ed.
Everything® Baby Shower Book, 2nd Ed.
Everything® Baby Sign Language Book with DVD
Everything® Baby's First Year Book
Everything® Birthing Book
Everything® Breastfeeding Book
Everything® Father-to-Be Book
Everything® Father's First Year Book
Everything® Get Ready for Baby Book, 2nd Ed.
Everything® Get Your Baby to Sleep Book, $9.95
Everything® Getting Pregnant Book
Everything® Guide to Pregnancy Over 35
Everything® Guide to Raising a One-Year-Old
Everything® Guide to Raising a Two-Year-Old
Everything® Guide to Raising Adolescent Boys
Everything® Guide to Raising Adolescent Girls
Everything® Mother's First Year Book
Everything® Parent's Guide to Childhood Illnesses
Everything® Parent's Guide to Children and Divorce
Everything® Parent's Guide to Children with ADD/ADHD
Everything® Parent's Guide to Children with Asperger's
    Syndrome
Everything® Parent's Guide to Children with Anxiety
Everything® Parent's Guide to Children with Asthma
Everything® Parent's Guide to Children with Autism
Everything® Parent's Guide to Children with Bipolar Disorder
Everything® Parent's Guide to Children with Depression
Everything® Parent's Guide to Children with Dyslexia
Everything® Parent's Guide to Children with Juvenile Diabetes
Everything® Parent's Guide to Children with OCD
Everything® Parent's Guide to Positive Discipline
Everything® Parent's Guide to Raising Boys
Everything® Parent's Guide to Raising Girls
Everything® Parent's Guide to Raising Siblings
Everything® Parent's Guide to Raising Your
    Adopted Child
Everything® Parent's Guide to Sensory Integration Disorder
Everything® Parent's Guide to Tantrums
Everything® Parent's Guide to the Strong-Willed Child
Everything® Parenting a Teenager Book
Everything® Potty Training Book, $9.95
Everything® Pregnancy Book, 3rd Ed.
Everything® Pregnancy Fitness Book
Everything® Pregnancy Nutrition Book
Everything® Pregnancy Organizer, 2nd Ed., $16.95
Everything® Toddler Activities Book
Everything® Toddler Book
Everything® Tween Book
Everything® Twins, Triplets, and More Book

PETS

Everything® Aquarium Book
Everything® Boxer Book
Everything® Cat Book, 2nd Ed.
Everything® Chihuahua Book
Everything® Cooking for Dogs Book
Everything® Dachshund Book
Everything® Dog Book, 2nd Ed.
Everything® Dog Grooming Book

Everything® Dog Obedience Book
Everything® Dog Owner's Organizer, $16.95
Everything® Dog Training and Tricks Book
Everything® German Shepherd Book
Everything® Golden Retriever Book
Everything® Horse Book, 2nd Ed., $15.95
Everything® Horse Care Book
Everything® Horseback Riding Book
Everything® Labrador Retriever Book
Everything® Poodle Book
Everything® Pug Book
Everything® Puppy Book
Everything® Small Dogs Book
Everything® Tropical Fish Book
Everything® Yorkshire Terrier Book

REFERENCE

Everything® American Presidents Book
Everything® Blogging Book
Everything® Build Your Vocabulary Book, $9.95
Everything® Car Care Book
Everything® Classical Mythology Book
Everything® Da Vinci Book
Everything® Einstein Book
Everything® Enneagram Book
Everything® Etiquette Book, 2nd Ed.
Everything® Family Christmas Book, $15.95
Everything® Guide to C. S. Lewis & Narnia
Everything® Guide to Divorce, 2nd Ed., $15.95
Everything® Guide to Edgar Allan Poe
Everything® Guide to Understanding Philosophy
Everything® Inventions and Patents Book
Everything® Jacqueline Kennedy Onassis Book
Everything® John F. Kennedy Book
Everything® Mafia Book
Everything® Martin Luther King Jr. Book
Everything® Pirates Book
Everything® Private Investigation Book
Everything® Psychology Book
Everything® Public Speaking Book, $9.95
Everything® Shakespeare Book, 2nd Ed.

RELIGION

Everything® Angels Book
Everything® Bible Book
Everything® Bible Study Book with CD, $19.95
Everything® Buddhism Book
Everything® Catholicism Book
Everything® Christianity Book
Everything® Gnostic Gospels Book
Everything® Hinduism Book, $15.95
Everything® History of the Bible Book
Everything® Jesus Book
Everything® Jewish History & Heritage Book
Everything® Judaism Book
Everything® Kabbalah Book
Everything® Koran Book
Everything® Mary Book
Everything® Mary Magdalene Book
Everything® Prayer Book

Everything® Saints Book, 2nd Ed.
Everything® Torah Book
Everything® Understanding Islam Book
Everything® Women of the Bible Book
Everything® World's Religions Book

SCHOOL & CAREERS

Everything® Career Tests Book
Everything® College Major Test Book
Everything® College Survival Book, 2nd Ed.
Everything® Cover Letter Book, 2nd Ed.
Everything® Filmmaking Book
Everything® Get-a-Job Book, 2nd Ed.
Everything® Guide to Being a Paralegal
Everything® Guide to Being a Personal Trainer
Everything® Guide to Being a Real Estate Agent
Everything® Guide to Being a Sales Rep
Everything® Guide to Being an Event Planner
Everything® Guide to Careers in Health Care
Everything® Guide to Careers in Law Enforcement
Everything® Guide to Government Jobs
Everything® Guide to Starting and Running a Catering
    Business
Everything® Guide to Starting and Running a Restaurant
**Everything® Guide to Starting and Running
    a Retail Store**
Everything® Job Interview Book, 2nd Ed.
Everything® New Nurse Book
Everything® New Teacher Book
Everything® Paying for College Book
Everything® Practice Interview Book
Everything® Resume Book, 3rd Ed.
Everything® Study Book

SELF-HELP

Everything® Body Language Book
Everything® Dating Book, 2nd Ed.
Everything® Great Sex Book
**Everything® Guide to Caring for Aging Parents,
    $15.95**
Everything® Self-Esteem Book
Everything® Self-Hypnosis Book, $9.95
Everything® Tantric Sex Book

SPORTS & FITNESS

Everything® Easy Fitness Book
Everything® Fishing Book
Everything® Guide to Weight Training, $15.95
Everything® Krav Maga for Fitness Book
Everything® Running Book, 2nd Ed.
Everything® Triathlon Training Book, $15.95

TRAVEL

Everything® Family Guide to Coastal Florida
Everything® Family Guide to Cruise Vacations
Everything® Family Guide to Hawaii
Everything® Family Guide to Las Vegas, 2nd Ed.
Everything® Family Guide to Mexico
Everything® Family Guide to New England, 2nd Ed.

Everything® Family Guide to New York City, 3rd Ed.
**Everything® Family Guide to Northern California
    and Lake Tahoe**
Everything® Family Guide to RV Travel & Campgrounds
Everything® Family Guide to the Caribbean
Everything® Family Guide to the Disneyland® Resort, California
    Adventure®, Universal Studios®, and the Anaheim
    Area, 2nd Ed.
Everything® Family Guide to the Walt Disney World Resort®,
    Universal Studios®, and Greater Orlando, 5th Ed.
Everything® Family Guide to Timeshares
Everything® Family Guide to Washington D.C., 2nd Ed.

WEDDINGS

Everything® Bachelorette Party Book, $9.95
Everything® Bridesmaid Book, $9.95
Everything® Destination Wedding Book
Everything® Father of the Bride Book, $9.95
Everything® Green Wedding Book, $15.95
Everything® Groom Book, $9.95
Everything® Jewish Wedding Book, 2nd Ed., $15.95
Everything® Mother of the Bride Book, $9.95
Everything® Outdoor Wedding Book
Everything® Wedding Book, 3rd Ed.
Everything® Wedding Checklist, $9.95
Everything® Wedding Etiquette Book, $9.95
Everything® Wedding Organizer, 2nd Ed., $16.95
Everything® Wedding Shower Book, $9.95
Everything® Wedding Vows Book, 3rd Ed., $9.95
Everything® Wedding Workout Book
Everything® Weddings on a Budget Book, 2nd Ed., $9.95

WRITING

Everything® Creative Writing Book
Everything® Get Published Book, 2nd Ed.
Everything® Grammar and Style Book, 2nd Ed.
Everything® Guide to Magazine Writing
Everything® Guide to Writing a Book Proposal
Everything® Guide to Writing a Novel
Everything® Guide to Writing Children's Books
Everything® Guide to Writing Copy
Everything® Guide to Writing Graphic Novels
Everything® Guide to Writing Research Papers
Everything® Guide to Writing a Romance Novel, $15.95
Everything® Improve Your Writing Book, 2nd Ed.
Everything® Writing Poetry Book